A TORY SEER

A TORY SEER

The selected journalism of
T. E. UTLEY

Edited by Charles Moore
and Simon Heffer

Hamish Hamilton · London

HAMISH HAMILTON LTD

Published by the Penguin Group
27 Wrights Lane, London W8 5TZ, England
Viking Penguin Inc, 40 West 23rd Street, New York, New York 10010, U.S.A.
Penguin Books Australia Ltd, Ringwood, Victoria, Australia
Penguin Books Canada Ltd, 2801 John Street, Markham, Ontario, Canada L3R 1B4
Penguin Books (N.Z.) Ltd, 182–190 Wairau Road, Auckland 10, New Zealand

Penguin Books Ltd, Registered Offices: Harmondsworth, Middlesex, England

First published in Great Britain 1989 by Hamish Hamilton Ltd

Collection copyright © Charles Moore and Simon Heffer 1989
Foreword copyright © Margaret Thatcher 1989
Introduction copyright © Enoch Powell 1989

Cataloguing in Publication Data is available from the British Library

0–241–12728–9

Typeset at The Spartan Press Ltd, Lymington, Hants
Printed & Bound in Great Britain by
Richard Clay Ltd, Bungay, Suffolk.

Contents

Foreword

Few people have possessed such a complete understanding of the central tenets and principles of Toryism as Peter Utley. Certainly no one has articulated them with more eloquence. He stood in the tradition of the great Tory philosophers – Hooker, Burke and Lord Salisbury. Drawing on that tradition, he delivered powerful and incisive judgements on leading political, social and moral issues over a period of more than forty years. Though his range was remarkable, questions affecting the Anglican Church and the unity of the nation always had pride of place in his work. He was, quite simply, the most distinguished Tory thinker of our time.

It was his profound Toryism which led him to the conclusion in the late 1960s and early 1970s that the Conservative party should strike out in a new direction in order to reverse the nation's decline. He was one of the first to appreciate the need for 'a radical policy of economic liberalism', as he put it. He always said that the ultimate test of a Tory in politics is not his ability to frustrate change, but his capacity to recognize the need for change.

He was a man of immense intellectual generosity. He was always ready to put his knowledge and insights at the disposal of politicians, fellow writers and personal friends. I remember particularly vividly our last meetings just before his death last year when we discussed at length the ideas which I intended to use in my speech to the General Assembly of the Church of Scotland.

I was greatly honoured when the Utley family asked me to

become Patron of the fund that has been established in his memory. Every year an award will be made to a political writer, aged under 35, whose work shows particular promise. That is a fitting memorial to a man who gave such generous encouragement to young journalists throughout his career. I am very glad, however, that Charles Moore and Simon Heffer, two of the younger writers who learned so much from him, have provided this further memorial by compiling a selection of Peter's own writings. This volume shows why Peter Utley made such a profound impact on the discussion of political ideas in this country.

Margaret Thatcher
17 July 1989

Introduction

It is the pride of British politics, though not necessarily a pride
to be claimed exclusively by British politics, that we have had
men in every generation who exercise a dominant sway over
the political thought and movements of the time by their
writings in the newspapers and other periodicals. The roll of
honour, in which his mourning friends inscribe the name of
Peter Utley, comprises such names as Walter Bagehot,
William Hazlitt, William Cobbett and – dare one stretch a
point and add? – Samuel Johnson.

An Englishman who has the fire of politics warming his
entrails will normally, with Disraeli's Coningsby, decide that
'public life is a noble career and a seat in Parliament an
enviable distinction'. He will take up his stand on a barrel
wherever he can find one and solicit the votes of his fellow
citizens while expounding to them his political philosophy.
But that imperious impulse is not universal. Others imbued
with no less political passion address their fellow countrymen with the pen from vantage points just as dangerous and
exposed. These latter have the compensation that their
words, once printed and read, may come to be reprinted and
reread and thereby reach a wider audience over a longer
time.

It was to this band that Peter Utley belonged. Not that he
shrank from the hustings. In fact, he came forward to brave
them in, of all places, Northern Ireland; and I have no doubt
he would have acknowledged himself no less grateful for that
practical experience than Edward Gibbon notoriously was for
his brief service with the Hampshire Militia. Yet he was, and
everybody who knew him knew that he was, by nature as well
as by personal circumstances, by destiny as well as by
endowment, the natural writer-fighter. The calls to which his

spirit and intellect responded were the deadline and the feature story of the day. He rose to them as other politicians rise to catch Mr. Speaker's eye. His business in the newspapers was always the true politician's business of teaching, inspiring, leading, his fellow countrymen.

After he died, we politicians who had known Peter Utley were all of us of a single mind: we 'would not willingly let die' the ardour and the insight of his writings nor leave them scattered over the newspapers and periodicals of close on fifty years. There are some people (of whom Utley was one) whose true biography consists in their own writings. The pages which follow are in effect the biography – some might call them the testament – of a politician whose influence on his country's affairs exceeded that of most of those who held even high political office during the same period.

The most casual reader cannot fail to be aware that Utley was a congenital High Tory, in the specific rather than the vulgar headline usage of that term. He constantly looked to society, and to the particular society of his own country, as the framework within which the endeavours and ideas of individuals made living sense. He was prone to believe that the past had been as wise as the present and that the general instinct of men making up a society guides them more reliably than the intellects of the specialist and the academic. All his thought and all his writing – one might say, all his personal life – were imbued with that philosophy, for the application and exposition of which a rising generation in politics became accustomed to look to him.

It aligned him firmly with those of us for whom R. A. Butler, despite his quirkinesses and his compliances, continued to represent the natural rallying-point and the best hope of the modern Conservative party, the man whose instincts and philosophy would ensure that he struck the authentic Tory note on the platform and at the dispatch box during the years between 1945 and 1965. It is the same note which reverberates through everything, even the most ephemeral pieces, which Utley wrote as a journalist.

All journalism is in the literal sense ephemeral (*eph hēmeran*, 'for the day'), as the etymology of the word journalism itself warns us. Every piece reprinted in this book

had its transitory context, which was often a specifically party
political, not to say electoral, context. The perceptive
reader, however, will be able to disengage the content from
the context. When he does so, he will find, as in the output
of only the rarest of journalists, that the abiding outlines of a
political theory and a philosophy of life disengage themselves. I say philosophy of *life* rather than of *politics*. Utley's
thinking was integral. It embraced his religion and his family
and personal relationships as well as his professional writing.
This was the quality by which he created and held together
his continuing group or seminar, a phenomenon otherwise
unknown to Fleet Street and likely to remain (alas) unknown
to Docklands, but which links Utley's influence in the twentieth century with the coffeehouse institutions of the eight-
eenth century. It is a phenomenon which ought surely before
long to find its historian.

The primary arrangement of this book is by subjects.
Given the philosophical predisposition of the writer, that
was not an unreasonable decision.   On the other hand, within
each subject the order of pieces is strictly chronological. This
tends to obscure a fact about this book which will probably
prove to be its most important quality. The book is, just
because of the penetration and freshness of Utley's running
commentary upon events, a commentary which 'looks
before and after', in fact, a unique history of our time. I
predict that somebody some day, possessing a copy (or
rather, two copies), is going to cut it up and repaste it all
together chronologically. The result will be a contribution of
the highest quality to the history of post-Second World War
Britain. It will be true history and not chronicle; for Utley
the journalist was also Utley the historian, digesting events
and personalities as they were fed into his mind and redis-
playing them with the excitement and the dramatic flair of
historical imagination. Strands in the fabric of events, connections of cause and effect, become visible down the years
behind the confusing screen of passing events which are the
pabulum of journalism.

There could be no more striking testimonial to the quality
of Utley's mind and the importance of his lifework than that
his writings read as history. *A Tory Seer* will deserve to stand

among its peers on a shelf of the books from which posterity will learn what the British did, thought and suffered in the second half of the twentieth century.

J. Enoch Powell
June 1989

Editor's Preface and Acknowledgements

This book is our selection from all the journalism that T. E. Utley published under his own name, in a career stretching from 1941 to 1988. It does not include, because most of this is untraceable, the anonymous material – mainly leading articles – which he also wrote in large quantity. All the pieces are reprinted in full and with their original titles, except for one extract from Utley's pamphlet on Ulster. We have kept editorial comment to a minimum, believing that the articles need little explanation.

We are grateful to *The Times*, *The Daily Telegraph*, *The Spectator* and Conservative Central Office for permission to reprint these articles and for the assistance of their staff in tracing them. We should particularly like to thank Lara Tankl for her help in the research for this book.

All profits from this book will be paid to the T. E. Utley Memorial Fund, established to reward young writers who raise the quality of political thought in their journalism. For future enquiries about the fund please write to The Secretary, T. E. Utley Memorial Fund, 60 St Mary's Mansions, St Mary's Terrace, London W2 1SX.

Charles Moore
Simon Heffer
London, July 1989

This book is dedicated to Peter Utley's widow, Brigid

1 · What is a Tory?

*The loss of the will to govern has often been cited as the cause of
the downfall of the Conservative Government in 1964. More
than five years earlier, Utley identified this problem in a
trenchant article which gives the measure of his own precise
brand of Toryism.*

Toryism at the crossroads

The Daily Telegraph, 18 February 1960

The Tories have shown that they can win General Elections;
have they still got a philosophy of government? This is the
question which nags the conscience of many a faithful
Conservative inside and outside Westminster.

The election was won not by truckling to the Left but by
competent administration; in so far as ideology entered into
it, the experience of most candidates was that full-blooded
Conservatism was infinitely preferred to any of the
watered-down versions. Tories were expected to believe in
honest money, freedom at home and strength abroad.

Yet, on the morrow of victory, the Conservative party, for
all Mr. Macmillan's glittering triumphs in different parts of
the world, is as much the captive of its confused and
sentimental Left wing as ever in its history.

How then shall the years of Tory ascendancy be used?

A negative answer to the question has already been given.
Power is not to be handed over to the 'lunatic fringe' who
have been waiting their chance. Those who believe in holding
the Colonies, thrashing the young and smashing the unions
are not to be allowed to consume the fruits of office earned by
the tact and diligence of the moderates. All this is implicit, it is

said, in the appointment of that archangel of moderation, Mr. Butler, to the chairmanship of the party.

What, then, has Mr. Butler to offer? I understand that he has already got to work on the re-organisation of the Conservative Research Department, the scene of his most brilliant triumphs during the period of opposition. A group of its abler young men is to be formed into a special department dedicated entirely to thought and to be relieved of the duty of looking up facts for MPs.

This inner cabinet of the party bureaucracy will recall the great days when Iain Macleod, Enoch Powell and the rest plotted the downfall of Socialism. The question is, what are their successors going to plot?

It is a hard one; it will not do simply to review all the useful things that have been done and all the pleasant things that have been promised and to consider whether anything in the party's past pledges happens to have been overlooked. Although there are some differences about how to apply it, the party's formula for running the economy has been vindicated and approved; elections cannot be won by simply repeating it. The issues on which politics now depends are not economic.

Normally, one would expect this to put the Conservative party at a great advantage. Apart from maintaining the Queen's Government in times of crisis, its *forte* is the conservation and improvement of institutions. It is to this traditional task that Mr. Butler's young men must apply themselves. Under this general heading there are one or two fairly obvious sub-heads: highest on the list, as Mr. Macmillan is now aware, is the Commonwealth. Not to put too fine a point on it, is there still a case for this institution? If so, what is it?

The Conservative answer is no doubt an automatic 'yes'; but what are the implications of this affirmative? In the multi-racial dependent territories, Britain is faced with the task of holding the ring in one of the fiercest of human conflicts, the conflict of the races.

She needs to know not only exactly when to abandon power but also how to maintain it until that time has arrived. Exercising ultimate authority from London over the affairs of countries like Kenya and the Federation of Rhodesia and Nyasaland is a formidable business, demanding an instructed public opinion and a carefully thought-out technique.

It is a long time since the assumptions of national educational policy were seriously examined from the Conservative point of view. Can we really be satisfied that an increasing number of universities and an ever-wider access to the kind of higher education now available is all that is needed?

The defence of the Constitution is one of the traditional preoccupations of Conservatism; just because the immediate peril of a spate of Socialist legislation rushed through a virtually one-chamber Parliament has disappeared, it does not follow that the notion of a balanced Constitution is out of date, and Tories ought to be considering how it can be realised in modern terms.

Just because no one proposes to destroy the trade unions by legislation, it does not follow that their place in society and particularly the impact of their internal arrangements on personal liberty ought not to be considered by legislators.

One of the features of post-war Britain is supposed to be the birth of a Conservative intelligentsia; but this appears to be exclusively represented at present by a society of young men and women known as the Bow Group, whose beliefs are hardly to be distinguished from radical liberalism and sometimes even from Socialism.

The chief interests of most of them appear to be abolition of the death penalty, legalisation of homosexuality and instant release of anyone who happens to be in prison for subverting order in any part of the British Commonwealth – interests not necessarily un-Conservative, but not the natural preoccupations of a Tory intelligentsia at present, nor the dominant interests of those who returned Mr. Macmillan to power.

All this is particularly important for Mr. Butler. He is, in fact, the best of Tories, exhibiting exactly that balance between principle and expediency which is essential to that philosophy; but circumstances for which he is not absolutely to blame have put him at the centre of the party's cliché-ridden progressive wing.

If he is not careful he will get identified with those who have identified themselves with him, and he has already once lost the leadership of the Conservative party through irritating its Right wing.

For example, the impression has been carefully fostered that Mr. Butler is the captive of his penal reforms and that as Home Secretary he turns for advice to that self-appointed aristocracy of social workers, psychiatric specialists and pontificating juvenile magistrates who have nothing to tell him but that punishment can never deter.

I do not believe that these accusations against Mr. Butler are just, but I do believe that they are damaging. The Left wing of the party has had a monopoly of attention for too long; any renaissance of Conservatism will now come from the sane Right.

Lord Hailsham is no longer in the ascendant, but it should not be forgotten that it was he who convinced the rank and file of Conservatism, at a critical moment, that the party still had some distinctive convictions. Who in the party leadership today makes that as plain as Lord Hailsham did?

Eleven years of Tory rule

The Spectator, 10 May 1963

How the reputations of governments are made and destroyed will always remain, in the last analysis, a mystery. It is certain, however, that from time to time and often for no easily apparent reason other than general boredom the publicists conspire to declare a government's policy bankrupt.

This has been the recent fate of Mr. Macmillan's administration. Scorn had been poured upon it for the last six months from right and left and as a result, rational argument upon its achievement, let alone dispassionate judgment of its quality, is far from easy.

I believe that three-quarters of both cases against Mr. Macmillan and his colleagues rest on unproved assumptions and mere misrepresentation of fact. I hold that, within the limits of political possibility, the Tories over the last 11 years have done markedly better than could reasonably have been expected of them and demonstrably better than the Labour party would have done. To establish this point, however, I must begin by trying to state as forcefully as possible exactly what is alleged by their critics.

The prevailing impression of Conservative policy over the last 11 years is one of extreme incoherence. The Tory party has, it is alleged, lived from hand to mouth. It has occasionally checked but has never fundamentally reversed the trends towards national bankruptcy and imperial and social disintegration which were going on when it came to power. Essentially, we remain in much the same position as we were in 1951.

This represents the common element in the criticisms of both Right and Left and, it must be admitted, it probably also represents at present the average independent view of the period.

Within the limits of this general condemnation, two broadly opposite lines of criticism can be distinguished. The critics from the Right – generally the more venomous – contend that they have been deceived. In 1955, they accepted the Government's explanation that it had had to spend four years in establishing confidence and providing first aid to a country ravaged by Socialism. They hoped that the second term of Tory rule would see the Government at work restoring the foundations of a Tory society; they looked for vigour abroad and economy at home. In 1959, they were willing to renew their act of faith on the understanding that the Tory party was now controlled by Mr. Macmillan, a man of the Right who, by his zealous support for British intervention in Suez, had established himself as a devotee of the imperial cause.

Soon, however, they found that they had been deluded. Mr. Macmillan, like General de Gaulle, had seized power with the aid of the Right only in order to betray the Right. In Africa he embarked on a policy of indiscriminate surrender; towards America he showed that he was willing, in the last resort, to accept the role of European agent; at home he treated full employment and the preservation of the Welfare State as aims which should take precedence over the revival of enterprise and the defence of the pound. Such is the

gravamen of the charge made by discontented Tories and
Liberal converts.

Criticism from the other side is also formidable. The most
telling Socialist complaint is that 11 years of Tory rule have
seen no fundamental improvement in the country's economic
position. On the contrary, it is said they have been marked by
a series of alternating booms and slumps, directly caused by
Government policy. One minute we appear, at long last, to
have started to climb the broad and sunny uplands of
prosperity; then, there is usually a general election and, when
the Tories are safely returned to power, they calmly tell us
that we are back on the brink of ruin. More than once during
these last 11 years the country has seemed, in respect of the
balance of trade and its effect on the national reserves, to be
almost precisely where it was in 1951. If it has had a share in a
general rise in the standard of living elsewhere, its rate of
economic development has been far slower than that of other
countries, and most notably than that of the rest of Western
Europe. Further, Socialists argue that the country as a whole
has not benefited equally from this rise in prosperity, but that,
on the contrary, the least productive sections of the community have done best. Britain, they say, has become a
gambler's heaven; the people's welfare is built on private
debt. The Tories have favoured personal consumption by the
rich, at the expense of public investment in fields like
education, health and industrial modernisation, and, by so
doing, have hindered the growth of productive capacity.
Their economic policy has been as objectionable on grounds
of efficiency as on grounds of social justice.

Admittedly, it is hard to discover any consistent theme in
Left-wing criticism of the Government's policy abroad. Since
the death of Mr. Gaitskell, however, something like a
coherent line of attack has emerged; it is obviously strongest
in relation to defence, where the Government has been
forced to abandon the development of a succession of
extremely expensive weapons. One after another, they have
been hotly defended and promptly renounced. The moral
now drawn by the Labour party is that it is idle for Britain to
go on competing in the nuclear race as an independent power,
that her efforts should be mainly concentrated on making a

proper contribution to the conventional strength of NATO, and that she should in general bravely accept the inevitable role of a junior partner in the American alliance. The Government, it is alleged, cannot overcome these facts, and obstinately refuses to face them. Similarly, it is said, efforts, foredoomed to failure, to slow down the pace of constitutional development in the dependencies have robbed us of the chance of appearing as genuine liberators.

Such is the picture presented by the Left. The charges which it carries certainly cannot be refuted merely by arguing that they are cancelled out by those advanced from the Right; indeed, up to a point, they are not. All the critics are at one in seeing Tory rule as a succession of muddles and makeshifts, hesitations and evasions. Can this indictment really be met by anything but an appeal, which is certain to fail, to blind loyalty and deep-set fear of Socialism?

Essentially, the Conservative party has been faced, during its whole period of office, with precisely the same general economic and political problem in relation to home policy as confronted the Socialists between 1945 and 1951. It has had to try to reconcile the conflicting demands of the public for full employment, extensive social services, constant economic expansion, unrestricted trade unionism and stable prices.

The Socialist way of approaching this dilemma was to maintain a high level of public expenditure and a high rate of direct taxation and to try to check the rise in prices by straightforward administrative controls. By 1950 that policy had failed and had, indeed, been repudiated by the electorate. Before making way for the Tories, the Labour Government was far advanced on the road towards its complete abandonment. This failure was due fundamentally to the Labour Government's inability to make direct controls at once strong enough and sensitive enough to stop the rise in prices. The most important of commodities in this respect, human labour, remained uncontrolled. Its price went up, and with it the price of everything else.

In theory, two extreme possibilities have confronted every British government since the war. The perennial dilemmas could have been overcome by simply giving up the task of trying to reconcile the people's conflicting claims, and preferring one set of claims to another. In theory, full employment and the growth of the social services could have been sacrificed to stable prices and economic expansion. Some Western European countries, faced by the challenge of war-time devastation, did precisely this, and are now reaping the benefit. In theory also, the policy of total control, rejected by Labour, could have been applied.

In practice, no British government was ever confronted by this clear choice between opposite policies. Not only would neither policy, if frankly professed, have been swallowed by the electorate, but either could have been effectively vetoed by organised labour at a moment's notice.

One of the persistent errors of Right-wing critics of the 11 years of Tory rule has been the belief that a Tory victory at a general election gives the party for five years the same kind of power as a surgeon wields over a patient who has been successfully anaesthetised. The fact that, under parliamentary democracy and free trade unionism, the patient remains free to kick the surgeon whenever he threatens a move which may cause pain or inconvenience is widely forgotten.

The Tories had already embraced full employment. They therefore had no difficulty in accepting Mr. Gaitskell's definition of 3 per cent unemployment as constituting full employment, and since at no time under their rule, apart from the recent winter, has unemployment exceeded this figure, remaining more or less constantly at about 2 per cent, they can claim to have kept their word.

They also professed, however, to be able to stop inflation, to preserve and increase the rate of growth in the social services, and to raise the national standard of living as a whole, ensuring, in the process, that all classes had a share in the result.

Their main instrument in trying to fulfil these pledges has been the discredited policy of 'stop-go'. When economic activity has shown signs of lagging they have stimulated it by tax concessions, by lowering the Bank rate and by boosting public expenditure; when expenditure has threatened to outstrip resources they have reversed these policies, always, however, treating income tax concessions as sacrosanct.

What matters is that some version of the policy of 'stop-go' is an absolutely inevitable feature in the running of a modern economy. In the dark days of pre-Keynesian economics, 'stop-go' took the form of a devastating series of economic blizzards, ruthless and impartial in their effects and not directly attributable to the actions of any government. Under Socialism, it took the form of a little more or a little less on the clothes ration, a few more houses built, or a few more housing projects abandoned.

The measure of the Conservative party's success or failure is the extent to which its own version of 'stop-go' has been consistent with reasonably stable development. At no time since the war has the gross national product declined in any year. Between 1951 and 1962 it rose from £12,926 million to £24,824 million. The words 'stop' and 'go' relate, it should be remembered, not to economic activity itself, but to the policies which the Government uses to control it. In its effort to fight inflation, the Government has sometimes deliberately restricted the rate at which economic activity has been increasing; but this is quite different from restricting the rate of economic activity itself. Britain as a whole cannot be said, in any accepted meaning of the words, to have suffered a slump at any time since 1951.

It is equally incontestable that the increase in national wealth has in some measure benefited nearly everyone in the community. For every shilling prices have risen in the last 11 years wages have risen by two shillings and pensions by 2s. 1d. The average level of salaries has also exceeded, though to a less startling extent, the rise in prices. The total effect is that the average person's standard of living has gone up by 40 per cent in 11 years; we have gone a long way, therefore, towards fulfilling the Government's aim, commonly derided when it was announced a few years ago, of doubling the standard of living in a quarter of a century. In terms of real earnings, the lion's share of this improvement has gone to wage-earners and the holders of stock; salaried employees have done relatively well, the self-employed professional classes, though their impression of steadily increasing poverty is false, have benefited only modestly; professional pensioners such as retired army officers have benefited very little.

One of the most suspect of Conservative claims has

certainly been thoroughly vindicated. There has been a steady and vast increase in the size of the social services. This is nowhere more startling than in relation to education. The Tories have built 6,000 schools since they came to power; their annual average of primary schools has been about 300 compared with Labour's figure of about 100; their annual average of secondary schools about 200 compared with Labour's figure of about 25.

The catalogue of improvements in welfare could be extended tiresomely, and Mr. Powell's ten-year programmes of hospital-building and local health service improvements supply one of the most striking recent additions to it.

All this, it may be said, bears the mark of party propaganda, and leaves unanswered the question of whether more could have been achieved by another government, or whether Conservatives can reasonably claim that some specifically Conservative element in their policy has alone enabled them to accomplish it.

Up to a point at least this claim is clearly justified. What has been going on has not been a uniform expansion of the social services on the Labour model, but an expansion directed in accordance with strict Conservative principles to satisfying particular needs. The Tory view that the Government's first task is to help the people look after themselves, and that it should assume responsibility for looking after them only when for one reason or another direct help is essential, has in fact and to an ever-increasing extent been the guiding light of welfare policy. Housing is an obvious case in point; the first task was simply to build houses to meet the desperate demand which Labour had failed to satisfy. Once the target of 300,000 was achieved, it was possible to embark on a rational and long-term housing policy designed mainly to meet the housing needs of those who genuinely could not afford to house themselves. The Rent Act introduced a long-absent note of economic realism. By relieving private landlords of some of the necessity of subsidising their tenants, it undoubtedly created many cases of hardship, but it also brought more houses to let on to the market and ensured that relatively well-to-do tenants should in future have to pay something more nearly approaching an economic rent for the privilege of being comfortably housed. The next stage in the operation was to challenge the principle of indiscriminate housing subsidies for council house tenants by encouraging local authorities to adopt differential rent schemes. At the same time, the Government has continuously and successfully striven to make it easier for the relatively poor to buy their own houses. The effect of these policies is to enable public expenditure on housing to be concentrated as never before on the really urgent task of wiping out the slums. Right-wing critics should remember that in relation to housing and the social services generally the Government inherited from its predecessors a country thoroughly obsessed by the idea of uniform, indiscriminate public welfare. That idea has been nowhere more disastrous in its effects than in relation to housing; slowly, and in the face of much criticism, it has been exorcised from housing policy. Had it remained, the Government's vast success in housing the people would certainly not have been achieved without inflation and the diversion of resources from other urgently needed forms of capital expenditure such as road building.

The accusation that under Conservative rule Britain has oscillated violently between frenzied economic activity and almost complete paralysis is obviously untrue. The accusation that the rich and the relatively rich have alone benefited from increasing prosperity is equally false. Given the national income during this period, it may be regarded as certain that any substantially greater increase in the social services than that which has occurred could not have been financed without inflation. Given this degree of expenditure on welfare as the upper limit, it may be said with some confidence that its distribution between different kinds of beneficiary has been about as equitable as it could have been. To this extent, the Tory record is impressive.

One charge, however, cannot be wholly refuted. The economy has not developed at the pace set by the other economies of Western Europe, and their comparatively late start after the war does not supply a full explanation. The impression remains (and the Government has scarcely denied it) that the spirit of British industry is intensely conservative. It may be said that more could have been done by special incentives to the export industries, and by a deliberate diversion of resources from consumption to capital investment. What is certain is that the indiscriminate encouragement of expenditure, such as has been persistently advocated by the Opposition, would have revived inflation.

The British economy has desperately needed a stimulus from outside. The Government tried to provide that stimulus by its application to join the Common Market, but the *deus ex machina* failed to appear for reasons for which no one blames Mr. Heath. Whether in fact, had it appeared, it would have done its job, is open to a good deal of expert doubt. It is certain that the chances of getting some sort of association with Europe on terms acceptable to both sides in British politics would have been infinitely better had Britain responded, between 1945 and 1951, to European initiatives.

With Europe for the moment closed to us, however, are we thrown back on the policy of 'stop-go', which has proved consistent with increasing national prosperity but has failed to develop our competitive power?

The Government will, no doubt, seek general tariff reductions, but so it always has done in recent years. It knows, and its informed critics also know, that increasing trade within the Commonwealth is not an effective alternative to more trade with Europe. It must look round for some other source of economic stimulation.

The idea of a combined effort by employers, trade unions and government to plan production and to remove obstacles to its growth has for long belonged to the realms of pious platitude. An institution, the National Economic Development Council, now exists to embody it. A dignified body setting targets for production, making lofty recommendations for the improvement of management and the elimination of restrictive practices by labour and seeking to co-ordinate private and public investment plans is not in itself an answer to an economic crisis. Few of Neddy's admirers will go so far as to predict that it will succeed in doing more than increasing the national sense of inadequacy; without an unprecedented degree of co-operation between capital and labour it cannot do more. On the other hand, if that co-operation were forthcoming, it could lead to a smooth and rapid development of the economy.

Precisely the same applies to the National Incomes Commission. The only merit that can honestly be claimed for it is that it exists and contains revolutionary potentialities for good. At any moment since the war the appearance of two bodies expressly charged with the task of guiding national economic development and setting out to achieve agreement between government, employers and unions on the pace and direction of this development would have been inconceivable. At the end of 11 years of Conservative rule it has become possible.

The kind of Britain which has emerged from these 11 years certainly does not conform to any blueprint of the Good Society. In terms of competitive capacity, it has yet to vindicate its right to survive. It has its spivs and its Lucky Jims, as communities differently organised have their corrupt and power-seeking bureaucrats; it has the vices of a community dedicated chiefly to the enjoyment of wealth; since it must perforce produce more wealth, and since these vices are a stimulus as well as a hindrance to production, they are not likely to be removed by any process of moral regeneration which it is in the power of politicians to start. It is also a society in which vastly more people own property than ever before, and in which, in general, the connection between ability and reward is closer and more obvious than it has been hitherto. It is, above all, a society which, while refusing to abolish its traditional institutions, has exposed them effectively to the test of usefulness. If, for example, the public schools survive, it will not be, for all radical critics may say, because they provide those who go to them with a monopoly of top jobs, but because they foster qualities which parents are prepared to pursue for their children at considerable sacrifice to themselves; if these establishments prove in reality to be nothing more than breeding-grounds of a trivial, even if innocent, kind of snobbery, they will die a natural death.

As far as the main item in British foreign policy is concerned, relations with Russia, the Government has been relatively free from major criticism from any quarter since it came to power. It can claim to have taken the initiative in 1955, and again in 1960, in reopening top-level contact with the Soviet Union. It has continued to play its part in containing Soviet expansion, and for several years Soviet expansion has been successfully contained. Exactly what measure of diplomatic freedom could be achieved within the limits of the American alliance, on which, in the last resort, we depend for our existence, is open to endless dispute, but that a substantial measure of freedom has continued to be exercised without impairing the alliance will not be denied by anyone. Whether Mr. Wilson would be better or worse than Mr. Macmillan in influencing and making friends with Americans is at present a purely speculative question, but it is certain that he would operate essentially within the same framework of necessity, and in doing so would use essentially the same methods.

In one fundamental respect, however, the Conservative party's policy abroad is, now for the first time, being seriously, and more or less unanimously, challenged by the Opposition. The impression that defence policy has been a muddle is, indeed, fairly widespread in all political parties.

Britain, it is argued, has failed to make an adequate contribution to conventional armament in the West. She has also wasted millions of pounds on producing and discarding nuclear weapons.

Clearly, any large increase in expenditure on conventional armaments could be made only at the cost of nuclear armament or of a substantial reduction in social services, and would certainly involve the re-introduction of conscription. Just as clearly, it is economically impossible for Britain, like the US, to experiment simultaneously with the production of a large number of nuclear weapons. Any choice between the alternatives open to her that she may make is liable to be outdated before or soon after the weapon is produced. Since we cannot produce any nuclear weapon without the US's help, our choice, as the affair of Skybolt showed, is still further limited.

Essentially, therefore, the Government's policy stands or falls by the crucial issue of whether, at almost any cost, Britain should insist on having some sort of nuclear deterrent, as up-to-date as possible, under her control at all times.

Already, it may be said, British foreign policy depends on a gigantic bluff, the assumption that Britain will be ready to engage in nuclear war, necessarily involving her own destruction, fortified only by the thought that she will be promptly avenged by her American ally. How much larger is the bluff implied in the notion that Britain will be prepared to enter a war without the assurance of American aid, on the assumption that if the enemy should deliver a nuclear attack against her, the loyal commander of a British Polaris submarine will mark his indignation at the destruction of his mother country by delivering a missile, large enough to cause considerable inconvenience, on the Soviet Union?

The calculations on which nuclear strategy now depends are indeed grotesque in character. Nevertheless, these calculations have provided a deterrent for several years. I can certainly think of no government, however radical, including any of those of Mr. Gladstone, which would have stripped this country of the only conceivably effective retort to a threat of extinction, yet it is precisely this that Mr. Macmillan is being urged to do.

Whether or not Britain is, or can remain, a great power is the subject of morbid and not very fruitful speculation. Under Tory rule she has preserved a measure of independence much greater than her material strength would, on the face of it, seem to justify; it is not easy to imagine a foreign policy which would have achieved more.

At the end of 11 years of Tory rule, Britain is neither a gambler's den nor a country in which the self-respecting, self-supporting middle classes are being subjected to a slower and more humane version of what happened to the kulaks. It is a country where ownership is more widely distributed than ever before, where there are more educational opportunities for more people than ever before and where there is a higher level of employment than anyone thought possible when the phrase 'full employment' was invented. We are still at peace and we are still playing a leading part in the diplomatic process by which peace is being maintained. It is almost arithmetically demonstrable that if the Labour party's declared policy at home had been pursued in the last 11 years, we would be in a condition of roaring inflation as fatal to the chance of preserving the social services as it would have been to the chance of increasing production. Nothing, I believe, but the frenzied boredom of political commentators with the task of describing the same men tackling the same problems for over a decade could even momentarily obscure these facts.

Enoch Powell, whose Toryism was in many respects identical to Utley's, was interviewed by the author as a prelude to the Conservative party conference that was to be diverted by Macmillan's resignation and Home's accession to the premiership. Powell, along with Iain Macleod, resigned his post of Minister of Health in protest at the treatment of R. A. Butler, whom he supported to succeed Macmillan.

Toryism for tomorrow

Interview with Enoch Powell: *Sunday Telegraph*, 6 October 1963

When I went to talk to Enoch Powell, Harold Wilson's programme for the New Britain was still ringing in my ears – harnessing Science to State, and harnessing State to Socialism, setting up five new Ministries, multiplying civil servants, and making Britain, as Richard Crossman nearly had the courage to point out, a land fit for bureaucrats. I could not help thinking as Enoch Powell and I talked, that in him I had in front of me the complete embattled opposite of the Wilson approach.

Enoch Powell is the philosopher statesman who, while relishing the bread-and-butter business of administration and politics as much as any of his colleagues, not only finds time but feels the need to think about the permanent meaning of what he is doing and to measure it by defined standards of political prudence and morality.

He begins with the doubts: 'I am worried, deeply worried,' he says, 'by two widely made assumptions which seem to dominate our thinking today in a way which they did not 10 years ago. The first is reflected in the mood of national self-abasement and pessimism typified in the July number of *Encounter*; the second is the habit of looking automatically to government for the solution whenever confronted by any kind of problem.

'Through these attitudes we can so easily slide into thinking that the only way to be rescued from ruin is by stripping ourselves of all our inherited characteristics, jettisoning all typically British methods of conducting life, abandoning all our proven systems of selection and decision-making, and consigning our destiny to the hands of a few omniscient technocrats.

'These attitudes are, in fact, ready-made instruments of persuasion at the disposal of the Labour party to further its electoral prospects. They oblige even Tory Governments to operate within the framework of an implicitly Socialist public opinion.'

This, as Powell sees it, is the Tory dilemma and the Tory challenge.

National self-depreciation, he contends, is pandered to by the habit of using deceptive or at best irrelevant statistics as whips with which to scourge ourselves. There is, for instance, no revealing conclusion about national decadence to be drawn from the fact – in which Left-wing economists now luxuriate – that Britain's percentage of world trade has declined in the last 10 years.

As the European nations have been recovering and new nations entering the arena of world trade, what other statistical effect do people expect? The same arithmetical process has been going on since the beginning of the century and before. And anyhow, what on earth is a percentage share of total world trade supposed to prove about a country's prosperity, progress and well-being?

Another trick of the purveyors of gloom is to record only the depressing aspects of every elementary fact about Britain's geographical and economic position in the world. 'They observe,' says Powell, 'that we are a large population packed into a small space. For them this means that we can easily be destroyed by a ruthless enemy whom we have failed to deter from attack. It never means, what is equally true and far more pertinent to the present, that we have the outstanding economic advantage of having all our resources, human and physical, in close proximity.'

But even if the mood of self-depreciation were well founded, where is the warrant for the belief that State direction is the path of salvation? That this is so prevalent is due to the superstitious reverence with which the technocrats have succeeded in investing themselves. If our progress is to be unfavourably contrasted with that of Germany, might it not be relevant to add that Germany is dedicated to a free enterprise economy? Many people, however, are prepared to believe the technocrats even when what they serve out is against their direct personal experience:

'The people chose,' says Powell, 'to live in the South rather than the North of England: they flocked in obedience to their own calculations of advantage southwards. They were proved abundantly right; they became in consequence richer than they ever had been before, and enjoyed better conditions of life. But now the technocrats say that they ought not to have done it at all, and the people meekly agree.

'Nothing can be more certain than that if the distribution of our population had been planned by a central authority 50 years ago we should have been infinitely worse off than we are now.'

The essence of the Tory faith, says Powell, is the conviction that salvation lies within the grasp of the people themselves, that, by their unhampered pursuit of their own insights, we shall forge ahead in the future just as we advanced in the past.

The State can and must maintain the value of money; it can legitimately pursue a foreign trading policy; it must finance defence and other national and public purposes out of taxation; and it may promote welfare services to modify the harshness of life, and secure basic but rising standards of material comfort to all people. But the State ought not to will specific economic development; it cannot will the good society. It can only set the framework within which society evolves according to its own genius and by means of an infinite series of private decisions directed to private ends but tempered by a rational patriotism and taken in the light of as much accurate information about the nation's activities and their total effect as central agencies like the NEDC and the NIC can supply.

How then does the Minister see the possibilities open to a
Tory in 20th-century government?

He knows that politics is the art of the possible and that
institutions which the nation has evolved must be respected
even though they arose in part from false doctrine. He is no
liberal radical wanting to scrap all the apparatus of government
control and start building a free society from scratch. But he
believes that two ideas are contending for the soul of Britain;
the idea of State Socialism and the idea of freedom, and that,
within the limits of what is possible without a counter-
revolution, the Government can encourage the forces of
freedom. He also sees the politician as a teacher who, by
constantly attacking false assumptions, can over the years help
to change the climate of opinion.

'Today,' says Powell, 'the Ministry of Health is perforce the
central spending authority; I must try to use the power that falls
to me as Minister as rationally as I can and with what little
foresight is ever vouchsafed to a planner. But I do claim that I
have used this power in a way different from that in which it
would have been exercised by one of other convictions.

'I have tried to build up and strengthen local agencies within
the national system; I have done all that lies in me to strengthen
and encourage voluntary effort and the voluntary bodies. I
have gone, some would say, to the length of adulation in
commending the activities of such independent bodies as the
King's Hospital Fund and the Nuffield Trust; I have jealously
guarded the frontiers between administration on the one side
and the territories of professional knowledge and skill, of
scientific research and of commercial enterprise on the other.'

What about education? That, in Powell's opinion, presents
far more difficulties than health.

'It is unnatural to the Tory to have to work on the assumption
that this activity, which of all others should be an expression of
spontaneous national character, can be directed from above; it
is repugnant to have to pretend to know the answers to such
fatuous questions as how many theologians Britain will need in
1985, and what proportion they should bear in the interests of
popular happiness to the number of physicists. Yet the State is
the main spending authority, and must seek to spend rationally.

'It is well that the State education policies should be controlled by men whose creed teaches them to respect local, professional and parental opinion and even the hopes, tastes and desires of the students and pupils themselves.'

But here Powell allows himself to wonder whether administrative ingenuity may one day devise a method of directly endowing students and allowing them by the free use of their endowments to take an active part in determining the content of university education.

Powell's convictions are unshaken by the suggestion that it may be difficult to win an election in the next year on the basis of a philosophy which deliberately eschews a programme of bigger and brighter Government intervention all round. He will not be bludgeoned by the argument that we have proceeded so far on the road to Socialism that efficiency demands we go the whole hog. 'Victory will be valueless unless we have chosen rightly the ground on which to fight.'

Here, then, is the making of a Tory manifesto. Before it is written off as more in keeping with the age of Peel than that of Macmillan, let us remember that it is essentially what won the last three elections and what, announced with the greater stridency and somewhat less elaborate syntax of Lord Hailsham, rescued the party from the trough of depression in 1957.

Once the Tories lost power in 1964, an ideological debate began on the role of government – a debate which would not be decisively resolved until 1979.

Planning or freedom first?

The Daily Telegraph, 28 January 1967

Which way will the Tory party go – towards a revival of the Macmillan policy of comprehensive planning 'based on consent' or towards a considerably freer economy, with the

State maintaining the framework, making *ad hoc* interventions to achieve particular objects and, especially, offering discriminatory social help to the needy?

The formulas of Conservative policy are at present so constructed as to allow either interpretation. No doubt, there must be divergent elements in any Tory programme which stands a chance of success, but what are their relative proportions to be?

Early last year, the Conservative Political Centre published on the same day two pamphlets – one by Sir Edward Boyle and one by Mr. Russell Lewis. Sir Edward's sketched a policy of Tory planning based on intimate co-operation between government and industry and the maintenance of a wages policy; Mr. Lewis's offered a recipe of radical reform for the economy, including the scrapping of wages policy, a wholesale reform of the social services and a ruthless attack on restrictions even of so cherished a kind as those on the sale of alcohol.

Both programmes are reconcilable with the broad principles of Conservatism as currently defined; but this is a criticism of the principles, for, in practice, the differences between Mr. Lewis and Sir Edward are at least as wide as those between Sir Edward and Mr. Stewart.

To which pronouncement should be the political commentator, anxious to assess Mr. Heath's mind, attach the more weight? Sir Edward is deputy chairman of the Policy Advisory Committee; Mr. Lewis is Mr. Heath's choice as Director of the CPC, the main source of sophisticated Tory propaganda.

Even more striking of course are the apparent differences between Sir Edward and Mr. Enoch Powell. Mr. Powell regards it as his appointed function to criticise the heresies absorbed by the Conservative party during the Macmillan administration. He is now commonly regarded as a pure exponent of the philosophy of Adam Smith, as one who would jettison all controls and virtually dismantle the State in its economic aspect. Can there be a place for such a man in the modern Conservative party? Would even Sir Robert Peel, let alone Disraeli, have put up with him?

The answer is, surely, that Powellism, the most valuable single ingredient in Conservatism today, is 'not so much a programme, more a way of life'. For most of the time Mr.

Powell is attacking doctrines, not policies. He has, more skilfully than anyone else, pointed out the immorality of bringing moral pressure to bear on the public to co-operate in the carrying out of controversial policies not authorised by law. He has cast useful doubt on the actual economic advantages to be derived from trade union membership. He probably speaks more persuasively to a wider audience than any of his colleagues.

When it comes to the point, however, the actual deviations in policy which Mr. Powell recommends are, with one exception, of comparatively small importance. If his plans for a radical reduction of overseas commitments, in respect both of defence and economic aid, were accepted, the country's economic position would be revolutionised. Short of this – and it is the aspect of Powellism which attracts least attention – the practical differences between him and his colleagues do not seem insuperable. Even Powellism would be consistent with a small amount of *ad hoc* first aid to the afflicted regions of Britain; it would surely also be consistent with a general policy of fostering restraint in wage claims, provided of course that this was not described as wages policy.

Mr. Powell, as his recent book on health shows, does not seriously believe in the possibility of reform. Like Prof. Oakeshott, he thinks we live in the best of all possible worlds and that everything in it is a necessary evil.

Fundamentally, the choice before the Tories is between a policy which assumes planning and makes concessions to freedom and one which assumes freedom and holds the power of the State in reserve to correct its excesses. It is the second kind of policy which Tories want.

In one respect the party, under Mr. Heath's leadership, has moved significantly towards it. It has attacked compulsory wage control and offered the trade union movement freedom and responsibility within the limits of the law in exchange for privilege in relation to their members plus subjection to Government. This, Mr. Heath's major strategic decision, could win the support of many natural Labour voters. To my mind, it matters very little that this move has been combined with a careful preservation of the right to urge, not to force, wage restraint.

In the most crucial area of policy revision – the reform of the social services – on the other hand, progress has been dangerously slow. The formula is clear enough – help given to those in need and denied to those who are not, and reasonable choice between different types of service. The first point has been partially but timidly accepted, the second is still shunned in terror.

Short of a revolution in defence policy, to which the party will not commit itself, what hope is there of offering those large tax incentives to effort, which represent the Tories' chief promise, without some curb on public expenditure in fields like education and health? What chance is there of ever having adequate services in these fields if provision continues to depend almost wholly on what can be spirited out of the taxpayers' pocket?

Above all, how can the Tory party, without grotesque hypocrisy, preach the gospel of personal independence and family life while continuing to withdraw all major decisions about personal welfare from private hands? Yet, among articulate Conservatives, Mr. Geoffrey Howe is almost alone in systematically advocating a fundamental reform of welfare.

There are schemes in plenty, and with respectable expert support, for adjusting welfare provision to need and making it compatible with personal choice (for instance, the educational voucher plan, the numerous proposals for changes in the finance of medicine and the idea of subsidising householders rather than housing). Official Conservatives (with the significant exception of the astute and imaginative Mr. Macleod) offer not the least encouragement to such thinking. While Socialism challenges the last strongholds of independence in education, for example, Tories have to content themselves with the bland reservations of Sir Edward Boyle, whose social philosophy is barely distinguishable from that of Mr. Crosland.

In a scarcely less important sector – that of State action to increase competitive efficiency in the economy – the party is equally out of touch with reality. Such concrete thinking as is done is due entirely to the personally financed exertions of Mr. Ernest Marples. No doubt, here as elsewhere, the Tory party has access to 'experts', but I suspect that too many of these advisers wear the compulsory pink of the academic establishment.

Welfare reform and the encouragement of productive efficiency are the two most glaring gaps in Conservative policy formation. If, from his still unchallenged position as leader, Mr. Heath could fill them, he would do much to restore confidence both in the authenticity of his Conservatism and in the breadth of his political imagination.

He has already done more than his critics are prepared to concede to modify the Macmillan inheritance. He is manifestly a revisionist, and it is no criticism of him that he is not by temperament an evangelist like Mr. Powell.

The fact remains, however, that the process of revision is proceeding far too slowly. It is still not clear to the country what kind of Conservative party we have or with which ear Mr. Heath is listening more attentively.

To command the economic heights . . .

The Daily Telegraph, 28 July 1967

And so the shuttlecock of British post-war politics comes to rest – or does it? Today, the public sector of the British iron and steel industry is formally vested in the control of the British Steel Corporation under the chairmanship of a relatively young merchant banker, Lord Melchett.

Of course, roughly the same thing has happened before. On 15 February 1951, the State took over steel much more comprehensively than it takes it over today.

The difference was that the Labour Government of that day had only a minute majority in the Commons and was living under what was virtually sentence of death. Nothing was more certain than that within a few months the Tories under Churchill would have returned triumphantly to power and that, at the earliest opportunity, they would return steel to private ownership. In 1953, the Iron and Steel Act, which provided for the resale of the industry to private purchasers was law.

By 1960 all the steel companies with the obstinate – and, as it was proved, permanent – exception of Richard Thomas and Baldwins, were back in private hands.

Today, the outlook is very different. A more than comfortable Labour majority is likely to be in possession of power for at least another three years. The new Corporation will at least have time to alter the structure of the industry radically – for better of worse.

On the face of it, however, the Tories remain implacably opposed to steel nationalisation. At Llandudno in May, Mr. Heath declared roundly that the industry would be denationalised again by the next Tory Government. On the second reading of the Steel Bill, which is now an Act, Mr. Anthony Barber made what was essentially the same point in somewhat more circumspect language:

> We shall therefore repeal this Bill and we shall denationalise the industry to whatever extent is necessary and practicable to conform with the principles which I have mentioned and to provide the disciplines of competitive enterprise.

Clearly, the extent to which denationalisation proves practicable will depend in the first instance on the ability of a future Conservative Government to persuade people to commit their private fortunes to the steel industry. In a few years from now, who will want and have the means to buy Lord Melchett out? In 1951, prospective shareholders in a restored private industry had only to wait their moment. Today, it is impossible to foresee how great or slight will be the investor's demand for a stake in a future privately owned steel industry.

If nationalisation appears, in commercial terms, to have succeeded, the demand will no doubt be proportionately greater than if it seems to have failed. By the same token, however, the political case for denationalisation will have been weakened.

The point is crucial. The Tories are not a doctrinaire party. Three-quarters of their more popular arguments against steel nationalisation have indeed consisted of self-congratulatory reflections on the superiority of the practical to the theoretical approach. If the steel industry were to appear to be prospering under its new régime, the case for reopening the controversy would be seriously damaged.

Shrewd doubts may exist about the likelihood of the Tory party's being subjected to this particular embarrassment. Steel exports are at present extremely high, but steel imports also are running at an unprecedented and dangerous level: hence the Corporation's decision to offer its British customers a bribe in the shape of a substantial discount available to all users of wide strip steel who will agree to buy these products exclusively from it.

In general, it may be assumed that Mr. Marsh was showing no more than ordinary prudence in remarking in the Commons last January that '. . . the Corporation's initial results may well be rather depressing.'

Little is yet known about the industry's future structure. It will be divided into four parts, and these regional groups will be encouraged to compete with each other in everything except prices. In practice, however, how much autonomy will they have? In strict constitutional terms, none whatsoever, since those directing them will simply be the employees of the central body.

Then again, the relations of the public and private sectors have yet to be worked out in practice. In terms of crude steel production, of course, the private sector is a pathetic remnant. It is also the public sector's chief customer and its dependant in respect of many essential common services. In terms of the production of special steels, however, the private companies will still be responsible for a quarter of outside sales (calculated in monetary terms) and will therefore be powerful competitors with the Steel Corporation.

In short, within the terms of the act which is now its charter, the steel industry may develop into a monopolistic giant or, if relative wisdom prevails, may continue to display many of the characteristics of a privately run industry, including a diffusion of responsibility and a measure of competitiveness – but not of course including the most essential characteristic of all, a financial discipline arising from a genuine liability to bankruptcy.

In one respect of supreme importance, the role of steel in British politics is now bound to change. In the forties the steel industry represented the frontier post between two types of socialism – the type that would have confined public control to service industries and that which demanded the nationalisation of manufacturing industry as well. The Rubicon has now been well and truly crossed. In 1965, the public sector of the British economy as a whole (including, of course, such State activities as education) accounted for 45 per cent of gross fixed capital formation and 23 per cent of all workers. This trend is bound to continue.

If the Government now gives itself enabling powers, as it seems certain to do, to acquire shares in private industry, the whole question of steel's future will be set in a new context. Steel will be only one element in a rapidly expanding public sector into which the other remaining 'commanding heights' (chemicals, oil and electronics, already largely dependent on the State) will be increasingly drawn. The Tories will have a far broader target to attack than the nationalised steel industry.

By the same token, Labour, equipped with subtler and for that reason more dangerous means of extending public control, will be less inclined to fight to the death for nationalisation as an institution. A future Labour Government, inheriting a denationalised steel industry from Tory predecessors, will not conceive itself to be under an absolute obligation of honour to renationalise.

What is more, the formula of mixed ownership (though intended to promote the cause of Socialism by stealth) cuts both ways. It should make it easier for a future Tory Government to sell the steel industry back to private hands in a gradual and piecemeal fashion.

A straightforward denationalisation of steel might well embarrass the Tories, making them look as pedantic and dogmatic as their opponents and as indifferent to constitutional continuity. Logically, of course, there is no reason why it should. There is grave danger in the view (already being canvassed, incidentally, in relation to the future of the public schools) that, when one political party insists on permanently lodging in its programme a thoroughly misguided and not particularly popular proposal, decency requires the other to 'take the issue out of politics' either by acquiescing or by agreeing to some ludicrous compromise.

In the case of steel, however, I predict that no such dilemma will arise. In short, tomorrow's battle will be on a far broader front – the aim will not so much be to restore steel as to preserve the pathetic vestiges of a free economy and turn back the tide of collectivism.

What is more, the Tories will not be defending the steel industry as it existed until last night – itself a relic of the restrictive, semi-socialist Toryism of the thirties – but the concept of a new industry not controlled by Government so much as forced by Government to be competitive, and shaped in such a way as at least not to hinder Britain's entry into the Common Market.

Vesting day closes a chapter in the political history of Britain. In the chapters that lie ahead, the Tories will not be preoccupied with the defence of a particular vital area of the economy but rather, uncongenial as the thought may be to some, with the advocacy of principles for the reform of that economy as a whole.

The upsurge of interest in Enoch Powell that followed his 'rivers of blood' speech in April 1968 led to Utley's writing a book on a politician whose style had become increasingly fascinating to him. These two articles are extracts from that book, Enoch Powell, the Man and his Thinking, *published by William Kimber.*

Enoch Powell: for better or worse?

Sunday Telegraph, 8 September 1968

Enoch Powell's first intimation of the interest aroused by his Birmingham speech on immigration on Saturday, April 20, this year, was a telephone call from Mr. Heath at nine o'clock on the following evening dismissing him from the Shadow Cabinet. He was, he professes, wholly astonished at the stir he had caused.

Mr. Heath read Powell's speech for the first time in the form in which it was reported in the Sunday Press. By lunchtime he had summoned the Chief Whip, Mr. William Whitelaw, from Cumberland and himself driven up from Broadstairs to his flat in Albany. By nine o'clock his mind was made up, and an hour later he publicly announced his decision to sack Powell for a speech which was 'racialist in tone and liable to exacerbate racial tensions'.

In the West Midlands, Powell's speech appeared to be a vigorous though not particularly shocking or even particularly original contribution to a familiar debate. To almost all the political and journalistic establishment elsewhere, it was instantly apparent that it was dynamite. Friends, enemies and neutrals all immediately recognised it as a challenge either to the authority of Mr. Heath and the Shadow Cabinet or even to the whole politics of consensus on the racial issue.

Powell was throughout convinced that his speech was wholly consistent with the doctrine of his party. May he not in retrospect have underestimated the extent to which by dramatising that doctrine and drawing out what he thought to be its ultimate implications, he was making an important impact on politics and taking a decisive step in his career?

What gave the speech its special flavour was the technique which Powell chose to employ of allowing his constituents or their friends to speak for themselves through direct quotation. He could rationally claim that by reproducing these striking passages he was not expressing his own feeling or even reporting his own observations but simply providing evidence of the strength of feeling among the white inhabitants of the Midlands.

The hard core of his argument depended upon one statistic supplied by the spokesman of the Registrar-General's office. It was that in 15 or 20 years there would be three-and-a-half million Commonwealth immigrants and their descendants in the United Kingdom. The value of this statistic was at least disputable. In October, 1967, Mr. David Ennals, of the Home Office, computed that in 1985 the coloured population would be nearer two-and-a-half million. The Commonwealth Immigrants Act of 1968, by cutting down the hitherto unrestricted inflow of Kenyan Asians to only 1,500 a year, ensured a further reduction. In order to enforce his argument Powell undoubtedly chose the highest estimate available. It was almost certainly a false estimate.

What is most remarkable, however, is the extreme generality and unoriginality of the practical conclusions about future policy to which this analysis led Powell. On the future level of immigration, he concluded that 'nothing will suffice but that the total inflow for settlement should be reduced at once to negligible proportions, and that the necessary legislative and administrative measures be taken without delay.' On the case of dependants, he stated, philosophically, 'It can be no part of any policy that existing families should be kept divided; but there are two directions in which families can be reunited, and if our former and present immigration laws have brought about the division of families, albeit voluntarily or semi-voluntarily, we ought to be prepared to arrange for them to be re-united in their countries of origin.'

The Tory party had already committed itself to the principle that future immigrants, before being admitted, should be obliged to state how many dependants they had who might eventually wish to follow them. It was also committed to the view that generous financial help should be given to any immigrant who wanted to return to his own country.

Powell might well claim that he was doing more than putting the most stringent possible interpretation on his party's commitments. What he cannot be acquitted of is the charge of skirting round the one major moral dilemma which has perplexed the Tories in their consideration of this problem for the past year or so.

It is one thing to recommend a drastic reduction in the number of immigrants to whom work vouchers should be granted. It is also morally easy to refuse work vouchers to immigrants who are likely to bring a large number of dependants in their train. It is quite another matter for a party which is fond of preaching the sanctity of the family and the honouring of pledges to assert that immigrants already established here (who came on the assumption that their relations would be allowed to follow them) should be told that in future they are forbidden to bring dependants over.

That dilemma cannot be solved by suggesting that the

immigrants should go home and be helped financially to do so. Suppose they decline to go home: are they to be deported? Or are they to be allowed to remain only on condition that they accept continued separation from their families? Powell's words suggest that it is this second alternative which he is recommending, but a certain amount of ambiguity is allowed to remain.

Powell is emphatically not a racialist in the only intelligible meaning of that expression – one who believes in the natural inferiority of some races to others and in the justice of legal and social arrangements designed to register that inferiority. He may fairly be described as a nationalist in the sense that he believes that a degree of cultural homogeneity is necessary to the stability of society. To that extent he believes (and who can rationally gainsay him?) that the cultural and racial composition of the community and the speed with which that composition changes are proper concerns of government.

To neglect these concerns, he is passionately convinced, is to endanger the survival of the State, the security of the rule of law and the sacred convention of equal respect for different cultural groups within the State's jurisdiction. Had they been stated thus abstractly, Powell's beliefs might have been dismissed as a collection of tired platitudes. As it was, his dramatic rendering of them turned British politics upside down.

Why was this moment chosen for what was evidently a carefully if subconsciously planned explosion? Ever since 1962, when Mr. Macmillan's Government imposed limits on the rights of citizens of the Commonwealth to enter this country, the trend in all parties has been towards an increasing recognition of the fact that Commonwealth immigration into Britain constitutes a serious social problem.

On the whole question of immigration, the Conservative party suffers an acute and perennial *crise de conscience*. Both its liberal and its imperialist wings have special reasons for supporting the concept of the multi-racial society. Many Conservatives, for one reason or the other, were reluctant to oppose the second Race Relations Bill of February, 1968, extending the legal protection afforded to immigrants.

A reasoned amendment to the Bill, implying sympathy with its aims but belief that the means proposed for achieving them would be ineffective and harmful, was drafted by the Shadow Cabinet, and Powell voted for it in the Commons after his Birmingham speech.

There can be little doubt that this decision of the Shadow Cabinet was a signal victory for what may roughly be described as the Right wing. Had Powell's speech not been made, the party's handling of the Bill would almost certainly have been interpreted as proof that at long last Heath had been captured by the Right. In the event, this triumph of the Right was gratuitously thrown away.

There is little doubt also that Powell's speech angered, perplexed and disturbed in various degrees almost all his colleagues in the Shadow Cabinet. It also enabled Heath to do what the evidence suggests he would have gladly done at several points in the last two years – remove Powell from the Shadow Cabinet.

Possibly because he is the first Conservative leader to owe his position to a free election among back benchers, Heath has been exceptionally sensitive to the least suggestion of criticism from his colleagues. Powell's speeches, mainly directed towards advocating the merits of a wholly or almost entirely free economy, seemed to Heath to be driving the Conservative party too far and too fast along a dangerous road. Outright condemnations of incomes policies in any form and strongly implied criticisms of regionalism particularly rankled. More than a year ago he was in the habit of saying that 'the less Enoch talks the better.'

Powell has achieved a style of oratory which marks him out as one of the most forceful of present-day parliamentarians, though it does not quite place him in the historic ranks of the great. As a speaker, the most that can be said of Heath is that his patient and undistinguished discourses give his audiences the impression that he is a man who understands his subject; it would be too much to say that, when he sits down, his audiences also understand.

Powell's reputation has rested in recent years on the sustained talent for exaggeration; Heath's on an infinite gift for understatement. Powell more easily hits the headlines than his leader does. A breach between the two men was inevitable.

From this breach Powell has derived certain clear advantages and disadvantages. On the debit side, he is now effectively removed from direct influence on the strategy and tactics of his party. In Parliament, his position has on balance been weakened. In the country, it has been improved to a positively revolutionary extent.

Powell has a surprising and not easily explicable knack of appealing to working-class audiences, particularly in the Midlands. He is also meat and drink to the journalists. Among a section of the politically articulate young, particularly in the universities, he has fervent admirers.

It must have been painfully apparent to him, however, by April of this year that reasoned expositions of the fallacies involved in Prices and Incomes policy, humorous assaults on the questionnaires sent to hotel keepers by the Board of Trade and learned dissertations on the need for a floating pound were not likely to make him into a popular political hero. Certainly, his advocacy of withdrawal from foreign commitments is not the kind of aphrodisiac to which Tory-minded working men traditionally respond. Immigration is the one note which Powell has struck in the hearts of the people.

It has been the dream of many Conservative politicians to forge a genuinely democratic Tory movement, to rise to power on a wave of evangelical enthusiasm, to present themselves not in the characteristically Conservative role of safe men with their feet on the ground but in the role of prophets expressing the native sentiments of simple people in vigorous and intelligible language. Such was the ambition of Lord Randolph Churchill and that of Joseph Chamberlain.

It is a kind of ambition which is particularly repellent to the ordinary run of Conservative politicians, who prefer to think of themselves as divinely commissioned to control rather than to express popular enthusiasm. Over and again, however, the Conservative party has been revived by movements of this kind and to their exasperation, the more conventional Conservative leaders have been forced to try and contain these movements within the party's framework.

Certainly, the signs are that it is for such a role that Enoch

Powell is cast and that the chief internal problem for the Tory leadership during the next decade will be that of containing and taming his disciples. What kind of a man is the author of this challenge to Tory orthodoxy? What is the precise nature of the challenge? What are its potentialities for good and evil? These questions may prove to be of far more importance to the country's and the party's future than speculations about the succession to the leadership.

John Enoch Powell was born in the Black Country on June 16, 1912. Both his parents were schoolteachers, and he was a child of extreme intellectual precocity and phenomenal industry.

These qualities have borne fruit in a career probably of more varied distinction than that of any other contemporary British politician. Educated at King Edward's, Birmingham, one of the best of ancient English grammar school foundations, he went as an open scholar to Trinity, Cambridge, took a brilliant degree in Classics and collected a glittering array of academic awards including Cambridge's blue ribbon of classical scholarship, the Craven prize.

He has been a Fellow of Trinity, and a Professor of Greek at the University of Sydney. During the war, he rose from the rank of private to that of Brigadier in the Royal Warwickshire Regiment and became a member of the General Staff. He was a member of the committee which laid the foundations for the reorganised defence forces in India and Pakistan. He collaborated in the production of a major work on strategy, 'War in Three Dimensions'.

He has held Wolverhampton South-West for 18 years, in the process converting this largely working-class constituency into a safe Conservative seat, refused office in Governments three times, held two junior Ministerial posts, been an outstandingly successful Minister of Health, and served in one Cabinet and two Shadow Cabinets.

He has translated the 'Historia' of Thucydides and large parts of Herodotus, edited an ancient Welsh manuscript (learning the language for the purpose), published three books of verse in English, collaborated in the production of a history of Britain, completed much of a history of the House of Lords, written a book on saving and innumerable pamphlets on political, social and economic subjects. He was once an interpreter in Urdu.

It is not surprising that such a man should have become a myth in his own lifetime. 'Vast intellect and phenomenal industry' – these are the qualities which friends and critics alike concede, with only slight and somewhat peevish reservations on the part of the more intellectually gifted of his political colleagues.

Powell's contemporaries at King Edward's recall him as a pale youth with stooping shoulders, almost wholly devoted to his books. He avoided games and his only relaxations seem to have been the clarinet and gymnastics. In this last activity he was, to the unending amazement of his schoolfellows, astonishingly proficient. It had the merit of providing healthy exercise and was not open to the charge of frivolity.

Powell seems to have inspired awe but remarkably little hostility in his schoolmates. They included many who have since achieved outstanding distinction, but even they seem to remember him over the years with a touch of trepidation. They find his public demeanour now almost incredibly human. Nothing, however, has surprised them more than their old schoolfellow's brilliant military career. At school, Powell never joined the Officers' Training Corps and is said to have held schoolboy soldiering in undisguised contempt.

A man who was somewhat senior to him at King Edward's and who is now a distinguished scholar and churchman remembers Powell as one of the youngest but quite the cleverest member of the classical Sixth. He also remembers feeling obliged, as secretary of the King Edward's Old Boys' Association at Cambridge, to visit the prodigy on his arrival at Trinity. He found him, on a bitter November morning, in an attic room in New Court. There was no fire in the grate and Powell, covered in an overcoat and rugs, was reading Thucydides.

His visitor asked him if he would care to come to tea: Powell simply replied 'No.' In a renewed effort to break the ice, his school friend sauntered across the room and lit a cigarette. 'Please don't smoke,' said Powell. This was the last time the two men exchanged words for getting on for 20 years.

The next occasion was a visit by Powell to a university where the distinguished churchman now held an eminent post. Powell chatted affably and had almost dissipated his host's sense of awe when, learning that he was now a standing authority on an obscure aspect of Biblical scholarship, he asked him whether he had ever read an unusually obscure work on that subject by a Levantine scholar. With a chagrin from which he has never recovered, the churchman was forced to confess that he had never heard of it. Powell himself knew it intimately.

There can be no doubt that at this stage Powell's imagination was fired by the current idea of what the true classical scholar was like. Its chief ingredients were industry, detachment and terseness – the uncharitable would say positive rudeness – in the conduct of personal relations. Powell seems to have done his best to live up to this image. His ambition was to be the greatest living authority on Thucydides and few of his contemporaries doubted that he would achieve it.

It was the war which changed the course of Powell's life. It confronted him for the first time with the need to apply his formidable intellect and his astonishing memory to practical problems of organisation. It was not long before he had brilliantly vindicated the proposition that a classical education is a training for most things. His part in the organising of supply lines in the Middle East won golden opinions, but it was his transfer to India which made the decisive difference.

He saw in India a unique example of the power of a minority, united by a strong national tradition and equipped with the hereditary skills of a ruling class, to produce a deep and beneficent influence on a distant and alien land. He was fascinated by the love-hate relationship which seemed to bind rulers and ruled inextricably together. The vision of the Indian Empire appealed as much to his reason as to his romanticism; it was a unique example of the potentialities of the political art.

When an account comes to be given of the evolution of Powell's political ideas, the full extent of the impact of his Indian experience will be clear. It explains the highly distinctive character of his Toryism. Paradoxically, it also explains the strong anti-imperialistic flavour of his current thinking about defence and foreign policy. The premise of Powellism is quite simply that the Indian Empire has been lost.

Meantime, his whole personality was being modified by the experience of military service. It is impossible to be a recluse in the Army. It was equally impossible, however, for Powell to develop overnight into a genial messmate.

He once had to spend several days crossing the desert in a three-ton truck in the company of a typical cavalry officer – a characteristic product of the public school system and a man of fairly exalted social rank, but of only modest academic attainments. Powell put the occasion, he says, to the best possible use by giving his companion a concise course of instruction in Greek and Roman history in return for a detailed description of the appurtenances of an English gentleman.

Both felt themselves to have benefited immensely from the exchange. In particular, it gave Powell his introduction to the theoretical principles of foxhunting. On his return to England, he soon joined a hunt, travelling to its meets on the Tube.

Powell is almost entirely destitute of social self-consciousness and is wholly free from anything which might be stigmatised as snobbery. He has, however, a detached and almost scientific interest in the traditions and customs of what used to be called the English ruling class. The romantic elements in his philosophy of politics still consist largely of admiration for the techniques of social and political leadership which that class evolved.

The most important factor in the humanisation of Powell, however, was his marriage in 1952 to Pamela Wilson, once his secretary at the Conservative Research Department and a soldier's daughter. Innumerable stories are told of their courtship, which did not run smooth. There was the initial difficulty that Powell seldom if ever addressed his secretary for any other purpose than to give her an instruction. She is alleged to have taken bets with her colleague on how long it would be before she could induce him to bid her good morning.

When marriage came it produced an instant and dramatic effect on Powell's character. His austerity diminished; his essentially friendly nature became more obvious even to casual acquaintances; he ceased to be a total abstainer from alcohol and graduated via an occasional glass of sherry to an appreciation of wines. He was said by those who knew him well to be 'greatly relaxed'. He has remained a far more domestic animal than most politicians. Much of his work is done from home, his wife still often acting as his secretary. He is a conspicuously devoted father of two daughters.

At a deeper level, it may be supposed that the development of Powell's personality since before the war has been influenced by his conversion to the Anglican faith. He is a punctilious churchman. As a young man he was a confirmed atheist. His moral convictions were humanist and Hellenic. He was also considerably affected by his reading of Nietzsche. His critics have been delighted to discover these lines in a poem which he published in the 1930s:

> I hate the ugly, hate the old,
> I hate the lame and weak.
> But most of all I hate the dead,
> Who lie so still in their earthen bed,
> And never dare to rise.

Many a young man who has afterwards progressed to unchallenged respectability has written as wildly and as culpably before. Yet, it would be idle to maintain that these lines convey no clue to the character of Powell. He still believes in the inevitability of conflict between nations and men and, in certain fields, in the positive fruitfulness of such conflict.

The final result of all this is a character strikingly different from the conventional idea of what a politician is like. He is almost wholly destitute of smoothness. It is not only his carefully prepared political speeches which are rigorously classical in structure and remorselessly precise in expression. Even his casual conversation has these qualities. He seldom talks for the purpose of clarifying his own thoughts. They have already been thoroughly formulated and documented long before they are expressed. The intellectual wrapping in which they are presented is often so impressive that the flaws in the argument only become clear, to the infinite frustration of his adversaries, long after the argument is over. 'Powell,' one of his former Cabinet colleagues remarked, 'has the best mind in politics until it has been made up.'

Two mutually inconsistent views of Powell's character remain to be explained. In the first place, there is the impression, which is certainly his greatest political asset, that he is a man of 'extraordinary integrity'; that he consults only his principles and that no consideration of mere expediency will divert him from the duty of stating and supporting them to the best of his ability.

Insofar as this implies that Powell is indifferent to the consequences of his political actions, this is an almost fantastically false view. Few men calculate more closely the effects of their words and actions. Insofar as it means simply that Powell considers deeply the moral implications of what he is doing, it is undoubtedly right.

While being praised by the Press for his integrity, however, Powell has more than once been accused by his colleagues of showing less than total loyalty. Many of those who have worked closely with him have carried away the view that his actions are unpredictable. The most recent and outstanding example of that view was the reaction of his Shadow Cabinet colleagues to his speech on immigration.

How are these apparently opposite reputations to be reconciled? The key, I believe, is to be found in the solitariness which even now is one of Powell's most outstanding characteristics. The Army, marriage, religion and politics have transformed Powell's personality beyond instant recognition, but they have not destroyed his ultimate detachment. His colleagues say that in Cabinet and in committee he talks comparatively little. When he does it is to announce and defend with precision conclusions at which he has already arrived in private. Most men's minds are formed in conversation with their peers; Powell's is not.

Much that passes for loyalty and comradeship in politics depends on the observance of a convention of relaxed and even slovenly conversation. Men win trust by seeming to have nothing to conceal and by conducting their thinking in public. The very qualities which make Powell an awkward colleague also unfit him for conspiracy. What is more, his unsparing intellectual honesty leads him, both in public and private relations, to a more systematic, carefully thought out definition of his moral obligations than most men are capable of. It is the very rigour and exactness of that definition which often arouse the suspicion of those who work with him.

He is, as a consequence, never wholly absorbed in a team; his relations with others are systematised on the basis of a precise casuistry from which he never deviates. He knows, to his own satisfaction, exactly what candour requires him to reveal to his colleagues and what he is justified in keeping to himself. Inevitably, his own ideas on this point sometimes prove different from theirs. On these occasions, he is often genuinely surprised and injured by the ferocity of their reactions. Yet, the impact of the shock, one suspects, is generally reduced by Powell's lack, rare in a politician, of any conspicuous wish to please. Generous, affectionate and almost imperturbably (one might say complacently) tolerant by nature, Powell's loyalty is, nevertheless, primarily to principles. Men with far less exacting consciences and infinitely slovenly minds have a larger capacity for political friendship.

This temperamental isolation, and the strength and weaknesses which go with it, may well prove in the end to be the decisive factors in Powell's political fate.

How strong is the Powell challenge?

Sunday Telegraph, 15 September 1968

Enoch Powell entered the House of Commons in 1950 as a distinguished member of the Butler kindergarten. He had worked in the Conservative Research Department. He was of comparatively humble origin. His war record was outstanding.

In all these respects, he was typical of a group of young men who, it was thought, were designed to propel the Conservative party into the 20th century. They would re-interpret Conservative principles. They would put an end to the notion that the Conservative party was an upper-class institution controlled by the stupid. They would provide an intellectually valid answer to Socialism.

Powell's own contribution to their restatement of the principles of social and economic Conservatism was recognised as outstanding. Yet he remained intensely preoccupied with imperial affairs, and in particular with the destinies of India.

It is said that while he was working for the Conservative Research Department in the years before he entered Parliament he was sent to see Winston Churchill to assist in the preparation of a speech on India. When the interview was over, Churchill rang up the Research Department to ask, 'Who is that young madman who has been telling me how many divisions I would need to re-conquer India?'

Powell bitterly opposed the decision to set a date for the ending of British rule before agreement had been reached on what was to follow it. He passionately believed in the duty and the possibility of preserving the Indian Empire until eventually it had evolved into a stable and self-governing part of the Commonwealth. The abandonment of India seemed to him to be as much an act of self-mutilation as the abandonment of Kent might have seemed to others.

What has to be explained is the almost incredible contrast between Powell in the early 1950s and Powell today. In home policy, the moderate Butlerite, the defender of a tempered form of capitalism, has become the apparently fanatical advocate of a *laissez-faire* economy in which the State is limited to the function of an overall monetary regulator and a keeper of the general rules. In foreign affairs he is now, at least by reputation, the ruthless advocate of a policy of withdrawal from distant overseas commitments and total concentration on the defence of Europe.

He is now disposed to argue that the British Empire always cost the people of these islands more than it was worth. It was a burden to be borne from duty. Freed from it, we are at liberty to rethink our defence and foreign policies starting from the assumption that their aim is simply the defence of these islands.

This transition in Powell's thinking is characteristic of his mind. He is not a man who starts out from abstract principles which he proceeds to apply to changing situations. Equally, he does not believe that politics is a hand-to-mouth affair, a succession of expedients to meet unforeseen and unforeseeable situations. In his mind, circumstances are almost everything, not only because they limit the possibilities of action but also because they positively indicate the kind of action required.

To him any given set of historical facts points to a policy. There is a latent order in human affairs which it is the business of statesmanship to perceive and realise. Politicians, he believes, are always free to ignore the intimations of history, but they do so at their own and at their nation's peril.

The starting-point of his political thinking is that Britain must in future regard herself as a European power. It is on the Continent of Europe alone – or almost alone – that she can effectively apply force. By concentrating all the force she has there, she can maximise her influence in the world. Hence, the total reversal of Powell's position in this field.

Powell's capacity to pursue the two distinct roles of prophet and administrator simultaneously, exemplified by his vigorous tenure of the Ministry of Health from 1960 to 1963, is undoubtedly one of the main sources of the distrust and bewilderment which he often inspires. He administered energetically not only because he believed that the Health Service as it was constituted demanded such treatment, but also because he loved administration. How long would his convinced liberalism – his passion for individual freedom and his deep scepticism of the beneficence and efficacy of government – last if he were ever effectively in charge of a government?

Of the popular illusions about Enoch Powell none is more obstinate than the notion that he is primarily an intellectual and only secondarily a politician. He has, indeed, a greater volume and variety of knowledge than most other politicians, but he will sometimes be found (as in his famous speech on immigration) to be subordinating logical rigour to the demands of style, a fault not uncommon in classical scholars who readily equate the balanced period with the indestructible argument.

There are some kinds of political activity at which he is not adept. He does not flourish in close oligarchies; he is not skilled at making subtle personal alliances; he lacks the humility or subtleness necessary to successful intrigue. His code of political loyalty is rigidly reasoned out and strictly observed, but it does not include some of the woollier conventions of camaraderie which are important to his colleagues. Though not cold, he is detached to the extent that his principles are thought out in advance of being stated and are not easily modified by contact with the opinion of others. His contribution to the work of any team, therefore, is bound to be strongly distinctive.

It is this fact, no doubt, which explains why in some quarters he has recently acquired another kind of reputation which is almost fantastically false, that of being some sort of fascist or semi-fascist demagogue who is appealing over the heads of the political establishment to the prejudice and violence of the mob.

A more ludicrous distortion is hard to imagine. Powell is by nature a parliamentarian. By conviction, he is at least as much of a Whig as of a Tory. He is by instinct as well as doctrine a libertarian, sometimes to the point of fanaticism. He believes, as a good Whig should, in political hierarchy. He has been less inclined than many of his colleagues to enlist popular passions in support of his opinions or his ambitions. The kind of activity in which Mr. Quintin Hogg indulged, for example, at the Conservative party conference of 1963 (the occasion, it will be recalled, on which he 'sacrificed' a peerage for the service of his country) would not come easily to him.

In the accusation of demagogy, there is this much and only this much truth: Powell, like many others, has observed the increasing gulf which is developing between the politicians on both sides and the mass of the electorate. He has tried, on one crucial issue, to bridge it.

In selecting, consciously or otherwise, immigration as the point at which the bridge was to be built, he was, up to a point merely reflecting the views of his own constituents. Yet, there was plainly more in it than that: his speech came at the climax of a campaign mainly dedicated to winning public support for carefully reasoned economic doctrines which, as stated by Powell, had little emotive appeal. The people may be tired of bureaucrats and oppressed by taxation, but the law of supply and demand does not seem to them to be pure poetry nor capitalism a 'gift of the Holy Ghost'.

Like other politicians, Powell has achieved the strongest
response when giving vent to one of the less important of his
convictions, wholly sincere though it is. There are dangers in
this, but they do not justify the charge that he has whipped
up racial hatred for the sake of political advantage.

Three years ago Mr. John Biffen wrote:

There is no tangible evidence of the effect of coloured
immigration on the voting habits of the electorate, but it is
possible that Tory attitudes on immigration will strike a
working-class response and replace the old-style imperialism that traditionally attracted, say, the Lancashire working-class to the idea of Tory democracy.

The analogy which this suggests between Joseph Chamberlain and Powell is, I believe, helpful to an understanding of
Powell's position in politics today. Chamberlain's mission
was to convert the Conservative party to a doctrine and a
policy – to imperialism and to a vigorous and radical concern
for social reform.

Powell also conceives himself to have a mission – the
conversion of the Conservative party from an outmoded
imperialism to a realistic patriotism, and from a largely
dirigist and paternalistic view of economic policy to a radical
policy of economic liberalism. He is seeking, as Joseph
Chamberlain sought, to alter the nature of the Conservative
party – to transform it from a 'safe' party, to be turned to for
sound administration in a crisis – into a positive and dynamic
party with a defined political and social faith.

Chamberlain never became leader of the Tories. In a
supreme national crisis he might have done, and so might
Powell. Certainly, the view that Powell's principles are so
rigid that he could never achieve the capacity for compromise indispensable to the effective leadership of the party is
not borne out by his career. His lust for political and
administrative activity is at least as strong as his intellectual
consistency. The probability must remain, however, that
Powell will not lead the Tories, a probability which he would
certainly admit himself and which I suspect causes him no
special anguish.

Chamberlain was an adept party manager; Powell is not. Yet, it is undeniable that Powell appeals as Chamberlain did to powerful popular sentiments which the Tory leadership will neglect at its peril.

What is more, Powellism, like Chamberlainite imperialism, offers the Tory party a rare chance to achieve a permanent and solid foothold in areas of society which are assumed to belong by right to its opponents – in other words, among the working classes.

One measure of a politician's skill is his ability to gather together in a single package a miscellany of popular ambitions and grievances which left to themselves conflict with each other. Powell offers the middle classes a free economy; he offers working-class opinion not only or primarily resistance to immigration but also resistance to incomes policy; he thereby effectively exploits the central weakness of Labour – the tension between its philosophy of State control and its dependence on the trade unions. One may even add to this list Powell's advocacy of a foreign policy more independent of the United States, and his zeal for the reduction of foreign commitments. In these respects, his programme might in practice be more congenial to many a Leftist than is that of Harold Wilson. Like the young Disraeli, Powell is attempting nothing less than a drastic political re-alignment of the classes, a new version of Tory democracy.

This is something more and something less than a challenge to the leadership of Heath. Powell has been and remains scrupulously determined not to be involved in plans for a palace revolution in the Conservative party. He has bigger fish to fry than that. He is challenging not the leader, but the party's fundamental habits of thought.

What has given the impression of a challenge to Heath is the intrinsic weakness of the Conservative leadership at present. That weakness is not due solely to Heath's limitations. The party has not yet recovered from the effect of two leadership crises which rapidly followed each other. It has not even recovered from the transformation of the whole concept of the leader which came about as the result of the adoption of an elective system.

It is, and it ought to be, profoundly disturbed by the

evidence that its leader continues to be widely unpopular in the country at a time when the party's fortunes are so dramatically improving (evidence, surely, that it is benefiting chiefly from disillusionment with Labour). At the same time, it is wholly conscious of the dangers of any attempt to change the leadership yet again in the absence of any acceptable alternative to Heath.

This last fact confers considerable strength on the leader, but it is a strength which at any moment may disappear. His task, like that of all party leaders, is to hold a coalition together. For that, there is much in Heath's make-up to commend him. As a Chief Whip, he had the reputation of being as gentle as a dove and as wise as a serpent. He used at least to be gifted with the capacity for compromise. He is an empiricist unencumbered by rigid doctrines, a man who might be expected successfully to hold the balance between opposing views.

Yet, it is precisely this that, on a large variety of issues, he has failed to do. The rigid discipline which he has sought (though often conspicuously failed) to impose on his Shadow Cabinet is not fitting to a party in Opposition. He has helped to stultify the process of re-definition which his party has urgently needed from 1963 onwards. He is suspected increasingly of depending on the counsel of a few congenial men who in turn are suspected by large sections of the party of being out-moded relics of the Macmillanite conception of progressive Toryism.

Those suspicions were strengthened by Heath's recent decision not to oppose the Race Relations Bill on its Third Reading in spite of having opposed it by a reasoned amendment on its Second Reading. The importance of that issue and of the rebellion in the Tory party to which it led were both exaggerated by the Press. Nevertheless, Tory discontent with the leader on this occasion was due in part to the feeling that Shadow Cabinet policy had suffered in clarity and constancy from Powell's dismissal. That feeling may well grow dangerously in the months that lie ahead.

The strength of Powell's position, however, does not arise from any capacity or inclination on his part for intrigue at Westminster. It consists precisely in the strength of his ideas.

They offer the Conservatives a unique opportunity for positively restating their philosophy and appealing to feelings in the country which in the long run cannot be ignored with impunity.

Containing Powellism, if not Powell, will, I believe, be the main preoccupation of Tory internal politics for the next decade at least. By impetuously dismissing Powell from the Shadow Cabinet (though the action was not unprovoked), Heath has for the moment declined that task. That was a serious mistake.

Is it irreparable?

John the Baptist

Sunday Telegraph, 20 April 1969

After at least a year during which the public has been bombarded by an incessant series of brilliantly reasoned opinions from Mr. Powell, the time has come to ask the only relevant question about him. Is he to be taken seriously?

The question which has been most insistently asked – is he making a bid for the leadership of the Conservative party? – is the most staggeringly irrelevant of all. What backbench member of the Tory party, in his daydreams at least, is not making such a bid? Who would refuse the great offer if it were made?

What is certain is that Mr. Powell lacks not only completely, but also ostentatiously and deliberately, all the qualities which are necessary to the accomplishment of a successful palace revolution in the Tory party. He talks only briefly and precisely to his colleagues; he does not form or even join dining clubs; his interest in and capacity for intrigue – the most important qualities for a prospective Tory leader – are negligible.

Powell's bid is for something much larger and more majestic than Mr. Heath's post. It is for the soul of the Conservative party and indeed, as the latest collection of his speeches (*Freedom and Reality*, edited by John Wood, Batsford, 35s.) shows, for the soul of the country itself.

The most revealing section of the book is the last, which is called 'Myth and Reality'. In it Powell, who is generally less given than other politicians to criticising his compatriots, accuses us of being a dithering nation which cannot accustom itself to its new role in the world. We are the victims of hallucination. We think that we can govern Central Africa when we manifestly cannot; we have the attitudes and aspirations of an imperial power when we are clearly a small island off the mainland of Europe whose future depends on its ability to think of itself as a part of Europe.

In our domestic affairs, we are simply the victims of a vast heresy which teaches us that national wealth and happiness are the products of organised, State-directed activity, when they are really the products of private effort, regulated and curbed where necessary by government.

This is not mainly an indictment of Mr. Heath, or even of Mr. Wilson, but of public opinion as a whole. It is a call not to a palace revolution but to an act of national regeneration: it is John the Baptist, not Machiavelli.

Does this mean, then, that Powell is a doctrinaire – a man with his eyes fixed on perfection who is really not operating within the field of practical politics at all? And who, in that he continues to present himself to the public as a politician, must himself be regarded as the victim of hallucinations no less grotesque than those which he believes to afflict the rest of us?

I think not. The recurrent, implicit theme of all these speeches is that Powell is stating the assumptions of ordinary people, that he is attacking not the beliefs and behaviour of the majority of his compatriots but the imposed and artificial conformities of consensus politics. When we speak as politicians, he seems to be saying, we are subject to powerful inducements to talk rubbish: his claim is that he is inventing a language of politics which will bridge the gulf between government and ordinary humanity.

Powell's style, it is true, is that of the doctrinaire rather than the demagogue. Nevertheless, his ideas are sometimes simple to the point of pathos. His economic doctrines are full of tacit and challengeable assumptions – the assumption that any State interference must lead to all State interference, the belief that people have rights as consumers but never as producers.

He would not dare to proclaim them in so naked a form in one of his other natural environments, a Cambridge combination room. His skill in defending them against Professor Galbraith mainly supplied evidence about Professor Galbraith. These ideas are deployed for a political purpose. They are not intended as intellectually viable statements but as general descriptions of the trend which he wishes to foster in politics – and, as such, they are legitimate.

Powell consciously uses his intellect as a source of political glamour. When the present Archbishop of Canterbury was Bishop of Durham, it was said of him that he got on very well with miners because he behaved towards them like a scholar trying to be a scholar rather than like a scholar trying to be a miner. Powell's popular success arises largely from his grasp of the same secret.

His aim remains essentially practical. It is to create a Tory party fundamentally different from that which exists at present – a party cured of the illusions of Empire and resolved to concentrate on the defence of Britain's military interests in Europe, a party committed not simply to limiting the advance of Socialism but to reversing it by creating an economy in which competition is assumed to be the norm and control has to be justified on its merits.

It would be absurd to deny that this campaign – a carefully calculated political campaign, not a mere free-lance exercise in prophecy – has derived some impetus from what is clearly the temperamental and intellectual incompatibility between Mr. Powell and his leader. Why else the special zeal and questionable logic with which Powell applies himself to attacking savings as a substitute for taxation just at the moment when Mr. Heath has recommended them?

It would be sycophantic to deny that Powell's pre-occupation with immigration (natural as it is for a Wolverhampton member and a believer in the nation state) owes something to his knowledge that this is a compelling popular theme, more so than the virtues of free enterprise or the need for a realistic defence policy.

It is in relation to defence and economic policy, however, that the true challenge of Powell and Powellism consists. Do we want the Conservative party to maintain its characteristic contemporary role as a brake on the excesses of collectivism, or do we want it to emerge as a radical party dedicated to the re-creation of a free economy tempered by that strong element of compassion which makes Powell one of the firmest champions of the essentials of the Welfare State?

By slow, painful and graceless steps, the Tory party has conceded on a variety of subjects to the views of this self-appointed prophet. Powell is no madman but a master of a particular form of political tactics which he has chosen to adopt. He has made himself clearer and more generally intelligible than any other contemporary politician.

He may receive the traditional prophet's reward – death or exile; if precedent is a guide, he is certainly unlikely ever to lead the Conservative party. Yet the likeliest prediction is that Powellism (tempered by prudence and muddle-headed-ness) will prove to be the most powerful single element in mid-20th-century Conservative politics. Whether in British politics as well depends on the speed and agility with which the Tory leadership completes its own conversion.

How Tory are Young Tories?

The Daily Telegraph, 25 September 1969

'The youth of a nation,' affirmed Disraeli, 'are the trustees of Posterity.' If the patron saint of modern Toryism could survey the various movements and organisations which claim to speak for Conservative youth today, what would he make of their stewardship?

It was from him that the modern Conservative party derived the myth which, until yesterday, enabled elderly English Tories to transmit to their progeny a tradition of political behaviour to which the political atmosphere in Britain during the past 100 years has become increasingly uncongenial. Disraeli's gospel of 'Young England' had almost everything which an upper-class young man with political ambitions and a generous heart could need for his nourishment. It reconciled radicalism with conservation by representing social reforms not as leaps into the future but as reversions to a glorious and forgotten past.

Under the guise of being a Disraelian Conservative, you could be something very like a thorough-going Socialist, provided you remembered to stigmatise the rich as a Whig, Venetian oligarchy which had usurped the rights of the English yeomanry. You could justify almost any proposal for the extension of bureaucracy provided you remembered to defend it (at least in your own mind) as an application to modern industrial life of the principles of paternalist government for which Charles I was beheaded.

So it was that many a young man (a Macmillan or Hogg, for instance) was able to live out his political adolescence safely within the family fold, earning the patronising plaudits of his elders as a 'stormy petrel' but one whose heart could be trusted to stay firmly in the Right place.

There have, of course, always been disadvantages in Disraelian double-talk. It has encouraged the Conservative party to swallow and indeed to promote many a policy utterly alien to its interests and principles; but Disraeli's formula for keeping the young happy has also had its merits. Language is the master as well as the servant of thought. The idiom in which the Young Tories of the 1920s and 1930s expounded their heresies left behind it a solid and valuable deposit of principle – belief in the nation, in the equal importance of social cohesion and social variety, in the duty of paying due respect to whatever has endured for long.

Those nurtured in Disraelian radicalism could usually be trusted to mature into sound, Burkeian characters, statesmen who thought of themselves as gardeners rather than architects or demolition experts.

Yet the Disraelian brand of romantic Tory idealism specially designed for the requirements of the under-30s was plainly best adapted to the needs of a political aristocracy, or at any rate to the needs of those who could convince themselves that they belonged to such an aristocracy. It is hardly surprising that it has failed to capture the imagination of the mass youth movement which the Conservative party set out to create after the Second World War. It is hardly surprising that the average Young Conservative today has never opened the covers of *Sybil* or *Coningsby* and, if he did, would be disposed to regard their contents as a load of codswallop.

The Young Conservatives, successors to the frivolous, self-consciously bourgeois Junior Imperial League, are a serious mass movement which grew with immense speed to staggering dimensions. They have proved to be a particularly effective instrument for practical purposes such as canvassing.

They have, of course, their pastimes – their dances and their country rambles – and, in the suburbs particularly, they are said to provide an excellent marriage bureau. As advertisements for Conservative virtue, they stand well in the esteem of their elders.

Yet, as befits the contemporary young, they are becoming dissatisfied. Some of them allege that they are not given a fair say at party conferences and, indeed, that the whole hierarchic organisation of the Tories is urgently in need of reform. One group has claimed that the party chairman should be elected by the conference.

But to what great political end is this influence sought? To judge from the resolutions of their various conferences, the majority of the Young Conservative movement in no way differs fundamentally in outlook from the Shadow Cabinet.

There are, of course, vocal minorities, such as that most ably and stridently represented by a young married couple, Eric and Lynda Chalker, of the Greater London Young Conservatives. Lynda says: 'We are determined to shake off the pin-stripes, bowlers and anyone-for-tennis image.' Her Young Conservatives have prepared a 'Bill of Rights' embodying 15 freedoms including 'freedom of sexual expression' and 'freedom to take addictive drugs'. Eric demands that cannabis should be legalised unless proof can soon be found that it is harmful.

YCs increasingly demand permissive legislation, many of them regarding it as an actual extension into the moral sphere of the principles of economic liberalism. In this respect, Mr. Powell has unwittingly done his young admirers a power of harm: they understand his economic liberalism but fail to understand his conservatism and nationalism. He is helping to rear a generation of Benthamites, bent only on individual competition, oblivious of the distinctive maxims of traditional Conservative thought.

Among the élitist sections of Young Tory opinion – the undergraduates and graduates represented by the Bow Group and the body called Pressure for Economic and Social Toryism – the outlook is scarcely more inspiring. Founded in 1950, the Bow Group has lived up to its original concept of a Right-wing Fabian Society. Its members – mostly extremely able and hard-working young men and women from the professions – write careful, moderate, statistically well-informed research studies into current political questions. (For instance, last May there was a 60-page pamphlet on developing the ocean bed).

Mr. Simon Jenkins, the excellent editor of the group's magazine *Crossbow*, is typical: once a Fabian Socialist, he became a Tory on the ground that enlightened administration and social progress were more likely to come from the Conservatives than from Labour.

Little wonder that some should have felt the need for a more activist organisation and formed themselves into PEST. PEST has collective opinions and is known as a ginger group, though that quality is not instantly apparent in the conversation of its civil, judicious, extremely moderate and very able chairman, Gary Waller. The group, consisting largely of undergraduates, sees itself as the private intellectual army of Sir Edward Boyle, its patron. It is particularly concerned to defend the cause of comprehensive education (with, of course, 'safeguards') and to press, in general, for a strategically planned economy based on consent.

Of course, if you are a young and warm-hearted Tory and find all these alternatives a bit dismal, you can join the Monday Club, but only at the cost of belonging to a somewhat intellectually unsophisticated and largely middle-aged organisation whose members tend to conceive Toryism as a conglomeration of arbitrarily associated panaceas such as the birch and a presence East of Suez.

Is it surprising that an increasing number of fervent Young Conservatives seek self-expression in working for extra-political organisations such as Shelter, which have hitherto tended to be monopolised by the Left?

Perhaps this is no bad thing, for who would want the Young Conservatives to show the same degree of enthusiasm as Young Liberals used to? Yet, the fact remains that the Tory tradition is no longer transmitted to the young, that they have rejected (probably because they have never been offered) both its idiom and its substance, and that for many of them the Conservative party is not a vehicle of social idealism but a source of efficient administration and a hopeful way of 'getting into' politics.

The two electoral defeats of 1974 prompted a slump in the Conservative party's self-confidence and were to lead to the replacement of Mr. Heath by Mrs. Thatcher in February 1975.

'Left', 'Right' – or simply Tory?

The Daily Telegraph, 14 November 1974

On the rare and painful occasions when the Tory party feels constrained to re-examine its role in British politics, it normally starts its thinking with the assumption that, whatever other characteristics it should have, it should above all else be a party of 'balance' and 'moderation'. This imposes on it the need to postulate an 'extreme Right' and an 'extreme Left' between which a middle course must be steered.

Even experienced politicians sometimes become so obsessed by these spatial analogies as to allow themselves to be transported into realms of fantasy which in other walks of life would be seen as evidence of a propensity to hallucination. Only a few days ago, at Worcester, for example, Mr. Heath affirmed that 'the Socialists think equality the be-all and end-all' while Liberals 'believe that freedom is the overwhelming objective.' Though this provided an excellent cue for saying that the Tories believe a bit of both philosophies, this was achieved at the cost of converting the Liberals (the one party which favours a full and immediate statutory incomes policy and shares almost without qualification Labour's egalitarian policy for education) into a party of freedom fanatics.

With the same sort of breathtaking distortion, Mr. Peter Walker now seems to conceive his mission to be the protection of the Tory party against the infection of certain Cobdenite heresies which, in their pure form, have not been seriously represented in British politics for at least half a century.

The invention of these hypothetical dragons, to be slain or compromised with, is only one of the troubles about this way of not thinking about politics. The more serious objection is that the words 'Right' and 'Left' continually change and even reverse their meanings. This in itself would not matter but for the fact that politics is full of people who find it necessary to their spiritual comfort to regard themselves either as Right or as Left without much reference to the connotations which those words have come to acquire. By this means political allegiances come to be determined not by reason or honest prejudice but by the obscure murmurings of ancestral voices.

Before 1914, and indeed for most of the inter-war period, a Right-wing Tory was a man who believed in the Empire, in strong national defence and in the State's having a reasonably active role in co-operation with industry in the running of the economy.

Today, the Empire has gone, national defence has lamentably ceased to be a national preoccupation and all that is left of this brand of paternalistic Toryism – belief in the positive role of the State in running the economy – has been appropriated and expanded by what now calls itself the Left of the party.

By the same token, what used to be regarded as Left or Centre Toryism (i.e. liberal Conservatism with an anti-paternalistic flavour and a strong bias against governmental activity in economics) has become the property of what is now classified as the party's Right.

The truth is, as Lord Hailsham pointed out years ago, that the Conservative party is at times a party of authority and at times a party of freedom. Which of these two complementary principles should receive more emphasis at any given time is a recurring question which permits of no permanent answer. At a time when world-wide slump was the order of the day in economics and when the relationship between money supply and unemployment was ill understood, it was natural that the party of conservation should have looked to the State to protect society against the extreme hazards of competition. When the most conspicuous evils are stagnation and restriction, it will be the Tories' instinct to preach freedom and private initiative.

It may be some comfort to reflect that the historic attitudes of radicalism towards liberty are no more superficially consistent than those of the Tories.

All this is very nice but not quite enough, since it leaves the Tory party in the position of claiming that it is gifted with an instinctive power to determine, without reference to any fixed principle, how much State regulation there should be in any society. In reality, all the diverse strands which go to make up English Conservatism have certain features in common, one of which is a totally different approach from that of all Radicals (whether collectivist or individualist) to the question of freedom. Here, then, is a series of maxims which, I suggest, most Conservatives in the party's authentic central tradition should find it possible to accept:

(1) Apart from securing the nation against foreign attack and maintaining public order at home (which objects should take precedence over all others) the chief function of government is to use its influence and, when strictly necessary, its power to maintain that minimum of cultural and moral unity within society without which a nation can be held together only by political tyranny. It is, therefore, proper for the State to seek to register and protect in its laws the community's accepted moral standards.

(2) In economic affairs, the 'public good' is not a thing to be defined and imposed from on high but a compound of private interests properly adjusted to each other. In a healthy society the economic activities of most men most of the time will be directed to furthering their own material interests and those of their families within a settled framework of law.

(3) The normal method of adjusting private interests should be that of free contract between individuals or corporations. Apart from protecting and enforcing these contracts the main duty of the State in relation to the economy is to maintain a sound currency without which a socially stable and prosperously employed community cannot be achieved or maintained.

(4) While it is not the business of the State to impose any scheme of distributive justice, it is its business to intervene in the economic process to ensure that all its subjects shall have access to minimum standards of welfare and security.

(5) The State is further justified in intervening to protect particular sections of the community (certain categories of producer or the inhabitants of certain areas) on whose interests economic competition is likely to operate too harshly or whose protection is seen to be a matter of special importance to the nation as a whole. These interventions, however, must be exceptional, directed to specific ends, and subjected to the strict control of Parliament, exercised with as little dependence as possible on administrative discretion.

(6) Of all the groups which the State exists to protect, none is of more fundamental importance than the family, and this institution depends for its survival on two others – on private property, and on a reasonable right of inheritance. It is therefore part of the business of government to ensure that ownership is distributed as widely as possible. It is also the government's duty to ensure not only that those who need help get it, but also that they get it in ways which do not rob them of choice, dignity and responsibility and which do not weaken the family.

These maxims do not provide the Tory party with a policy, but with the criteria by which, if it is faithful to its central tradition, it will determine its policy. There is scope for infinite debate about their application. No one has suggested, for instance, that it is feasible for government to revert overnight after years of inflation to a sound currency or to dismantle at one stroke the elaborate apparatus of a collectivist State. There may even be occasions when it is necessary to increase government intervention for the sake of eventually diminishing it.

The sting in the charge against the present Tory leadership is that it has abandoned these criteria, or anything like them, altogether; that it has substituted technology for philosophy and administration for politics; and that, by so doing, it has become virtually indistinguishable, save in the inferior consistency and integrity of its thought, from its Socialist opponents.

The rise and fall of Enoch

Sunday Telegraph, 1 May 1977

Who has lost more from the political decline of Enoch Powell, Mr. Powell or his country, and what lessons are to be drawn from the fate which has befallen him?

Those familiar questions are raised by yet another book published last week about Britain's top political maverick. Dr. Schoen's *Enoch Powell and the Powellites* (Macmillan, £10) is in one respect a very strange book. Its opening section and its concluding chapter are models of clear, unpretentious writing and acute historical analysis. The middle, on the other hand, consists of a farrago of sociological fantasies and murderous assaults on the English tongue, the contaminating influence of which should not be extended by unnecessary quotation.

What emerges clearly, however, is that Enoch Powell's rise and fall are not only inexplicable by any known scientific theory of politics (that applies to most political phenomena) but are a unique event in British political history.

What other British politician, not addressing the public from the front benches of a political party, has, in modern times, for so long sustained a massive personal following? What is more, in respect of at least two of the causes which Powell espoused, monetarism and immigration, his views, reviled and derided when they were first uttered, have to a large extent been incorporated (without acknowledgement) in the political consensus. Those who follow closely the affairs of Ulster can now discern at least some signs of the same success in relation to that tangled subject. On the face of it, it is certainly not a bad track record; yet it is not altogether surprising, or even necessarily a cause for deep commiseration, that it should have been rewarded by what looks increasingly like personal political annihilation.

British political history is littered with examples of men who have not realised their political ambitions in spite of being possessed of vast talent and outstanding personal magnetism. Powell would have no cause for chagrin at being relegated to the same category as, say, Randolph Churchill and Joe Chamberlain. Moreover, the explanation of this failure is boringly familiar. Powell defied the party system not, let it be observed, from being too inflexible (that charge cannot sensibly be levelled against a man who, in the course of his political development, sacked the British Empire, abandoned the Tory party, and moved from nervous support of the Common Market to fanatical opposition to it) but from failure to observe Burke's maxim that no man can 'act with effect' who does not 'act in concert'.

The party system rests on the assumption that what politics are about is who should govern. A man may be forgiven for deserting his party connection provided he acquires some other effective one as rapidly as possible. He will not be lightly forgiven for retiring in disgust from the fray while appearing to be determined to control the progress of the game from the sidelines, for deserting his life-long colleagues while refraining either from joining his opponents or from forming any new alignment capable of promoting his views. That, as Dr. Schoen points out, is precisely the pattern of Powell's career since February, 1974.

Had he been an enemy of parliamentary institutions, he would, in the late 1960s and early 1970s, have been in a far stronger position than Mosley ever was to assail them. The strongest ingredient in Powellism is disillusionment with our established arrangements; Powell, however, was and is the most staunch devotee of those arrangements. He is first and last a parliamentarian, and this in reality means in Britain a man who believes that government descends from above and is not a merely automatic means of registering popular sentiment. One of the consequences of that system is that those who wish to change the face of politics must be at pains to acquire a base (and a broader one than the Ulster Unionist group in the House of Commons) within the political establishment. That requirement Powell was not prepared to fulfil.

And so, from what the pompous call disloyalty and what can be more accurately described as lack of political sociability, Powell has been reduced to his present isolation, the saddest feature of which is his vulnerability to the unjust charge that his complex conduct can be wholly explained in terms of thwarted ambition and personal enmity towards rivals. Outside the narrow confines of Ulster, where he still disposes of influence (and exerts it most beneficently to restrain Protestant extremism) has he, in the past eight years, exerted any perceptible effect on the course of British politics? He may, as Dr. Schoen is inclined to believe, have helped Labour to return to office in February 1974; yet it is arguable that for several years the advocacy of all his great causes has been hindered rather than helped by the fact that he espoused them.

In so far as we have approached realistic policies on immigration, monetarism and Ulster, we have done so by the painful process of exhausting the alternatives, of committing and repenting the errors against which it was his mission to protect us; and the process has been the more painful and the more prolonged because of the ease with which most manifestations of sanity could be stigmatised as 'Powellism'.

That Powell, like Edmund Burke, will achieve immortality as a classic source of Conservative wisdom I do not doubt; it is equally sure, however, that he will stand as an example to the generations of one of the ways in which politics in Britain cannot be practised.

And yet the Powellite movement, at its height, still stands out as one of the great lost chances in the history of the Tory party – the chance of creating and sustaining a genuinely Tory democratic movement with a firm working-class base, of appealing more effectively than the Tory party has done for decades to the latent patriotism of English working men and of harnessing organised labour to the defence of capitalism by emphasising the inherent contradiction between Socialism and a trade union movement free to bargain for higher wages. Powellism, in its heyday, seemed a far more promising formula for achieving that miracle than the elaborate and often boring process of economic re-education to which the current Right wing of the Tory party subjects the electorate; for Powell, unlike many of his successful rivals, is pre-eminently a man of flesh and blood.

As Dr. Schoen insists, the fate of Powell is an extraordinary tribute to the continuing strength of British political institutions. It may also be a dire warning of the dangers of carelessly using that strength to frustrate genius.

Supermac and the super myth

Sunday Telegraph, 11 February 1979

You have to be at least 40, or to have been politically precocious, to retain any clear, direct memory of the character and performance of Harold Macmillan when he dominated British politics. Yet the Young Conservatives, whose annual conference he is addressing today, will approach the delectable experience which awaits them with the aid, or handicap, of a thoroughly established myth.

They will know from his television appearances that he must have been one of the most accomplished stars ever to appear on the British political stage. Indeed, they may be inclined to exaggerate his past prowess in this field, for they will make totally unnecessary allowance for the decline which any other artist would have suffered between the ages of 70 and 85. They will see him, as his contemporaries were taught to, as a representative of a bygone era in which political leadership was the prerogative of a political élite, an age in which policies were formed, successions determined, downfalls contrived by the operations of a 'magic circle', a phenomenon which, after the war, did not, in fact, exist at all, save as a comforting illusion in the public mind. They will see him as the perfect Tory romantic, combining what, in most Young Conservative minds, are the equally venerated virtues of arguably plebeian origin, an aristocratic marriage and a perfect assimilation of the style of the governing class.

What a contrast they will observe between him and most of those upon whom the burden of Tory leadership now falls! What a contrast between those deep, mellifluous, port-sodden tones, those exactly-timed hesitations and lapses into calculated improvisation, and the desiccated monotony of the generation which modelled itself on Mr. Heath or, indeed, the scrannel piping of some of the agitated economists who surround Mrs. Thatcher!

But what did this wizard actually stand for and achieve in politics, and what message has he for the future? Here, again, the myth supplies the answer, and it is at least substantially true. Throughout his active career, Macmillan was an imperial statesman of vision, anxious that his country should cut a good figure in the world, and deeply convinced that, for this purpose, diplomatic skill could make up for the deficiencies of material power. He had a passionate and profoundly personal concern for the poor, and with it the zeal of a reformer. He was, particularly in his later years, a supreme exponent of the politics of reconciliation, believing that the business of a statesman was not so much to define and answer questions and to choose between incompatible courses as to blend opposites and strike balances. Like a good Burkeian, he believed in the merit of continuity and, when he could not achieve that, in the therapeutic value of the illusion of continuity.

But what did all this achieve? Among those who are over 40, you will find some who will tell you that Macmillan's gifts were purely of style and character and that their very brilliance operated malignly to render palatable and even bewitching a measured, elegant descent towards doom. Their case, let it be admitted, is formidable. Take all the miseries which now reasonably sadden this ageing patriot: who was the Prime Minister who, spurning 'a little local difficulty', sacrificed Peter Thorneycroft, Enoch Powell and Nigel Birch in 1958 to an inveterate (and apparently still active) personal preference for generous public expenditure rather than for sound money?

Who first brought into practical politics the notion, which has lain like a curse on all his successors, that the way to control trade union power was to trust wise men with the task of deciding what wages the nation could afford and then to appeal to the unions to heed their advice? Even Macmillan's solicitude for the unemployed eventually took the form of a fatally obstinate refusal to recognise that they had ceased to exist, and his reformism degenerated into an uncritical acceptance of the shibboleths of collectivism. His 'middle way' veered remorselessly to the Left.

The determinedly churlish find it just as easy to tarnish his record as a world statesman. How much of the expansion of Russian power which he now laments fed on the illusions fostered by his dedication to 'summitry'? True, he reconciled us to the extinction of the Empire, but how much did he also do to accelerate the Empire's demise, and what does he now feel about the 'wind of change' which is sweeping the African continent? True, he tried (and failed) to get us into Europe, but does he not also rank high among those who weakened British foreign policy, and made Dr. Owen a possibility, by allowing national defence to depend almost exclusively on the nuclear threat?

Of course, this long indictment is as unjust as it would be tasteless but for the fact that Harold Macmillan is so brilliantly alive as to make merely pious commendation of him an impertinence. He really cannot be held to blame for everything that happened during the period of his political ascendancy. Like other politicians, he did what he felt he could with the materials and opportunities at his disposal; he thought, like most Conservatives of his generation, that he was engaged essentially in a rearguard action, the kind of military exercise which is most congenial to the English Conservative mind; so congenial indeed as often to tempt Conservative politicians to invent the necessity for it. He plainly prided himself on his ability to recognise the inevitable, which is half the business of his craft but the other half – that of distinguishing between those tendencies in society which politicians can and ought to promote and those which they can and ought to discourage – exhibited him to less advantage.

Certainly, he practised the politics of reconciliation, but too often with the aid of the politics of hallucination, the gift for dressing up defeats as victories, for cloaking revolution in the ceremonial dress of tradition. Even now that talent has not deserted him. Remember the deft manner in which, the other night, he transported us from the present jungle into a world in which 'the masters' and 'the social reformers' would be able to get on with the Government and the unions, and in which that great estate of the realm, the Trades Union Congress, would unite with the Established Church in a concerted act of national moral regeneration?

But the jungle remains with us, and to find the middle way out of it is going to involve several sharp turns to the Right. It is even going to involve painful decisions, with unpleasing overtones of lower-middle-class stridency. If the operation is to be pulled off at all, those charged with it will, of course, have to show much of the skill, even the guile, of the great Macmillan. But the operation is no longer defensive; we shall even have to know with some precision where we are going.

So let the young relish their contact with historic Tory culture. For heaven's sake let Harold Macmillan perform not the least of the services of his career by teaching the Tory front bench how to make speeches. But when it comes to the diagnosis of our present ills and the fundamental remedies for which they call, I say to these innocent worshippers at Bournemouth, 'Beware the old magician!'

By 1981 the Thatcher Government was at its lowest popular ebb. 'Wets' were being sacked from the Cabinet; one of the most deflationary budgets of modern times helped send unemployment towards 3 million. Only the Falklands War, the following year, would initiate a change of fortune.

For God and the Right
The Daily Telegraph, 9 February 1981

We have heard a good deal in recent years about the 'new Right'. Like much else in the tool box of the political commentators, the concept is fairly vague. It includes a variety of converts from several types of Left-wing radicalism who have attached themselves to the bandwagons of Mrs. Thatcher and President Reagan, bringing with them many of the aesthetic and moral characteristics of their former beliefs.

An identikit picture of a member of the new Right (a picture, of course, which would not be a faithful reflection of an actual member) would be something like this: he is dynamic and strident, radical in the sense of wanting a total transformation of society, wholly libertarian, resenting not only the State's intervention in the economy but all attempts by society to temper the eccentricities of its members unless these can be conclusively shown to damage other people in a material manner. In his approach to religion, he is either an agnostic or some sort of synthetic deist with a world view favourable to freedom. He has a taste for seminars and for rather rowdy and over-crowded political cocktail parties which, in spite of the free flow of liquor, are infused with the moral seriousness of a meeting of the Band of Hope in the last century. He went to a grammar school, hates comprehensives and cannot abide Etonians. He stands for the small business-man and the 'career open to talent'.

Against these imaginary purveyors of 'new style Toryism' there is said to be arrayed the noble army of 'Wets' or, as in my boyhood they were more elegantly described, 'the great soft centre'. This section of the Tory party is deemed to consist of elegant but effete patricians more or less reconciled to the triumph of socialism, but bent on ensuring that the resulting monstrosity shall be managed by men of breeding and experience.

A caricature, but it contains an element of truth. You can fit a great many politicians and publicists, with only a modest measure of poetic licence, into one slot or the other. What is absent is anything which corresponds even remotely to the description of a traditional English Conservative as that phrase would have been understood right up to 1939.

It is this omission from most contemporary classifications of English Conservatives which gives special interest to the political aspects of Mr. Maurice Cowling's recently published book, *Religion and Public Doctrine in Modern England* (Cambridge University Press, £20). It is a very odd book indeed – written with all the thoroughness of a first-class technical historian; but no one would recognise it as, in the ordinary meaning of the phrase, a 'history of opinion'. In large part, it is simply an account of the extraordinary effect which certain brilliant men in the Cambridge of the 1930s and 1940s (Kenneth Pickthorn, Charles Smyth, Edward Welbourne and Herbert Butterfield for instance) had on the mind of an unusually intelligent undergraduate. As I was exposed to precisely the same influences at much the same time the book has for me the appeal of what the BBC would call 'a trip down memory lane'.

For the general reader, however, its importance is greater; for these men (whom Mr. Cowling still looks on, as I do, with the awe of youth) were all unconsciously engaged in giving intellectual expression to a brand of English Conservatism which now seems almost extinct among the articulate but, in those days, represented the unstated assumptions of many generations.

The dominant characteristic of that brand was that it was Christian. We were encouraged to believe that the State could not be indifferent to the moral assumptions of its subjects. Society rested on Christian foundations, and it was the positive duty of government to protect these foundations, largely through the agency of an educational system which could not be based on the illusion of ethical objectivity. Beyond that, we learned that the nation-state was probably the best means which human ingenuity had discovered of reconciling freedom with public order, that a government's principal task was to maintain the nation against the seldom distant threat of foreign aggression and the never absent danger of social disintegration.

Above all, we were taught to despise and distrust all forms of utopianism, socialist liberal or any other. It was presumption to believe that there was some single principle or simple body of principles on which human society could be reconstructed and sheer wickedness to be prepared to use massive public force for the sake of imposing such principles. I vividly recall the venom with which Kenneth Pickthorn used to protest against the attempt of the Left to capture the war, to imply that we were fighting not for the defence of our country but for a whole variety of social and moral purposes which could not be achieved by war, which it would, in any case, be immoral to pursue by war and thoroughly repugnant to many who were fighting it.

Now it is clear that this variety of English Conservatism has much more in common with the philosophy of the 'new Right' than it has with the sort of *dirigisme* by default, passive acceptance of the inevitability of collectivism, which dominated Conservative Governments from the late 1950s onwards. Pickthorn was by temperament a free trader and in his views on the economy accepted many of the assumptions of classical economics, but he certainly did not subscribe to any rigid dogma about the automatic harmony of interests which would follow from the operation of a free economy. State intervention was to be distrusted not because competition would produce perfection but because the results of all political action were so unpredictable and political action was itself so painful and potentially dangerous as to make the risks of planning intolerable.

This view, of course, was suitable to an age when the Conservative party was fighting a defensive action to protect the substantial areas of freedom which were still left to us. Mrs. Thatcher's task – that of re-conquering territory already lost to State intervention – may seem to call for a more messianic tone; but is it not arguable that the Government might have got further than it has done, and have found it easier to carry the public with it, if its approach had been a degree more sceptical and less doctrinal?

The contrast between the old and the new Right in respect of foreign policy is even more startling. Fresh from the appeasement controversies of the 1930s which had revealed liberal hypocrisy at its worst, Tories of Mr. Cowling's sort turned again to the wisdom of the great Lord Salisbury. Although they were far more conscious than most of their contemporaries of the strength of the Soviet menace, they did not believe that it was to be combated by a crusade for universal human rights. Those who set out with the view that foreign policy consisted simply in defending good causes would end by convincing themselves that all the evils which necessity obliged them to acquiesce in were morally defensible. As it was, in a wicked world, the most that a country could be expected to undertake was the defence of its own legitimate interests, the honouring of its obligations and a passive respect for the interest of others.

Where is the national dimension in Conservative thought today – the belief in a perpetual need to protect and foster the nation's sense of identity, to subordinate everything, including prosperity, to the need for adequate defence against foreign attack and disruption and disorder from within? Such themes occasionally make their appearance, in Tory oratory rather than in Tory policy, but they are rapidly swamped by animadversions on the relative importance of the M1, M3 and so on. Yet whenever these authentic notes of old-fashioned Conservatism are struck (as by Enoch Powell in the 1960s) the public responds. If only for crude electioneering reasons, Mr. Cowling's voices from the past deserve a hearing.

Bewildered but still loyal

The Daily Telegraph, 19 October 1981

The Tory party's 1981 conference has been so widely and comprehensively misrepresented that it may be permissible to exaggerate a little in order to restore the balance.

Consider, then, the picture that has been given. The party is rent by a white-hot controversy between the exponents of a monetarist theory of economics and the supporters of a Keynesian theory. The battle is being fought to the death not only in the Cabinet but in every ward-association throughout the kingdom. It is destroying friendships, splitting families, corrupting manners, creating mayhem at breakfast tables throughout the country. Every little Tory boy or girl that is born into this world alive is now either a little Friedmanite or a little Keynesian.

Soon the whole political system under which the country has been governed since time immemorial will collapse under the impact of this religious war. The armies are arrayed against each other and, behind the lines, guerrillas are operating with the aid of code words which can only be deciphered by expert political correspondents in consultation with each other. We are moving to a climax: it will not be long before Field Marshal Thatcher sues for peace and offers a safe conduct to an armistice delegation from the enemy. What will her surprise be to find that it is led by men with whom she has been rubbing shoulders and sharing bully-beef for months, men like Captain Heseltine and that 'best-type-of-staff-officer' Brigadier Pym?

Meanwhile disaffection grows in the ranks: Gilmour was humanely invalided out, but, only the other day, young Cranborne (who comes from an excellent stable) was heard muttering something mildly obscene about interest rates. As for the real rank-and-file, there is no means of keeping them away from seditious literature and broadcasts.

Certainly, there were those at Blackpool who would sagely nod and say that Heath was talking sense, though some would add that Margaret Thatcher was doing a good job. There were certainly plenty of people who would subscribe to the view that 'Howe had his head screwed on'.

What was harder to find was anyone who, if seriously pressed, would be prepared to admit that he had the smallest idea of what the row was about. It should now be revealed that this modesty is also prevalent among many of the leading protagonists: few of them, when talking in private, will fail to preface their remarks with a disclaimer of all knowledge of economics and any real understanding of what they are about to say.

The truth is that this whole business is damned difficult. Certainly no Tory can be happy about the current level of unemployment and all the rest of the surrounding gloom. But what is there to be done about it? Gilmour seems to say that you should spend just a bit more public money – but, then, if you only spend a bit more, won't the result in terms of employment and votes be fairly small as well?

Mrs. Thatcher says that you can't spend your way out of bankruptcy. Well, that seems common sense. It seems to follow that you must do your best to get the economy right, and grin and bear it in the meantime. Of course, we may not get the thing going by the election, but neither would Gilmour or Heath; one might as well, therefore, be hanged for a sheep as a lamb. Anyway, the woman knows her mind and the other lot tried their prescriptions before without producing anything much like miraculous recovery.

Of course, this simple wisdom does not exorcise all doubts. There are some very puzzling aspects of the discussion: it is a puzzle, for example, how Gilmour (in his smart way) can say that he is not asking for much more money to be spent than Howe already overspends every year (or that is what it sounds like); because if that is so, how can it be that Howe is some sort of manic flagellist who enjoys bleeding the economy to death just for the sake of religion?

Then, again, if Howe is really spending so much (and Ministers last week never tired of giving accounts of the vast sums they had blued on things like nationalised industries of which they disapprove), how can we be in such a mess and how can we be so courageous as Margaret Thatcher says we are? And, what's more, if there is all this money going begging and the private sector is really starving to death, why not stop ploughing money into British Leyland, Steel and British Rail, which cannot even provide a buffet car on the train from Blackpool, and why not distribute the loot among worthier causes, such as a subsidy to any private employer who will take on anyone who is currently unemployed – just the sort of scheme that the 'Wets' like.

This would be something new and hopeful; and, come to think of it, was not hope the great message of the Tories at the last election? Weren't we all told 'yes; things will be hard but there will be opportunity for those willing to work and save and generally emulate the virtues of the Prime Minister's parents'? Wasn't the great difference between us and the Socialists that, while they were on about strength through collective suffering, we were on about strength through the alleged joy of hard work and high endeavour?

These are not only the views which I have heard; they are also the views which, ignoramus as I am, I share. They lead not to dissent, but to a kind of bewildered, desperate loyalty. That is the spirit of the Conservative party today.

As for discontent, there is that in plenty. It arises from the view that the Government is more concerned with book-keeping than with the preservation of the nation. The party is deeply angry about what it regards as a perfunctory attention to law and order, to immigration as well, and some are more than a little concerned about Ulster, to which the Prime Minister's references were brief and did not include a reference to the one example of 'inflexibility' (the handling of the hunger-strike) which has been indubitably successful.

My impression still is that Mrs Thatcher has failed fully to grasp one of the clearest truths about British politics in the 20th century – the truth that the British people are not that much concerned about capitalism (though they are perfectly happy to accept its advantages); in the abstract, they do not understand or like it. They only become enthusiastic for it when it is presented in a patriotic context.

Joe Chamberlain knew this; the last Conservative politician to have known it with perfection is Enoch Powell. After that came Margaret Thatcher. She also knows it. Why they like her is because she 'speaks for Britain', not because she is a very good economist (though she is probably as bright as any of that bunch), but because she expresses the sentiments and prejudices of the British people.

On Thursday, I went to a party of the Primrose League, founded 100 years ago in favour of the constitution, patriotism, decency and all that. The members are mostly very old and they have not got much money; but they speak more accurately in the voice of British Conservatism than anyone else. I know rather more young Conservatives than most people do and I think that this sort of thing strikes a stronger chord in their hearts than Monetarism v. Keynesism. What a wonderful thing if someone would try to revive the Primrose League to its former eminence. Think of the patronising remarks from Brian Redhead and the other media connoisseurs of Tory antiques. And think how reassured Britain would be!

The art of Tory politics

The Daily Telegraph, 14 May 1984

When I was a young man (as Aubrey used to say 'before the Civil War'), there used to be a favourite question for scholarship examination papers for the ancient universities. It ran thus: 'The characteristic vice of the Tory party is avarice; that of the Socialist, envy; that of the Communist, revenge.'

On this (or something very like it), bright sixth formers were invited to comment.

Even then, it seemed to me that there was much to object to in this formulation. Avarice is a pretty widespread vice, not particularly connected with political prepossessions. Most articulate Socialists did not seem to me to be inspired by envy so much as by moral arrogance, their bequest from the Liberal party.

No, it seemed to me that what was wrong with the Tories (and not just the bad Tories but the very good ones) was a kind of sophisticated timidity, a belief that the whole art of politics consists in concession, that the only thing which a really grown-up politician can do is to decide what he loves best and then consider how he can preside most elegantly and judiciously over its destruction, making that process as painless as possible, saving what he could from the wreckage and, if possible, convincing the world that nothing had happened by calling what was new by an old name.

All this is deeply written into the Conservative myth. Did we not learn, when we tried to stand up to the American colonies, what a mistake it was to defend one's national rights? Did not this lesson enable us to embark on the great process of creating an empire destined to achieve its consummation by being transformed into a commonwealth of free and independent peoples?

Is not the great merit of English Conservatism that it comes to terms with reality and the great merit of the Tory party that it confines itself to the role of a midwife to history?

In all this, there is nothing intrinsically immoral. There are no absolute and universal principles in politics, or at least so few and those so abstractly defined are not to make much difference. Circumstances are almost everything. Concession is a great part of wisdom. Keeping a nation together takes precedence over pursuing models of perfect justice. Given a choice between this body of clichés and the stringent coarse clichés of moralistic radicalism, I know which I prefer and which I think to embody the greater degree of wisdom.

Yet there are pitfalls in this beautiful, balanced, mature political philosophy. The chief of them is the assumption, typical of most Conservative Governments since the last war, that if one looks at the facts and considers the circumstances, the only course which it is ever worth following is that of controlled surrender.

One of the ways in which this error comes about concerns that sacrosanct word 'consensus'. Of course there must be a consensus if any society is to be held together without a grossly oppressive application of public force.

But Tories are constantly tempted to include in the notion of the consensus all manner of institutions and policies (for instance the Welfare State as defined by Beveridge) which have found no place in the settled affections of the people and which, therefore, could be modified without creating any sense of alienation between the rulers and the ruled.

I tremble to criticise Lord Hailsham in this or in any other context. His brilliant book *The Case for Conservatism* was the nourishment on which I was reared. But I would wager that there are few things that he cherishes more than the Book of Common Prayer, the gradual expulsion of which from the ceremonies of the Church of England he is prepared to accept on impeccably Conservative grounds – the need not to disturb what he believes (wrongly I think) to be the established relationship between Church and State.

Similarly, in 1969, he rightly advised the House of Commons that if divorces were made easier, they would become more numerous. Now he seems to me to have presided over legislation designed to make them still easier and more painless – again, on the characteristically Conservative but highly questionable assumption, that it is too late to put the clock back.

So I am a lonely figure in politics, repelled by the rhetoric of the New Tory Right but inclined on the whole to support what they want to do, and sympathetic to the Burkeian conservatism of the likes of Sir Ian Gilmour but deeply apprehensive of the causes to which they apply it. If Mrs. Thatcher could finally rid herself of the false impression that she is a radical and the equally false impression that the English like radicals, she would to my mind have achieved perfection; for she alone among our leaders seems to have grasped the truth that valour is sometimes the better part of discretion.

Monstrous invention

The Spectator, 9 August 1986

There is no such a thing as Thatcherism. The illusion that there is is in part a deliberate creation of Mrs. Thatcher's enemies. They have proceeded on the age-old maxim that there is nothing (certainly not private scandal) more likely to injure the reputation of a British politician than the suggestion that he has an inflexible devotion to principle. This maxim is only partly true, but it is an unshakably established belief, a fact which helps to make it truer than it otherwise would be.

The illusion is in part also the creation of a coterie of admiring friends by whom Mrs. Thatcher has been surrounded. Some of them, for cultural and sometimes ethnic reasons, have little sympathy with the English political tradition, which they regard as a fraud perpetrated on the people by an oppressive and incompetent political establishment. What the country needed, they argued, was someone who would sweep away all this rubbish about compromise and consensus and lead the country in a radical reconstruction of its habits and institutions. They easily identified Mrs. Thatcher as their man.

The illusion, however, could never have achieved its present proportions without some assistance from its victim. Mrs. Thatcher is not by temperament averse to the Messianic role. She also has a wish to be, and to be regarded as, something of an intellectual, and she has a passionate devotion to intellectual honesty. When she got into politics, she became an avid student of the writings of what is broadly and rather vaguely called the 'New Right'. In the press of public business, she still finds time to discuss at length such profound questions as why Britain 'lacks a free enterprise culture', and how this deficiency can be repaired.

At another level, however, she is an exceptionally astute politician and an accomplished party tactician. It is inconceivable that her devotion to doctrine would ever persuade her to do anything which was plainly politically suicidal.

Now, in all this, you may say, there is very little that is new. Many of her predecessors have had a taste for philosophy, and only a philistine would suggest that this taste has had no influence on their political conduct. All of them, like Mrs. Thatcher herself, however, have been practical politicians with a sense of the status of principles as guidelines, not absolute and literal moral imperatives.

This is so, but somehow in the case of others the reflective and practical ingredients in their natures have blended more easily. It sometimes looks as though she lives a completely compartmentalised life. When talking to her friends or addressing a party conference, she is the philosopher-queen, although the impression, as far as her public oratory goes, springs rather from the manner of its delivery than from its actual content; listen hard enough and you will always hear the qualifying clauses, often uttered rapidly and with an almost palpable physical revulsion. Then something happens in the real world – the need to bring the Rhodesian crisis to an end, the need to avoid a miners' strike before the Government is ready to cope with it, the need to placate a divided Cabinet over trade union reform – and Mrs. Thatcher yields to necessity, often swiftly.

Who can doubt, for instance, that Mrs. Thatcher is convinced that the Welfare State needs radical reform, that she would like to introduce educational vouchers, student loans, possibly even to make the relatively rich contribute something directly towards their medical care? But most of these projects have been quietly dropped, or put into indefinite cold storage in obedience to supposed political necessity.

Consider, then, the 'ideology' in which Thatcherism is supposed to consist. Its chief plank is the advocacy of a free and competitive economy, but that simply represents one more or less permanent ingredient in modern Conservative philosophy. It was on that principle that Churchill fought the 1945 election, having just read Hayek's *Road to Serfdom*; to judge from what is now said, one might suppose that Mrs. Thatcher had 'discovered' the great Dr. Hayek. What brought the Tories to 13 years of political supremacy in 1951 was the slogan 'Set the people free'. 'Under Labour there has been too much government interference in the day-to-day workings of industry . . . there has been too much government'; 'We will reduce and reform taxation, giving first priority to reducing income tax'; 'Our aim is to identify and remove obstacles that prevent effective competition and restrict initiative.' All those quotations are from Mr. Heath's election manifesto in 1970.

Lord Bruce-Gardyne, in his admirable book *Mrs. Thatcher's First Administration*, has suggested that the real difference between Mrs. Thatcher and the rest (particularly Mr. Heath) is the fact that whereas they regarded sound finance and free competition as means to an end, she regards them as moral absolutes to be applied whether they appear to work or not. For the reasons I have given above, I do not think this to be a wholly accurate description of her political behaviour; but the essential point, for the purposes of this article, is that there is absolutely nothing new about the doctrinal front that she presents on these matters. In 20th-century English Conservatism (I say 'English' because there are absolutely no authentically Conservative Scotsmen, Irishmen or genuine Welshmen) two schools of thought about the economy have existed side by side – the liberal school, to which Mrs. Thatcher belongs, and the 'corporatist' school, to which Macmillan and (now) Heath belong. Sometimes one is in the ascendant, sometimes the other. Neither ever captures complete sway over the party. Neither is taken wholly seriously by any of its apostles who are seriously engaged in practical politics. That is all there is to it.

As for 'privatisation', Mr. Powell proposed it in his famous

'Morecambe budget' speech in 1968. As for 'property-owning democracy', I believe it was Anthony Eden who coined the phrase.

There is an even stronger and more profound reason for supposing that Thatcherism does not exist: the Prime Minister likes to regard herself as an exponent of the 'politics of conviction', as distinct from the 'politics of consensus'. Now this is a silly dichotomy, invented by inferior journalists. Consensus politics is an intrinsic part of the art of government; one has to achieve a consensus with someone and no consensus embraces the whole of the community. But what this monstrous distinction implies is that Mrs. Thatcher, unlike other politicians, is in no sense a product of history, that she is starting from scratch, that she is not putting her ear to the ground to hear what is going on in the world and to decide how she can (however slightly) influence it, but that she is deciding what is the good society and how she can create it. It is hard to imagine anything further from the truth.

Mrs. Thatcher was produced by history. Her two major achievements – the control of inflation and the reduction of the trade unions to size – were simply the climax of a series of unsuccessful attempts by Labour and Tory Governments alike to cope with what were increasingly seen as the two most important evils from which the country was suffering. When Chancellor of the Exchequer (1974–79), Mr. Healey boasted that the Government to which he belonged was 'perhaps the first in Britain for many years which has given monetary policy the importance it deserves'. In 1976 Mr. Callaghan said to his party conference, 'Higher inflation followed by higher unemployment: that is the history of the last 20 years.' As for the trade unions, Mrs. Castle had tried and failed to curb them in the late 1960s. Mr. Heath tried again and failed in the 1970s. After 'the winter of discontent' Mrs. Thatcher came to power on a wave of revulsion from trade union arrogance and oppression which had been steadily growing for ages. Bureaucracy and inflation were equally out. If she had not existed, it would have been necessary to invent her.

The other element in Thatcherism is supposed to be the wish to restore Britain as a great power in the world. By this Mrs. Thatcher does not mean primarily a power devoted to the preservation of its own interests. She belongs to that militant Whig branch of English Conservatism which took over when Churchill became Prime Minister in 1940. This is to say that her view of foreign policy has a high moral content or, in other words, that she likes to devote herself to large and distant causes – the freedom of Afghanistan rather than the security of Ulster. She is suspicious about the Common Market, but seems prepared to swallow its consequences (e.g. the Single European Act) so long as the blame for them can be attributed to the Foreign Office. I believe that she went into the Falklands with reluctance and regret and that, having done so, she carried it off with a courage and skill of which no other Prime Minister, possibly including Churchill, would have been capable. In terms of theory, however, she has contributed nothing new to the discussion of Britain's role in the world.

Margaret Thatcher is a great Prime Minister, great by virtue of her courage and by virtue of what ideologues would often, misguidedly, describe as her 'low political cunning'. We desperately need her; the greatest obstacle to our continuing to have her is the belief that she is the inventor of a 'political philosophy'. She will not get all she wants, as no politician can or should, but she will get more of it than others would and she will in the end be content with the deficiency. But, please, no more talk about Thatcherism.

The tightening of the grip of ideology was never better recognised than by John Biffen, then Leader of the House of Commons, when he spoke early in 1986 of the party's need for 'a balanced ticket' in the future. His reward was the sack after the 1987 election, something Utley foresaw, as was clear from the tone of this article.

Commentary
The Daily Telegraph, 20 October 1986

Exactly when, I wonder, did this practice of politicians giving long semi-academic lectures about the nature of politics begin? I do not remember it in my politically precocious pre-war youth. I do not think my hero, Oliver Stanley, would have been seen dead on such a platform. Later on, I do not remember Oliver Lyttelton engaging in such exercises. No, I think it is a post-war phenomenon. They are all at it now: MacLeod lectures, Disraeli lectures, Churchill lectures – the lot.

After the war, a veritable factory of such lectures was set up in Lord Swinton's house in Yorkshire, the exercise being supported lavishly out of Tory funds. As a penniless Tory journalist in the 1950s, I used to go there a lot, grateful for a fiver and even more for lunch on the Yorkshire Pullman. In return, I would deliver an extremely solemn piece on some such subject as the relationship between 'liberty and law'. The formula was simple. There had to be a great display of academic obscurity, but there also had to be a political sting in the tail. I was not bad at it, and I am still available for such exercises: Frank Johnson (if I recall his words rightly) has described me as 'an itinerant, jobbing Tory philosopher', and I am content with these words as my epitaph. But I was nowhere near so good as the great principal of Swinton, Sir Reginald Northam.

He used to give a splendid piece called 'The Tory Faith'. This consisted of a brief review of the history of the Tory party, pointing out that sometimes it had supported authority and sometimes freedom, but bringing out the essential theme of consistency in all these policies – i.e. that it had invariably been right. Then, he would suddenly descend from the clouds and convey some eternal and homely piece of Tory truth. He would say that when he was a lad he had had to black his father's boots every morning and that, if the job were not properly done, his father would beat him. After that, there was not a single dry eye or silent hand in the hall. The perennial essence of Toryism had been displayed.

But enough of reminiscence. The point I am trying to make is that the mixing of high philosophy with practical politics does not really work, and is not a particularly good thing. Of course, there have been great practical politicians who have also been deep philosophers, but they have kept these distinct interests rather separate. The great Lord Salisbury wrote articles for the *Quarterly Review* and even, if I remember rightly, leaders for the *Daily Standard*. But political philosophy, as such men knew, is action recollected in tranquillity.

On the whole, I think that political philosophy suffers a good deal from being practised too ostentatiously and too often by politicians. I also think that practical politics suffer a good deal from being invaded by political philosophers. To be thoroughly nasty, the most expert practitioner of this kind of semi-intellectual politics was Joseph Goebbels, the Nazi minister for propaganda.

Now there is no one less like Goebbels than Mr. John Biffen, who has just delivered the Disraeli lecture on 'Tory Conviction Politics'. The lecture was a work of reconciliation between himself and Mrs. Thatcher. He has identified himself with the politics of consensus, she professes the politics of conviction: so it is necessary that the two things should now be seen to be more or less identical.

For a man of John Biffen's intellectual skill, this is not a difficult job. From 1979 (and indeed rather before that), Mrs. Thatcher pursued the politics of conviction (assisted, as he admits, by events), thereby creating a new consensus. So all we have to do now is preserve the consensus, while adding a bit more conviction to it in matters like education. In other words, we are all friends once again.

I do not think this would do for an inaugural lecture from a chair of political philosophy; and, though it contains much wisdom, I do not think it does as a political speech either.

In so far as there has been a consensus in British politics since the war, it may be thus defined: the people do not like high taxation but want high public expenditure; they dislike bureaucracy, but are happy with compassionate state intervention. They do not care a row of beans for monetarism, which they think has something to do with foreign economists; they like the idea of owning property, but are not altogether enthused about 'free-for-all' competition (British people have only been reconciled to capitalism by its association with more easily comprehensible ideas like imperialism): they believe in the nation, want criminals to be severely punished, and would like a strong foreign policy devoted to the protection of British interests, not to the ludicrous idea of enforcing human goodness in remote places 'of which, thank God, we know virtually nothing'.

The consensus is, in fact, self-contradictory. Skilful politicians have to manage it, in such a way as to promote, roughly, what they believe to be good for the country. Mrs. Thatcher has done this superlatively, as Mr. Biffen recognises. There is no politician to whom I wish better luck than John Biffen – though, I remind him, Mrs. Thatcher runs him a close second in this respect and has her sex going for her. I hope their reconciliation will last forever, but I hope they will both give up the habit of analysing it in long, academic addresses. Less examination of 'styles of politics', please, and more straightforward political speeches in which these styles will be exhibited: then indeed we shall have 'a balanced ticket'.

Too obsessed to be my guest

The Times, 27 July 1987

The other day I was woken up in what seemed to be the early hours of the morning by the languid voice of Mr. Julian Critchley, conveyed by courtesy of my bedside wireless, exposing a dilemma which went straight to my heart. He said that he had been elected to the House of Commons as a Conservative, and that, according to Mrs. Thatcher, he was now meant to be radical.

He found this very difficult indeed, since, in his day, radicals were nasty, dangerous people whom one did not have to dinner. Nevertheless, if Mrs. Thatcher said that he must become a radical, indeed that he was already a radical, a radical he would be.

Mr. Critchley did not go on to explore the deeper implications of his anguish. That is one of the nice things about him: he points us to matters of philosophical interest without laboriously exploring them. However, since laborious exploration now seems to be the order of the day, I will try to fill the lacuna. I shall ask such questions as 'what is a radical?', 'is

Mrs. Thatcher a radical?', 'should we all be radicals?' and 'how is it that infinitely pleasant people like Mr. Critchley and me find it hard to accept the description?'.

A radical (the sort of person who must not be asked to dinner) is a chap who wants to impose some rational order on society, be it an order in which every important decision is taken by central government or an order in which every decision is surrendered by central government to the whims of the individual citizens, these being expressed through the 'free market'.

He is also a chap who thinks that everything in the way of arranging political, social and economic institutions should ideally be the same everywhere in the world, and that we should do our best to make it so. He is also (and this is the crucial point of my thesis) someone who wants to liberate mankind even against its will – forcing it into the right direction, exhibiting total contempt for its sentiments and prejudices. Unlike a Tory, he does not start by looking at the country, trying to discover what its people want and trying to establish arrangements, bearing in mind the national tradition, which suit its particular requirements and which would stand some chance of becoming stable and of winning popular affection.

He is, in fact, a 'social perfectionist', assuming that his own definition of 'perfection' is accepted. These are the people whom Mr. Critchley and I were taught not to ask to dinner – no matter whether they were devoted to the principle of liberty or that of collective organisation.

But what I would say to Mr. Critchley is this: Mrs. Thatcher is conspicuously not such a person. She is a very cautious, sensible politician; deficient in imagination (a somewhat over-rated quality and one which in my youth was greatly discouraged), rigorously practical and inspired by a general desire to swim with the tide of history, but equally convinced that its direction can be slightly but significantly altered from time to time. That is why the electorate gave her a third term of office. This, of course, is not an interpretation of events which will appeal to her: she would probably prefer to think of herself as somebody who has changed the course of human history by her own volition; but, *au fond*, she knows that nobody ever has.

To get back to the main point: she is not liberating people according to some abstract theory and against their own will. She came on the scene at a point when the power of the State over our affairs had been increased to an intolerable extent. It had been increased in obedience to a theoretical, radical concept – that of distributed justice presided over by government. The real trouble was done by that latter-day saint, Attlee, between 1945 and 1950; then followed a period in which the frontiers of government were somewhat turned back, and we got 'the mixed economy' and all that lark, most incorrectly described as 'corporative'.

By 1979 the whole nation yearned for something to be done to take us back to a state of affairs in which government concentrated on maintaining a framework of law within which private interests could be pursued, subject to occasional interventions to meet intolerable evils.

By responding to this need, Mrs. Thatcher has not made herself into a radical. She does not challenge institutions, like the Royal Mail, which have a fundamental place in the affections of the people. Yet there are many institutions inflicted on us since the war which have no such place. Happily it is, for example, part of the consensus that everybody, however poor, should have access to the best medical treatment; and that everybody, however dim, should have access to the most appropriate form of education. This, however, does not mean that the Health Service and the education system must be maintained exactly as they are; in fact it means quite the opposite. Mrs. Thatcher is, in fact, doing far less to reform these institutions than she should be – ironically for fear of being regarded as too much of a radical.

Mr. Critchley and I should have no difficulty in supporting her or indeed dining with her. Our objections to her style are purely aesthetic, and it would be kind of her to stop describing herself so often as a 'radical'.

How the Tories do go on

The Times, 12 October 1987

Only one passage in Mrs. Thatcher's Blackpool speech (the best conference oration, I think, that she has ever given) caused me a short pang of discomfort. She had dwelt justly and not vaingloriously on the achievements of the Government. She had said that they consisted in putting certain simple, central truths back in the heart of politics – the need for sound money, competition and the opportunity to make adequate profits. She had gloated, in a reasonably good-natured manner, over the discomfiture of Labour and the Alliance. Then came the contentious passage.

'Our third election victory,' she declaimed, 'was only a staging post on a much longer journey, and I know with every fibre of my being that it would be fatal for us to stand just where we are now. What would be our slogan for the 1990s if we did that? Would 'consolidate' be the word that we stitch on our banners? Whose blood would run faster at the prospect of five years of consolidation?'

I had a minor objection of taste to these words. 'Consolidation' was the concept with which John Biffen identified himself, and he has suffered enough injury to make it gratuitous to inflict insult as well. Nevertheless, politicians cannot be expected to display infinite charity towards each other, and the Prime Minister has put up with a lot from Mr. Biffen. No: my main objection was of a more fundamental nature.

Mrs. Thatcher has cast herself in the role of a crusader and also (though you may think it paradoxical) of a progressive. The dilemma of progressives is that, by the very nature of their conviction, they can find no resting place. One object achieved, they have to embrace another. Great benefit sometimes arises from the display of this kind of energy in politics, but it is always an exhausting experience for the governed. After a spell of dramatic effort and high tragedy, they begin to pine for a spot of peace and even a touch of drawing-room comedy. One pines for precisely those things at the end of a Tory party conference. Indeed, a mildly disrespectful idea occurred to me as I listened. If Mrs. Thatcher's Utopia were ever to be achieved, how much would she enjoy it? Her aim is a perfectly self-regulating economy in which there is no further need for political intervention save of the most automatic kind. She wants a society governed by regular and general laws, within the framework of which individuals are free to pursue their own ends. It is, in principle, an excellent objective, but where would it leave the likes of the Prime Minister – politicians with a passionate sense of political mission and an obsessive desire to move forwards? They would be obliged to think up some other sort of Utopia.

No sooner had this thought occurred to me, however, than I became conscious of intense injustice. Had Mrs. Thatcher declared that she would stay put, rest on her laurels and the like, would I not have been the first to complain? She is right to believe that the most difficult tasks still wait to be accomplished or even embarked on. The Welfare State has to be reformed, not only to give those who want it the opportunity of choice but also to ensure that its benefits are not indiscriminately distributed to those who need them and those who do not.

Some stages in this operation are likely to prove painful and electorally unpopular. Indeed, considering the conference as a whole my main anxiety was that Mrs. Thatcher's colleagues in the Cabinet have still not got fully to grips with these formidable tasks. Mr. John Moore, on the Health Service, for instance, seemed to be rather less of a radical than he was a few days ago. I find few discerning people who are convinced that the 'opting out' principle in relation to education and housing will really achieve very much. Measures which, in the prevailing parlance, are regarded as 'even more radical' may well be needed.

Nevertheless, such measures (I have in mind, for example, direct charges for health care with, of course, generous provision for the needy) are more likely to be acceptable if they are defended on the ground of sheer necessity rather than presented as moral and doctrinal imperatives.

What then is needed? Above all, the indomitable spirit and energy of the Prime Minister; but should not this be tempered from time to time by some modest concessions to those of us – to be found in all ages and classes – who have a taste for understatement, stability and as quiet a life as we can get?

As I left the Winter Gardens, for a brief respite, on Thursday morning, a great gale was blowing, and I was struck on the head by a metal object, necessitating a short visit to an admirably conducted NHS hospital. The folklore says that my assailant was the C in Conservative that appeared on the legend adorning the Winter Gardens porch. If so, the conference must have ended as the *On*servative Conference. Could there be some sort of moral in this? I do not want to go 'on' for ever, particularly if I am to be hit on the head at every 'staging post'.

Peel's misplaced mantle

The Times, 9 February 1988

I have elsewhere, and I imagine more than once, deplored the increasingly fashionable practice of 'historical body-snatching'. Let me explain the phenomenon: whenever some anniversary of a great statesman occurs, there is a scramble to appropriate his memory for the benefit of some contemporary cause or more often for the glorification of some contemporary statesman. This does great violence to history and also introduces much confusion into present-day political discussion.

Alas! my protests have been in vain, as is vividly illustrated by the recent celebrations of the bicentenary of the birth of Sir Robert Peel. Last Friday, Mr. Douglas Hurd, speaking at Tamworth, and doing so with characteristic elegance, extolled Sir Robert's virtues and made a daring assessment of their contemporary relevance. With equal elegance, Mr. Paul Johnson pursued the same theme in these columns on Saturday. And what were their conclusions? On which contemporary British statesman has the mantle of Peel fallen? Well, no prizes for the right answer – on Mrs. Thatcher, of course, and on her brave, reforming colleagues.

Now I can see some resemblances, as one can see resemblances if one tries hard enough, between any two historical events or personalities, however disparate. Peel was a reformer, so is Thatcher. Peel liked facts and statistics, though happily for his generation there were relatively few of those about, so that they could not become, as they since have, a complete substitute for thought.

Peel was not quite out of the top drawer, though it was a good deal higher than that from which Mrs. Thatcher emerged (in any case, this sort of tiresome snobbery has, thank God, never had quite the importance in British politics which 20th-century journalists attribute to it). Peel came to be a free trader; Thatcher believes in the free economy.

All this I concede, but what was Peel really notable for? It was surely the perfection of what may be called 'concessionary' Conservatism. This is the concept that the highest virtue in politics is to resist change until change becomes inevitable, and then to concede to it with as little fuss and as much obeisance to tradition as possible.

So it was that Peel had almost convinced himself by 1832 that the Great Reform Bill was inevitable. He did not quite reach that point in time for an elegant surrender, but as soon as the battle was lost he reconciled himself to the result and, so the history books tell us, set about creating a modern Conservative party which could hope to woo the new middle-class electorate.

So it was that in 1846 he reached the conclusion that the Corn Laws were indefensible, abandoned protectionism and swam with the tide. The result was the break-up of the Conservative party and the building of a bridge over which most Peelites were eventually enabled to escape into the ranks of the Whigs.

Peel assumed, as most Conservative politicians until Mrs. Thatcher generally have, that his political opponents represented the future. Their excesses must be resisted, but most of their causes in the end would prevail and the business of the Conservative party was to make the transition as smooth as possible.

This is not a contemptible creed. It contains indeed a measure of the kind of practical wisdom which is part of the essence of politics. We have derived much advantage from it; but what on earth has it to do with Mrs. Thatcher? It is, surely, precisely the sort of thing to which she has put a stop, in so far as a stop can ever be put to it. Anyway, how could she now go about making judicious and timely concessions to the Labour party, since what Labour is trying to do remains deeply obscure.

If I was looking today for a spiritual heir to Peel, I think the right candidate would not be Margaret Thatcher, but Neil Kinnock. He now leads the 'listening party'. It is he who seems to assume that his opponents are on the side of history and he who applies himself to the task of absorbing as much of their wisdom as can be absorbed without undue violence to the socialist myth.

Why, then, has Mrs. Thatcher been so arbitrarily inserted into Peel's family tree? Well, the answer is plain to anyone who knows the elementary rules of 'historical body-snatching'. The others got Disraeli first. Disraeli has become a code name for 'collectivist' or, as they now put it, rather inaccurately, 'corporatist' policies. He is the mascot of the 'wets'.

This also is a grievous distortion of history. It is true that, in his romantic youth, he wrote the only phrase which the majority of his present-day admirers have ever read from his pen – about there being a nation of the rich and a nation of the poor. His paternalism, however, was superficial. In so far as he ever favoured authoritarian measures for the defence of what are now ludicrously called the 'under-privileged' he favoured them no so much in the name of abstract social justice as in that of national cohesion. What he believed in was the Nation which he tended in those benighted days to call the Race. This is his one, valid, surviving contribution to Conservative thinking. He was an imperialist.

How come, then, that it is the Left of the Tory party which now embrace him? If he were alive today what side would he be on over issues like the swamping of national culture by alien immigration and the surrender of parliamentary sovereignty to the EEC?

The answer is, of course, that he would be on whatever side

he thought would win, for, like Peel, he was fundamentally what they call a pragmatist. However, if the scriptures which he gave us are to be searched, it is clear that there is more in them to fortify Margaret Thatcher than in most of what Peel said and did. Disraeli claimed to want to 'put the clock back' to better and purer times; so does the Prime Minister. He stood for the Nation; so does Mrs. Thatcher, by comparison with most of her colleagues – witness the Falklands, her relatively tough stance towards the EEC and her off-the-cuff remarks on immigration.

To do Mr. Hurd justice, however, he only wanted to make a speech embodying a good Disraelian point – saying that freedom and prosperity are all very well, but that one also wants a cohesive society with some sort of communal ethos. Disraeli would have been a better peg for that message than Peel – but, after all, it was not Disraeli's 200th birthday.

By the way, the one thing that Tories of both traditions believe in is institutions designed to maintain the cohesion of society, and a good deal more thought on that matter would be welcome. Mr. Hurd clearly feels that as well – but I think he will have to offer us something a little more convincing on the subject than the statutory Home Secretary's castigation of clergymen, teachers and parents which he offered at Tamworth on Friday. Meanwhile, I boldly claim Mrs. Thatcher for the Disraelian tradition – and, of course, in strictest historical terms, that is a load of bunk as well.

2 · *Talking of politics*

This article was the first Utley ever published, while still an undergraduate at Corpus Christi College, Cambridge.

Young England

The Spectator, 4 July 1941

About a century ago, when the great question that agitated political discussion in England was whether or not the Corn Laws should be abolished, there developed inside the Conservative party a movement which called itself 'Young England', and which tried to revive those principles of Toryism that had seemed to be banished from English politics by the great Reform Bill. The movement started in Cambridge, and was led by George Smythe and John Manners, scions of two ancient houses. They succeeded in alienating every powerful interest in the State, and the interests they alienated have been multiplying and becoming more powerful ever since. The result was that the movement failed in its immediate purpose, and that historians have seldom alluded to it without ridicule. Indeed, their only reason for alluding to it at all is that it attracted the genius of Disraeli and provided the inspiration for his earlier novels. But immediate failure or even the ridicule of posterity is not in itself a condemnation or a proof that an enterprise is destined never to succeed, and a group of young men in Cambridge today are attempting to revive Young England and asserting, in face of the opposition of the Left (an opposition that is more noisy than numerous), the principles for which Young England stood.

The essence of the political philosophy of Young England was expressed in Disraeli's phrase, 'the King at the centre, the people at the circumference'. It is not, of course, suggested that the royal prerogative should be restored in its old proportions, or that the rule of 'benevolent despotism' could or ought to be revived. Disraeli himself substituted for kingly government the leadership of a governing class which should, nevertheless, represent something more than the interests of class, and the idea, translated into current language, is reform directed (but not imposed) from above. It derives from the patriot king of Bolingbroke, and Bolingbroke, it must be remembered, was a century before his time in advocating the extension of the franchise. In 1832, the mistake was not in extending the franchise, but in extending it only to one class, which was thenceforward in a position to dominate the rest of society and to regulate policy in its own interest. Disraeli saw the only hope of breaking that domination in an alliance between the old governing classes on the one hand and the people on the other.

It is the fashion, today, to assume that the ideal to be aimed at (although most people are willing to agree that it can never be reached) is absolute economic and social equality. Thus, when men defend inequality, it is commonly on the ground that it is inevitable rather than because it is right. Young England, on the contrary, asserts emphatically that differences in wealth and status are politically and morally necessary, and, although it is not pledged to defend every existing inequality, it is concerned to uphold the principle of inequality. Its social ideal is a small nucleus of hereditary privilege at the centre, continually reinforced from below. Believing, first, that heredity is not a myth but a scientific fact, and, secondly, that in the education of a governing class early training is of the utmost importance, it maintains that there must be some people, in any properly organised society, who are destined to lead. It is not supposed, however, that the principle of heredity can be applied to the exclusion of all other principles, and Young England would like to see a much larger measure of social fluidity than has ever existed since the age of 'enlightenment' and 'equality' began. The principle upon which we believe society ought to be organised is that of function, and, in our opinion, the object of the State should not be an approach to equality, which is the same thing as uniformity, but the maintenance of variety and the assigning of every one to that place in society for which natural talent and early education have suited him.

The next question is: What sort of reform would a governing class composed like this be expected to introduce? It is not the purpose of Young England to dictate policy to the Government, and it emphatically rejects the suggestion that wisdom and honesty are the monopolies of youth or even of that part of youth which happens to be at a university. Practical details are the business of the expert, but general principles are everybody's concern. The kind of reform in which the Young England of a hundred years ago was chiefly interested, and the kind of reform which its successor of today would principally advocate, would be that which is aimed at removing the worst effects of industrialism. Recognising, however, that life in an industrial town, even when enriched by all the adornments which science can provide, will not be either as varied or as free and healthy as life in the country, and believing that the land is the birthright of Englishmen, it would try to restore the balance which has been deliberately destroyed between industry and agriculture. This would not be because of a theory of economics, but merely because it is believed that the encouragement of industry at the expense of agriculture has been attended by a loss which, considered in terms of human character and happiness, has been too great to be justified by the increase and the diffusion of material possessions.

The criticism which is most often made of the movement is that it is trying to 'put the clock back'. The belief that it is either impossible or intrinsically wicked to try and restore anything which has existed before is a result of the Whig theory of progress, but we reject this superstition, which carries with it the slavish implication that man must always move along a predestined path. Such a theory denies free will as a factor in history, and, in its anxiety to prevent men from becoming slaves to the prejudices of their ancestors, enthralls them to the fashions of their contemporaries. 'Putting the clock back' is one of the oldest of human habits, and it might almost be called a regular part of the historical process. The essential question is not whether Young England is moving backwards or forwards (for such phrases are mere rhetoric), but whether it is moving in the right direction.

As I have said, it is not our purpose to dictate the details of policy, not because we despise such minutiae, but because we do not feel competent to fill the place of the expert. Our object is to give undergraduates who share our principles a chance of discussing, privately and without ostentation, the best way of putting them into practice. Slavery to principle is as bad as slavery to circumstance, and inevitably the amount that can be done and the nature of the things that ought to be done at the end of the war depend, to a great extent, upon factors which nobody can now foresee. But it is possible, and, indeed, one's duty, to prepare oneself to deal with those problems which are certain to arise, even though the exact form in which they will present themselves is still concealed. It may be well, therefore, to end by indicating, very briefly, the kind of reform which will commend itself to us.

These are some of the practical suggestions which have emerged from recent discussions among our members: – First, that the Spens Report should be the basis of the nation's education policy. This report recognises the principle of function, and aims at giving every one, not a uniform education, but the kind of training for which he is particularly suited and which will be of value to him in the place which he is going to fill in society. Second, with regard to agriculture, we do not look for a governing class based entirely upon the ownership of land, and we value competition in industry as one means of selecting leaders. But there would surely be nothing revolutionary or impracticable, for example, in a compulsory increase in the wages of the agricultural labourer, in order to make farming a more attractive pursuit, or in an attempt to prevent the spread of industry into districts like the Thames valley which are obviously more suited to agriculture. Third, Toryism, at a very late stage in its development, acquired from Liberal doctrine a bias in favour of private enterprise. The bias remains, but it has not been exalted into a principle. Thus, we maintain that an extension of public control is not in itself bad, but, on the other hand, we deny that nationalisation is a panacea for all evils. At the end of the war, it will obviously be necessary to regulate production more strictly, and, in this connection, some national control of investment has been proposed. All this is admittedly vague, and none of it professes to be new. It is merely included to give some idea of the spirit in which these problems are being approached by a less conspicuous section of the undergraduate community, and to show that it is not our purpose to prevent change, but to direct it along lines which are compatible with our national traditions.

Thinking and the Right

The Spectator, 19 October 1956

In the current number of *Encounter*, Mr. Wollheim has examined the familiar proposition that the intelligentsia is going Right and has found it, by somewhat ponderous arguments, to be untrue. Mr. Strachey in his recent book *Contemporary Capitalism* has given some attention to the same theme but his conclusion is different. With the aid of a quotation from a review of mine in the *Spectator*, he reaches the conclusion that young intellectuals who are politically free to speak their minds are these days often bitter critics not only of the Left but of democracy itself and he adds these significant words: '. . . these fatal characteristics of democracy have been discovered just at the moment when majority rule, working, as we have seen, almost as powerfully upon the party of the Right as on the party of the Left, is pushing the economy along paths profoundly unwelcome to "the 10 per cent."' This Right-wing reaction, according to Mr. Strachey, is the *avant-garde* of a bourgeois counter-revolution which it is the function of Socialism to anticipate, and obviously this is a convenient doctrine for a radical party which finds that it has few real abuses left to challenge and must justify its existence by inventing a threat to the established order. Mr. Strachey professes no doubt of the reality of this threat which he finds to come, at one extreme of years and distinction, from Lord Percy of Newcastle and, at the other, from me. He is convinced (and this is the important point) that it is essentially a threat from the intelligentsia.

Let me say at once that I do not share the almost morbid preoccupation of these two writers and many others with the supposed political opinions of 'the intelligentsia'. That preoccupation seems to me to be one of the hallmarks of Leftism; indeed, the assumption that it is important to have an intelligentsia at all is another such hallmark. An intelligentsia may be broadly defined as a class of people which claims distinction from other classes on the grounds that it is endowed with superior mental equipment, which is conscious of its identity as a class and which has a sense of having some sort of specific function to be fulfilled corporately in the life of society. I would say that we did not have the beginnings of an intelligentsia in Britain until the birth of the utilitarian movement; the belief of the early utilitarians that they were engaged collectively in building up an exact science of politics and morality, their passion for talking to each other and corresponding with each other, their zeal for starting reviews and giving lectures, all marked them out as an authentic intelligentsia; but they never achieved that remarkable degree of gregariousness which distinguished British intellectuals in the 1920s and early 1930s; members of the Victorian intelligentsia were capable of disagreeing with each other on fundamentals; their approach to life was eclectic; you could never be quite sure that because they believed one thing they would necessarily believe a whole lot of other things sentimentally though not necessarily rationally associated with it; like Samuel Butler, for example, they could denounce God without worshipping science.

Now it is clear that an intelligentsia in the sense which I have defined it is almost in its nature Left-wing, because its great binding link is the belief that life consists of a number of problems which will yield to an organised assault from reason, which assault the intelligentsia exists to deliver. It is also clear that it is possible to be an extremely intelligent man and an extremely learned man without belonging to an intelligentsia, without even finding the society of those who do emotionally tolerable. The late Lord Baldwin had a rather distasteful saying to the effect that the difference between an intelligent man and an intellectual roughly approximated to that between a gentleman and a gent, but I do not wish to introduce any judgement of value into the distinction I am trying to make. I merely wish to emphasise the fact that during the inter-war years when by everybody's admission the intelligentsia was Left, there were among the alleged mediocrities who governed us men of academic distinction like Lord Halifax or Lord Eustace Percy and there were also plenty of Chesterton's voluminous dons who in erudition certainly surpassed the editorial staff of any Left-wing paper and who habitually voted Conservative and never once wrote to the *Manchester Guardian* about the rape of Abyssinia. On the other hand, there was at the same time an intelligentsia which regarded itself as a sort of political technocracy, had a virtual monopoly of ephemeral political writing of the more sophisticated kind and was almost uniformly Left.

It is with the fate of this intelligentsia that Mr. Wollheim is concerned: he does not believe that most of his intelligent friends vote Tory; he concedes that a good many politically minded intellectuals have abandoned politics but denies that this is equivalent to moving towards the Right; he believes that the superficial impression of such a swing is created partly by the dilemmas which afflict the Labour party now that it has fulfilled that part of its programme which depended on moral intuition and has to calculate the consequences of its actions; and he sees no evidence of the emergence of a respectable and coherent Conservative philosophy.

Now I contend that what Mr. Wollheim is describing is the disintegration of an intelligentsia, but I think his prejudices obscure his mind concerning the causes of this movement. I certainly do not admit that it would be necessary to prove that most intellectuals vote Conservative in order to demonstrate a swing towards the Right in politics, and I think that the key to the whole matter is unwittingly provided by Mr. Wollheim himself in his account of the dilemmas of the Labour party: it is one of the privileges of the Left to describe its inadequacies as dilemmas and its mistakes as tragedies: where a Conservative would blush and be quiet, a Socialist is privileged to enter a stage of audible self-examination in which the responsibility for his own errors is subtly transferred to the rest of mankind. The alleged dilemmas of Socialism today are nothing more or less than the failure of the whole Socialist technique of arguing straight from abstract principles to policies, the whole heritage of political rationalism in the naive form in which it passed to the intelligentsia of the 1920s and the 1930s. The move towards the Right is a move towards empiricism, towards scepticism of generalities in politics, and towards the belief that sound political thinking must begin from concrete situations understood in the light of the history which created them. It is a repudiation of the tradition of the Encyclopaed- ists and of the French Revolution, the tradition to which doctrinal Socialism is the heir.

Mr. Strachey is quite wrong to see this movement as the stirring of the bourgeoisie: I would be at a loss, for example, to know what the precise views on British domestic policy of two of its eminent representatives, Dr. Talmon and Mr. Berlin, are, and if I asked that question of either of them it would be from the same humble curiosity which newspaper reporters seek to satisfy when asking great musicians if they eat cereals. An empirical approach to politics may result in a variety of practical conclusions, but it will not result in either the methods or conclusions which distinguished the Left-wing intelligentsia of the 1920s and 1930s.

Why does Mr. Wollheim not understand this? I suspect that it is because his mind in this respect is dominated by the Left- wing idea of the importance of an intelligentsia. One of the elements in that idea is the implicit and quite unwarrantable assumption that persons of equal intelligence and integrity will arrive at the same conclusions about politics.

Once intellectuals become empirical they cease to be organised. It is in this that the movement towards the Right, towards what is in reality if not always in profession a Burkeian philosophy of politics, consists: certainly it does not consist in what I suspect will prove to be the short-lived fashion of strident criticism of all aspects of the established order of which the most often quoted example today is *Punch*; that is mere Jacobinism and not particularly import- ant. What is important is that intellectuals are becoming sceptical and meditative about politics and as a consequence ceasing to function as an intelligentsia.

Will Parliament lose its sovereignty?

Sunday Telegraph, 30 September 1962

Although the Lord Chancellor's statement at Bristol last Thursday on the effect which membership of the Common Market would have on parliamentary sovereignty was not wholly wrong, I confess that it does seem to me to have been somewhat misleading.

Lord Dilhorne contends that if we join the Market we shall have to accept some diminution of the sovereignty of Parliament, but that this sacrifice will be worth while because of the diplomatic and economic advantages it will confer. To my mind, it is logically and legally impossible for Parliament by its own action to reduce its ultimate authority over the British people, as Lord Dilhorne himself admitted.

I have been talking to a number of distinguished academic lawyers who have for some time been studying the legal and constitutional effects of the Common Market. I find them almost unanimous in the view that parliamentary sovereignty, in the strict technical meaning of the phrase, cannot be affected by any treaty obligation we may assume towards the Common Market.

For over 250 years, the doctrine that Parliament can do anything it chooses has been unchallenged by English lawyers. This right has always been agreed to include the power to undo anything which has been done. If Parliament were to repeal the Act emancipating the American Colonies, no English court would declare this amendment to be contrary to the law of England. By the same token, Parliament would, in the eyes of the English law, remain free at any moment to authorise our withdrawal from the Common Market.

It is equally clear, however, as Sir Arthur Goodhart the distinguished American constitutional lawyer who presides over University College, Oxford, insists, that this doctrine has never been more than a legal fiction. What Parliament can do at any time is limited by innumerable considerations of practical politics.

Parliamentary sovereignty is in fact a convenient illusion, convenient because it is desirable in every community to have some authority which is recognised for practical purposes as having the last word. In Sir Arthur's view, however, Britain has often suffered grievously from treating this expedient lie as a sacred cow. So it was that we lost the American Colonies and nearly lost Canada. That the Commonwealth exists at all today is due, he says, to the boldness with which we renounced large hunks of sovereignty over a great part of the world's surface when the Statute of Westminster II was passed.

Among the practical limitations on the use of sovereignty, one of increasing importance in recent decades has been the steady growth of a body of international law. This law arises from voluntary agreements between sovereign States. Normally speaking, it binds governments, not peoples, but obviously it is always in potential conflict with the doctrine of national sovereignty.

Such a conflict would arise, for example, if Britain instead of joining the Six were to start bombarding them with rockets. By so doing, we should have committed a serious breach of international law, but I, as a citizen, would not, in the eyes of the English courts, be justified in expressing my distaste for the crime by refusing to pay taxes or sitting down on Air Force bases.

Complications arise, as Professor H. W. R. Wade, Professor of English Law at Oxford, points out, when national governments not only bind themselves by treaty to behave in particular ways but also actually undertake to allow their subjects for certain purposes to be directly controlled by alien or international authorities.

There is, however, nothing new about this arrangement. In medieval England, for instance, considerable powers, both legislative and judicial, were vested in the institutions of the Catholic Church. In modern times, institutions like the Postal Union have in practice wielded administrative powers in many countries.

Perhaps the most startling instance of this kind of international control today is that exercised by the European Commission on Human Rights. This commission was, until recently, presided over by the English lawyer Sir Humphrey Waldock, to whom I talked at All Souls.

Many countries, though not Britain, have agreed to accept as compulsory the jurisdiction of the commission in any case concerning the rights of the subject which may be brought against them. Here an aggrieved citizen is now entitled to sue his own government, or a citizen of one country who believes himself to have suffered injury from the activities of a foreign State may seek redress. In the judicial sphere, therefore, there are precedents for at least some of the provisions of the Rome Treaty.

In practical terms, what will happen if Britain joins will be this: over a wide but still carefully defined area of national life the British Government will undertake to frame its domestic policy within the limits prescribed by the European Economic Commission and the Council of Ministers. Parliament will then be called upon to pass whatever laws are necessary to enable this promise to be kept.

We shall have to change our Monopolies and Restrictive Practices Acts. We shall have to amend large parts of our commercial law, to alter, perhaps, some of the principles of our Law of Contract. We shall have to allow the Commission and Council of the EEC on some occasions to issue direct orders to British subjects. These orders will be enforced in the first instance in the English courts, but there will be an ultimate right of appeal to the European Court. To that extent, as Professor Emlyn Wade, the retiring Downing Professor of the Laws of England at Cambridge, emphasised, the House of Lords will lose its supreme appellate jurisdiction.

To Sir Arthur Goodhart, Sir Humphrey Waldock, Professor Wade of Oxford and his namesake at Cambridge, there is nothing horrifying in all this. They do not foresee the desecration of the monarchy, the dethronement of the immemorial Common Law, the pollution of private morals or the decline of cricket as the unavoidable consequences of these changes. They see no unacceptable extension to the sphere of international law.

Having made their point, they add, with astonishing unanimity and donnish detachment, that of course they do not know themselves whether we ought to go in or not; this is a matter for politicians.

Mr. William Pickles, senior lecturer in political science at the London School of Economics, takes a view at once more definite and more pessimistic. He points out that the institutions which wield power in the Common Market are at present the Council of Ministers and the European Economic Commission. Neither of them is constitutionally responsible to any European assembly, though an assembly with purely consultative functions does at present exist. To his mind, by joining we should be not merely diminishing the authority of Parliament, we should be giving power to unrepresentative bodies without any certainty about how it should be used.

Clearly, everything depends on the future development and political arrangements of the Common Market which are at present almost entirely fluid. Will it go in a federalist direction or not? Sir Arthur Goodhart agrees that it has some federalist ingredient, but neither he nor his colleagues will commit themselves further.

The French and the Germans, it is true, profess not to want federation, but how can the curious hotch-potch of institutions now developing in Europe work unless their constitutional development towards full federation is allowed to proceed, and how, in practice, could Britain ever withdraw from the Common Market if this prediction proved correct?

The lawyers maintain that membership involves no radical breach with the past, that it is all a matter of degree; but so, said Hilaire Belloc, is the difference between a blow and a caress. It may be right, wrong or merely inevitable (to use the most dangerous adjective in political discussion) for Britain to become part of a European State, but the decision is one which we must take with our eyes open.

Edward Heath's first year

The Daily Telegraph, 18 June 1971

A year is a short time in politics. That dramatic reversal of Mr. Wilson's famous judgement constitutes the only possible defence of Mr. Heath's Government.

A year ago today the Prime Minister came to power, asserting that to govern was to serve and that he proposed to abolish instant government. In that last ambition he has certainly succeeded. His predecessor's regime was distinguished by a series of dramatic gestures which promised to produce immediate and brilliant results and normally produced either nothing or disaster. Mr. Heath has so completely rejected this technique as to place himself almost entirely beyond the slipshod standards by which the efficiency of government is usually judged.

Under him, unemployment has increased, productivity has not and the economy continues to display that curious combination of maladies – fever and anaemia. Inflation goes on, but its compensation – a high rate of growth – remains strikingly absent. No one is yet conscious of having more freedom, more security or more prosperity than he had under Mr. Wilson. The electorate has been largely alienated; organised labour is up in arms; liberal sentiment has been affronted by an Immigration Bill widely denounced as tyrannical.

Yet the submerged Right (which might have supposed that its heyday had arrived) is no more content. Some of it fears that, by joining the Common Market, Mr. Heath is about to dismantle the nation; most of it finds the Industrial Relations Bill confused and morally ambiguous and feels that the Immigration Bill offers little substantial assurance of a reduction in the numbers of immigrants.

Had a highly skilled and experienced ex-Chief Whip with a malicious sense of humour attempted to devise a policy which would earn the hostility of the greatest variety of interests in the State in the shortest possible time, he might well have produced something like the recipe which Mr. Heath has followed.

Mr. Heath, however, has skill and experience but neither malice nor an extravagant sense of humour. If he has failed by almost all conventional standards, it is because he is trying to do things to which the accepted canons of political criticism do not apply. He is trying to govern without guile. This is a revolutionary experiment which distinguishes him as sharply from almost all other Tory Prime Ministers as it does from Mr. Wilson.

There is, of course, nothing new in the idea of a political leader who offers his followers suffering rather than gain. The inveterate masochism of the British electorate has for long demanded that every concession to popular greed and weakness shall be represented as a call to patriotic self-sacrifice. What is different about Mr. Heath is that he actually administers the medicine he advertises. Under him, the people really do suffer.

What is also different is that this suffering is not imposed for the sake of some glittering ideal of national greatness or consciously contrived social perfection. The object of all these exertions is not the New Jerusalem; it is the creation of a society whose members will have been trained thoroughly in the virtue and art of pursuing their own personal interests.

This, then, is the philosophy of the Heath administration, a philosophy which is being applied with relentless political courage. The Government has inherited a country whose habits and mental processes are conditioned by decades of collectivism. It is trying, by a rigorous and even ruthless therapy, to remobilise a crippled patient, to give him back the self-assurance needed to enable him to live in a competitive world.

The resulting policy contains two potentially incompatible elements – streamlined, efficient administration based on long-term planning by experts assembled in large Ministries and a deliberate attempt wherever possible is disengage the State. In both these respects, the Government, during its first year, has been outstandingly loyal to its mandate.

As far as disengagement goes, the budget has achieved the

largest reduction in taxation for several years and with it reforms in the taxation system, all directed to stimulating personal economic effort by reward. Real progress has also been made in the direction of concentrating public spending on those who are genuinely in need.

After some initial hesitation, the policy of not supporting industrial lame ducks and of forcing nationalised industries to behave like commercial concerns is now being pursued with something like doctrinaire purity. Pressure in favour of curbing rising prices by direct State action on wages is still being manfully resisted.

Yet this unprecedentedly bold experiment in government is exposed to certain growing dangers. Given that the Government is prepared to incur temporary unpopularity, do the measures which it introduces always justify the trouble they cause?

Doubt on that score must arise in connection with the Industrial Relations Bill with its weak-minded eleventh-hour statutory recognition of the closed shop in certain industries. Doubt of the same kind arises over the Immigration Bill. Doubt amounting in some quarters to near panic springs from the continuing failure of Mr. Heath's tough economic policy to restrain inflationary wage rises.

Can the policy succeed without far more radical cuts in public spending (which still increases, though the rate of increase has been reduced) and without a stricter control of the money supply? If the policy continues to fail, will not Mr. Heath and his colleagues be exposed to an irresistible temptation to use the vast administrative apparatus which they have created for the purpose of trying to achieve quicker results? Might not even they drift, via a wages policy, into something like the kind of economic régime from which they set out to deliver us?

There is an equally formidable danger of another kind. Mr. Heath rejects the classical principles of political behaviour. He despises compromise and loathes deviousness. He has rescued us from the genial atmosphere of muddled concession to supposed inevitabilities which distinguished the last years of the Macmillan régime.

But are not compromise and deviousness conditions of the

life of parliamentary democracy? Is there any principle of political action which permits no exceptions, any economic doctrine which ought not to be tempered sometimes by humanity and the instinct of political self-preservation?

There are certainly whole areas of political life to which the inherited political wisdom which this Government underrates is still relevant. The whole territory including Northern Ireland, which Mr. Maudling covers, represents one of these areas. In handling these questions this Government of administrators and economists has shown a lack of originality and even sometimes a lack of statesmanship.

It remains to be seen whether this same deficiency will apply to the Government's pursuit of the one remaining identifiable object of its foreign policy – entry to the Common Market. If Mr. Heath should succeed in this, he may well go down in history as the greatest of peace-time Prime Ministers. If he should fail, it is hard to see his experimental Government lasting long enough to distribute the fruits of the inconvenience it has inflicted. History might then see the Heath administration as an interlude during which a bunch of nature's company directors tried vainly to play a game which they never even began to understand and as a proof of the old-fashioned view that politics in Britain is the proper business of gentlemen and trade union leaders.

The aggressive tactics of Callaghan's Government in the Commons, masterminded by Michael Foot as Leader of the House, were to be revised two months later when the collapse of sterling, and the beginning of a rash of by-elections, plunged Labour into crisis.

The will of (some of) the people

The Daily Telegraph, 27 July 1976

Underlying the bitter and highly rhetorical controversies about the function of Parliament, the liberties of the Commons and Mr. Michael Foot which have lately been going on is a grotesque illusion to which both sides of the dispute tacitly subscribe. It is the illusion that there is such a thing as the British Constitution – that is to say, that there now exists in this country (as there used arguably to exist) a comprehensive body of convention about the use of public power to which it is possible to appeal for authoritative adjudications of conflicts between Government and Opposition.

The reality is very different. There are in fact two concurrent views about the nature of the Constitution, and they are wholly incompatible with each other. What is more, these views do not reflect the difference between Conservatives and Socialists but that between the Government, whatever its complexion, and the Opposition, whatever its character.

The first and older of these views (commonly adopted by all Oppositions) presupposes that the House of Commons is a genuinely independent assembly appointed to debate and remedy the grievances of the people. This view carries with it certain other archaic assumptions – that what is said in the Commons may conceivably influence what is voted in the Commons, that the Commons can make and unmake governments and that a majority of the Commons is not a mere registration of a party victory at a General Election but a wholly fluid quantity, the composition of which will change from day to day.

All that was true in the 18th century and it was still possible to believe it to be true until well into the 19th. From it derives the tradition of high-minded oratory about the rights of Parliament of which until recently Mr. Michael Foot was the best contemporary exponent and which his Tory critics like Mr. John Peyton sustain chiefly by quoting him. From it also derives the broad principle that there should be no limit on the power of the House of Commons to debate proposed legislation. Needless to say, this conception of the character and function of the Commons is quite incompatible with the doctrine of the electoral mandate.

If the Commons really consisted of 600-odd independent Members, it would be impossible for any of these to be bound by electoral pledges. They might make such pledges but in order to get anything done at all, they would have, on being elected, to strike bargains with their colleagues. In this kind of Commons, policy would be invented after elections and the MP would plainly be not the agent of his constituents but the trustee of their interests.

It is this grand (and wholly anachronistic) theory of the character of the Commons which explains the elaborate ritual governing its procedures and the high dignity which it claims and enforces. It is on this legend that the Tory Opposition now draws (and that Labour also drew when in Opposition) in order to castigate the Executive for its presumptuous encroachments on the liberty of Parliament – for curtailing the right of debate and for such other arcane monstrosities as attempts to pass off hybrid bills as public bills.

But there is another, more recent and increasingly realistic view of the Constitution: it is the doctrine that the function of Parliament (and pre-eminently of the Commons) is to enact the commands of the electorate, that these commands are embodied in the manifesto of the victorious party at a General Election and that the Executive is accordingly justified in using every necessary means to carry them into effect in the life of a Parliament. It is on this doctrine that Mr. Foot rested when he said the other day: 'We see a Labour Government as having a right and a duty to legislate against any attempts to frustrate us in the end from exercising our rights of legislation.'

It is, of course, true that the doctrine of the electoral mandate has no place in the law of the Constitution. It maintains a fragile and questionable existence on the periphery of that grey area known as 'the conventions of the Constitution'. Historically, the doctrine of the mandate has served two opposite purposes: it has provided a justification for the Cabinet whenever it wishes to curtail the rights of parliamentary debate in order to carry out a programme which has already been allegedly approved by the electorate, even though the 'electorate', under our present system, may represent only a minority of voters. On the other hand, it has supplied Oppositions with a weapon with which to attack Governments deemed either to be breaking their election pledges or acting on a mandate which has palpably been withdrawn by the people and doing one or the other without reasonable excuse.

Up to 1949, the Constitution provided a means by which such a Government might be brought to heel. The House of Lords had the power to delay legislation for two and a half years. It was a power which could be safely exercised only in extreme cases, but its existence provided a brake on any Government which, manifestly lacking a secure majority in the country, sought to impose radical and irreversible changes on society. Today, the Lords, with its delaying powers drastically curtailed, has almost entirely accepted the role of a merely revising Chamber, charged with rectifying errors and oversights in the bills presented to it.

So what does an Opposition do when faced like the present one with a mass of controversial Government legislation which it sincerely believes never to have been consciously approved by the people and to be repellent to a large majority of them? Its only recourse is to revert to the old, illusory notion that the House of Commons is still a genuinely independent assembly entitled to argue *ad nauseam*. Its only remedy is to obstruct. This is an unhealthy state of affairs and one which tends to bring Parliament into discredit. What constitutes obstruction will of course be a matter for debate, but an Opposition worthy of its salt will certainly not refrain from any use of parliamentary procedure calculated to destroy a Government which it believes to have lost the confidence of the people.

Of course, the ancient view of the Commons, as an independent assembly not of delegates but of trustees of the people, can some times be useful even to the Executive. Mr. Roy Jenkins secured the passage of a whole mass of 'permissive' legislation, almost certainly contrary to the popular will, by making it the subject of free votes in the Commons and therefore absolving the Government of responsibility for it. Mr. Heath secured the acceptance in principle of membership of the Common Market by a similar device. By contrast, Mr. Wilson kept us in the Market without undue embarrassment to his party by appealing over the heads of the Commons to a referendum, the most extreme expression of the doctrine of the mandate on record.

But none of this obscures the fundamental truth that, to all intents and purposes, we now live under a form of plebiscitary democracy the essence of which is that a Government once elected is there to carry out its programme come hell or high water. This doctrine of the mandate – once a classic heresy condemned by Edmund Burke – is now the basis of the Constitution in so far as such a thing exists. What is more, under our present system, the Government of the day is the sole interpreter of its mandate.

If we wish to end this state of affairs (deeply displeasing to all of us who were well brought up) we shall have to stop using tired rhetoric about the liberties of Parliament and apply our minds to how those liberties can be enshrined in institutions – notably, in a second Chamber with the moral and legal authority to stand sentinel over the people's interests.

Dyspeptic ghosts at the banquet

Sunday Telegraph, 5 June 1977

To understand the virtues of an institution, it is sometimes wise to look at it through the eyes of its enemies. Obligingly, the Left-wing intellectual establishment (as represented by the *New Statesman*) and the Left-wing underworld (as represented at its most malignant by the *Socialist Worker*) have provided us this past week with a rich miscellany of material for doing precisely this in relation to the monarchy.

Now I am not recommending devout monarchists (whether they be of the romantic variety or, like me, of the more empirical sort) to read this offensive trash. Much of it constitutes a serious health risk, some of it a potential menace to the Queen's Peace. The anger which it has aroused in me, for instance, were it not contained by grave physical disability, could easily express itself in violence. Rely on me, therefore, for your general impression of what this anti-monarchist propaganda is saying, and consider the extremely revealing light it sheds not on the deficiencies but on the merits of the Queen, her family and the institution which she adorns.

The least odious contributions to the miscellany are those provided by the spiritual heirs of Victorian intellectual radicalism who, let it be admitted, are as much authentic parts of the English scene as the free-thinking blacksmith and the village idiot used to be. They are a foil with which sanity cannot easily dispense. It would be unseemly if the ghost of Mr. Kingsley Martin were not present at our impending jubilations to contribute, off-stage, the sound effects of chronic dyspepsia.

In effect, all that these 'superior people' are saying is that the whole thing is a load of sentimental rubbish with which adult democrats ought to be able to dispense, that the Queen has no real power and no necessary function and that the causes of human dignity and public economy would be served at least marginally by the liquidation of her office.

This, at least, is what they are saying for most of the time. Now I confess that, although I abhor their conclusion, I think their reasoning reveals some of the defects of the orthodox defence of British monarchy, a defence which has survived virtually intact from the days of Bagehot. Roughly, this orthodoxy holds that the Queen's essential function is to make the lawful acts of her Government tolerable to its subjects by surrounding those acts with an aura of holy mystery; in other words, by convincing the gullible multitude that Government policy is not the work of a bunch of dreary and often manifestly subhuman politicians, but rather the emanation of a near-goddess.

Now, if this con ever worked, I very much doubt whether it still does, and I think there is a touch of absurdity also in the painstaking care with which a number of popular writers on monarchy set about explaining to the multitude precisely how they are being deceived and exactly why that is so good for them.

What is more, I also wonder whether, in what Lord Hailsham rightly describes as this 'elective dictatorship', there is all that much to be said for bolstering up the authority of Mr. Callaghan and Mr. Foot by pretending that it is really that of the Queen. I also observe that many of Her Majesty's most passionately loyal subjects, notably in Ulster and even in Rhodesia, have no difficulty at all in reconciling extreme contempt for the edicts of Governments and Parliaments with utter devotion to her person.

A monarchy is indeed more than a rubber stamp guaranteed to consecrate the ineptitude of politicians, and it is precisely because they perceive this that the sworn enemies of the national ethos mix their contempt for it with ill-concealed fear. That fear is apparent in the relatively decorous grumblings of the *New Statesman*, and is positively blatant in the crude graffiti of its less senile contemporaries. Rightly, these people see the monarchy as an obstacle to their ultimate aims, and they are the more terrified because they do not know precisely (any more than any of us can know precisely) how that obstacle would become effective if the chips were ever really down.

One obvious and continuous function of the monarchy is to confer approbation by word and deed on those things which, in the common judgement of most men and women of British stock, are still deemed honourable – the bonds of family love and loyalty, care for the unfortunate, respect for human personalities as distinct from dedication to the abstract rights of mankind, even hard work and enterprise. To the various scruffs who assault the monarchy these things are anathema either because they are incompatible with the total transform- ation of society they want or, at the very least, because they tend to make that transformation less urgently desirable than it otherwise might appear.

By upholding these simple pieties, which have worn thin among politicians, the Crown exerts a continuous subtle restraint on reckless and ruthless innovation. Hence the particular venom inspired among the dregs of radicalism by the Duke of Edinburgh, who can speak on such matters with greater freedom than the Queen and who wields that influence, not perhaps with unerring instinct, but with a beneficent effect which is the greater for not being muffled by immaculate caution.

Even more important than this, the Crown, in strict law, still retains vast powers – the power to dissolve or not to dissolve Parliament, to assent or not to assent to legislation, to appoint or not to appoint Ministers. It is inconceivable that those powers should ever be used against the deliberate will of a proven democratic majority, however evil or misguided. So to use them would be to destroy the monarchy.

But the British Constitution has often relied on the device

(the unreformed House of Lords is an example) of giving ultimate powers of veto to institutions which can act only at their own peril and which have therefore the best possible motives for acting only *in extremis*. Suppose that a revolutionary junta of corrupt obligarchy were blatantly to use the machinery of democracy to try to compass democracy's destruction. Would the Crown be wholly impotent? I do not think so.

Moderates can be a menace

Sunday Telegraph, 7 May 1978

In a startling manner, the deep sigh of relief from all 'responsible and right-minded people' which greeted the election of Mr. Terry Duffy to the presidency of the Amalgamated Union of Engineering Workers last week illustrates the stoat-rabbit relationship which now subsists between the trade union movement and the rest of the community.

There is, of course, nothing discreditable or strange about wanting the vast power now wielded by trade union leaders to be in the hands of moderates rather than extremists. In theory, no doubt, we live in a liberal democracy in which the elected representatives of the people stand supreme over all vested interests. In reality, however, this is not and never has been our condition. What is more, no State on earth has ever in practice possessed such absolute sovereignty over its subjects.

The most powerful and the most tyrannical of Governments is obliged to take into account the wishes and ambitions of the classes and 'interests' into which all societies are divided, and to live, in some degree, by playing them off against one another. Other things being equal, therefore, it is all to the good that powerful combinations of potential rebels should be under the leadership of men who are not actually dedicated to the destruction of society and who may even be prepared, from time to time, to subordinate the demands of their followers to the public good.

Mr. Duffy, we are told, is precisely such a man. He has already given evidence of the truth of that proposition by saying that he does not favour confrontation with Government, that he does not think wage negotiations can be conducted without any thought to inflation, that he is prepared to work hand-in-glove with Mr. Callaghan for the salvation of the country, and that he would not shrink even from consulting with Mrs. Thatcher if she were to become Prime Minister.

What is abundantly clear from all this is that Mr. Duffy, like other trade union leaders, has long ago ceased to regard himself merely as the authorised representative of a section of the labour force, employed to protect and advance its legitimate interests. Instead, he conceives of himself as an actual part of the machinery of government, entitled to a share in the formulation of general economic policy and probably also (since politics is one and indivisible) in the formulation of all other aspects of policy as well.

He remains, in fact, loyal to that almost unbelievably blatant violation of the Constitution, the 'Social Contract', the arrangement under which the Government largely abandons the role of governing in return for a partial abandonment by the trade union leaders of the function of wage negotiation.

Now it is obvious, from the Government's point of view and from the standpoint of preserving democratic control of the State, that this arrangement is something far more sinister than one of the innumerable examples in which history abounds of a technically omnipotent State exercising its power with a discreet regard for the need to keep on the right side of over-mighty subjects. It is an instance not of diplomacy but of surrender.

Since the assumption is that this new system for the ordering of our affairs can only function smoothly (and, probably, can only function at all) so long as a Labour administration remains in power, the effect is to import into the conduct of national politics a wholly new moral pressure in favour of permanent one-party Government.

To the extent to which the success of moderate trade unionists is a necessary condition of the survival of this condominium, I for one deplore it. Perpetual strife between Government and trade unions, continual disruption of industry, even public and humiliating defeats for political authority at the hands of the unions – all these awe-inspiring possibilities seem to me to be less dangerous to the cause of parliamentary democracy in Britain than the silent surrender of sovereignty which is now going on and which will increasingly reduce Parliament to the function of rubber-stamping agreements reached behind closed doors between the Cabinet and the TUC.

It is even arguable that there would be more ultimate hope for the free society in Britain if Parliament were formally to surrender its sovereignty to the General Council of the TUC than if it were to allow the present trend to continue unchecked. We should then at least know where we were going and the point we had reached.

But, *pace* Lord Carrington and his advisers, is there really a rational case for supposing that a major confrontation with certain powerful unions would unfailingly end in defeat for the State? As with all human conflicts, indeed, the outcome would be uncertain. It would largely depend on the skill of Government in selecting an issue in which it would have the moral advantage, in which it would be seen as defending its own legitimate authority rather than as seeking to trespass on the traditional preserves of the unions.

It may be that modern technology means that a handful of electricians can plunge the nation into darkness, bring industry to a standstill and slaughter hospital patients, though, if it came to all that, Lord Carrington's argument that the Army could not be used because this would fatally impair the fabric of society would begin to look somewhat *passé*.

What is certain is that, while the disaster continued, the strikers themselves would not be exempt from its consequences. Neither is it likely that they and their families would be altogether immune to the influence of social opprobrium.

The trade union movement is not in reality a monolith, but a conglomeration of mutually hostile interests perpetually torn between the ambition for political power and the pursuit of higher wages. Its moral disadvantages in any clear struggle against the community would be great – all the greater if its leaders were 'flagrant extremists' who had not learnt to mouth the deceptive platitudes of moderation.

Nationalisation of vice and virtue
The Daily Telegraph, 4 April 1980

It is some 40 years since C. S. Lewis reported the activities of Screwtape, the tutorial devil charged with the task of instructing his nephew, Wormwood, in the art of destroying human souls. There can be little doubt, however, that Screwtape's campaign continues, and there is even some evidence that it has been intensified. What is far more alarming is the possibility that the battle, at least in its Western sector, has moved on to new terrain of a kind vastly more favourable to the powers of darkness.

What I have in mind is the advance or drift of the Western world towards a form of organisation known as 'social democracy', the chief characteristic of which is to reduce the area of social life in which individuals make decisions for themselves in face-to-face relationships with each other, and to increase that in which decisions are made by remote authorities theoretically responsible to the entire people. This has led, in a considerable degree, to what may properly be called the nationalisation of virtue and vice, a change markedly favourable to Screwtape and his cohorts.

The process has been accompanied, and very largely caused, by a dramatic increase in the power of mass communication, from which also the 'Lower-archy' has derived great advantage. Instead of the gruelling task assigned to Wormwood, 40 years ago, of destroying individual souls one by one, and of subtly undermining the moral authority of firmly entrenched social conventions, all he has to do now (and it has proved astonishingly easy) is to secure a controlling interest in a handful of television companies or a few seats on the boards of public broadcasting corporations, in order to infect millions of people simultaneously with his spiritual poison.

Take, for example, one of the purposes dear to Screwtape in the 1940s, that of accomplishing the extinction of the human race by destroying its fertility. The best he could think up was to discourage women from marrying men with beards (beards being, in the extraordinary view which I suspect he has picked up from C. S. Lewis, proofs of virility). Today, it has become possible for the legions of Satan to mount a direct and wholly uninhibited attack on the cause of life itself. As the current controversies over sterilisation, abortion and euthanasia show, it has become the mark of a progressive man to favour, in almost all cases where a scintilla of doubt can be shown to exist, the destruction or prevention of life.

But the new political dispensation has produced consequences even more far-reaching than that. There is, of course, no reason for supposing that the practice of virtue is impossible in a collectivised democracy; but the kind of virtue for which such a system calls is so preternaturally exacting as to make vice an even more acceptable alternative than usual. Roughly speaking, social democracy may be defined as an arrangement under which we all largely cease to be responsible for our own behaviour and in return become responsible for everybody else's. The temptations which this way of doing things offers to synthetic anger, fraudulent penitence, all other forms of hypocrisy and the sheer evasion of duty are infinitely too strong for fallen man.

For example, what could conceivably be easier than to whip oneself up into an exhilarating state of moral indignation against the wickedness of a Cabinet Minister who is prepared to allow kidney patients to die rather than provide the money for kidney machines? If he replies by pointing out that those who will this end must also will the means to it – a heavy increase in taxation or a steep increase in inflation, or the neglect of many other equally deserving causes – he has already moved the controversy on to a level of complexity great enough to enable his assailants to retire gracefully from the scene, protesting that they are not experts but they do know the difference between right and wrong. What, indeed, could be easier than all that! Well, possibly one thing – the temptation to which Tories are exposed these days, that of saying that costly causes like this must depend on voluntary effort, hitherto the great glory of our people, and then, as individuals, doing precisely nothing to produce the effort.

Collectivism is full of built-in excuses for the evasion of

responsibility. It inevitably converts the moral life into a question of contract – a huge contract, the terms of which can always be conveniently, and often correctly, assumed to have been broken by others. Who would evade his tax if he could only be sure that it was not being spent on social security spongers? Who would sponge on security if he could only satisfy himself that the rich were not evading their taxes? Many perhaps, but without the comforting pretext which they now enjoy.

And the rot does not stop here. Even those who profess to be determined to destroy or reduce to proper proportions the whole collectivist arrangement show signs of hypocrisy. Do they really mean it, or is all this idealism about restoring responsibility to the individual a morally edifying camouflage for measures which are simply designed to get us out of a financial mess? If they do mean it, it is, on the face of it, hard to see why the Government, instead of embarking on a judicious reform of the Welfare State designed actually to encourage family responsibility, confines itself to haphazard economies which leave the established structure of social provision intact.

Hypocrisy is, of course, one of the built-in conventions of political life, relatively innocent when politics do not claim most of life and when millions of people are not daily invited to share its sham emotions. Certainly it is a healthy thing that opposing politicians, having denounced each other with untrammelled bitterness in parliamentary debate, should be able to meet privately to express mutual sympathy and even sly agreement. Only a small proportion of the public is in serious danger of falling into genuine anger and malice in response to political rhetoric. The danger is rather that these moral conflicts will not be taken seriously at all. Very few are even tempted to wonder, for example, how it can be (as the Tories maintain it is) that the policies of Dr. Owen in Rhodesia were so frightfully wicked, while the more vigorous version of them presented by Lord Carrington is so frightfully good. Constant exposure to the spectacle of synthetic anger and fraudulent self-congratulation on this scale can anaesthetise the moral sense of ordinary people.

So could it not be that the shrewdest blow to be delivered

against Screwtape today would be a determined effort to depoliticise our lives? There are still places, notably the family, where people drawn together by no set of common enthusiasms or necessary bond of economic self-interest meet in mutual love at the great Christian festivals. It is in such places, and not in parliaments or Cabinet rooms, that the seeds of national regeneration will be sown and in which Screwtape will find it hardest to keep up the battle he lost 2,000 years ago. Meanwhile, he will no doubt continue to derive some measure of satisfaction from the many eminent sermons undoubtedly to be preached today by which, however unintentionally, we shall be encouraged to seek salvation through politics.

Keep your insults in context, please

The Daily Telegraph, 11 June 1984

What is and what is not an insult (in ordinary human intercourse as well as in Parliament) depends, as Erskine May ruled and Mr. Speaker Weatherill has reiterated, on 'the context'. What is more, adjectives descriptive of political attitudes change their emotional content fairly rapidly.

Do I not recall that Mr. Gladstone took the gravest umbrage at being dubbed 'a democrat'? Certainly, the word 'Jacobin' must have been slanderous in Britain for much of the last century. The reason in both cases is the same: both words evoked memories of Robespierre, the guillotine, that vulgar little man Napoleon and of a vile tyranny from which England had gloriously saved Europe. So it is with 'fascist', particularly when hurled across the floor of the Commons on the eve of the anniversary of D-Day.

But suppose a man described me as a 'fascist' on some more sober, less emotive occasion – in the course, for example, of one of those ghastly philosophical seminars which the English have picked up from the Americans. I would think him a fool or, at any rate, a philosophical illiterate, but I would have some sympathy with the way in which he made his mistake.

Fascism, as a political theory, was always immensely confused and intellectually second-rate. (I will not trouble you with the very real distinction between it and Nazism, all to the discredit of Nazism.) Fascism's three salient characteristics, I make so bold to say, are:

One, the belief that every man owes a supreme duty, overriding all other duties, to the nation or race with which he, often fraudulently, has identified himself, and that therefore there is no 'international order' to which he can ever owe allegiance, other of course than an 'international order' based on the supremacy of what he claims to be his own ethnic community.

Two, the view that society should be organised as a rigid hierarchy in which all or most human relations are based on command and obedience.

Three, the view that the economy should be organised on a 'corporatist' basis, i.e., on planning arising from a partnership between employers, workers and the State.

Now every one of these propositions, like most heresies, is the corruption of a valuable truth. As a good Tory and a striving Christian, I cannot, of course, accept the view that I have no higher duty than to the nation to which I belong; but I do accept the view that, in normal circumstances, my first political duty must be to serve the legitimate interests of my country. I also believe that, in this imperfect world, foreign policy cannot consist in simply applying universal moral principles, but must aim at achieving some kind of tolerable accommodation between the opposing interests of nations which accept no common authority.

Of course, I do not believe in a rigid social hierarchy (what a horribly un-English idea), but I do believe that the welfare, the happiness and the civility of the nation depend on free and habitual respect for legitimate authority – on respect for judges and acquiescence in their judgements, on reverence for parents and elders, on ultimate deference by civil servants to their political superiors, on obedience by soldiers to their officers.

I certainly do not fancy corporatism as a method for organising the British economy today (or probably at any other time), but I would be far from regarding it as intrinsically, perpetually and ubiquitously evil, and I have to recognise that it has played an important part in the theory and practice of British Conservatism.

That other dirty word 'authoritarian' (happily too long and pompous for use at demos inside or outside the Commons) could still, I think, be rescued from total corruption. To achieve that depends on distinguishing between authority and power.

Authority is a moral concept, not to be confused with bullying; those who exercise it base their claims to obedience or deference, not on proud claims to personal superiority but on their own obedience to still higher authority. The centurion who, on behalf of his ailing servant, sent a deputation to petition Jesus did not describe himself as a man of great power and influence but as one 'set under authority'. A society from which respect for authority is absent can be held together only by naked power, precisely the kind of nightmare which the lunatic Left is trying to realise.

So please do not call me a 'fascist', but you are at liberty to describe me as 'an authoritarian', a paradox which is by no means insoluble. I do not suppose that Mrs. Thatcher would herself object to such a description, nor do I suppose that, if properly understood, it would do her much harm in the eyes of ordinary people who know by instinct that the most important question in politics, and perhaps in social life generally, is 'who guards whom?'

Commentary

The Daily Telegraph, 3 December 1984

What rational hope can today sustain an averagely ambitious SDP politician in his late forties (a man, for example, such as Dr. Owen or the exceptionally talented Robert Maclennan)?

I speak of the SDP rather than the Alliance, because Liberal politicians have little ambition in the normal and honourable political sense. They have become used to being a party of eccentrics and protesters, commenting from the sidelines. By contrast, the SDP is an offshoot of the Labour party and, therefore, has a tradition of government and political responsibility. It is about power.

On the face of it, there is virtually no hope for the SDP. In order to make any impact on the electorate at the next General Election it must offer itself as an alternative Government. That means that it must offer itself in total unison with the Liberals; but how can it risk association with this bunch of assorted oddities? Indeed, how can it reach agreement with them on any central issue like defence, on which the attitudes of the two parties are sharply divided – the Liberals veering towards unilateral disarmament and the SDP favouring (on the whole) an independent nuclear deterrent, though one less expensive than we are committed to?

SDP politicians are for the most part not fools. They have considered these questions and come up with reasonable answers. They assume, for a start, that Labour has virtually committed suicide and that there is, therefore, no danger of the SDP's splitting the Tory vote and putting Mr. Kinnock into power. They are also not excessively worried about the Liberal association.

In 1986, the Alliance intends to produce a long-term programme; assuming that hurdle can be crossed successfully, no further statements of policy will be issued independently by the SDP and the Liberals until the election. Then a common manifesto will be produced. However, they believe that this should not be too difficult, since the Liberal input will, according to the party's constitution, be settled entirely by David Steel, who is not a loony. Whatever may happen in such constituencies as are fought by Liberals, the Alliance manifesto will not be concerned with such peripheral matters as the promotion of homosexuality.

As for defence, the SDP hopes that the whole terms of the argument will soon be changed – partly by general and serious moves towards multilateral disarmament and partly by the discovery that Mr. Heseltine has assumed commitments for which the country has no hope of paying. All this, plus increasing middle-class disillusionment with Thatcherite remedies, might enable the Alliance to win enough seats to be the balancing force in a hung Parliament.

Well, it does not wholly convince me; but it does suggest to me that the Alliance, by virtue of its SDP ingredient, is a formidable challenge to the Tory party. That challenge cannot be effectively met by Tories building up Labour as the serious Opposition; the electorate sees through that sort of thing.

Mrs. Thatcher's best hope (and it is a strong one) at the next election is to ignore Opposition parties altogether and to concentrate on her own record and prospectus. The task of finishing off Labour belongs to her. The SDP's chance will come at the election after that, and some of its leading lights will still be young enough to take the opportunity.

*   *   *

This modern habit of exhuming Victorian politicians and forcing them to take sides in current debates about issues of which they knew nothing, and on which their thinking casts no light at all, is reaching truly obscene proportions. Poor Disraeli has been thus desecrated for a long time. A patriot, a nationalist, in the most favourable meaning of the term, a racist, he has been called in aid by almost every wet, drivelling liberal, cosmopolitan, bloodless politician in the Tory party.

Now, it is Peel's turn, because of the anniversary of the Tamworth Manifesto (well, not quite the anniversary, which will be 18 December, but it is too much to expect politicians to get that right). Sir Robert is being summoned to the aid equally of Thatcherites and anti-Thatcherites. On Friday Mr. Heath invoked his blessing on a general statement of all Mr. Heath's opinions, while Mr. Brittan finds him the prototype of Mrs. Thatcher, and, no doubt, of Mr. Brittan, since the distinction is one which he has always been anxious to obliterate.

It is 40 years since I could call myself an historian, but what I remember about Peel is that he first defended the Irish Protestants and then betrayed them, that he first attacked the Great Reform Bill and then grovelled to it, and that he first supported the Corn Laws and then abolished them. Perhaps he deserves the patronage both of Mr. Heath and of Mr. Brittan, but, in praising Peel, Mr. Brittan has no need to disparage Burke; even from the Home Secretary that is a piece of cheek which I will not tolerate.

What I seriously wonder, however, is what use politicians think that this kind of body-snatching serves. Mr. Heath, for instance, seems to think that Sir Robert believed in the Welfare State: if so, that great statesman was a man of even greater prescience than one had supposed!

Commentary

The Daily Telegraph, 27 May 1985

Dr. Owen, we are told, has not 'stooped' to reply to Mr. Kinnock's vitriolic personal attack on him. For this, we are invited to admire the doctor and we are also urged to regard Mr. Kinnock as a man who has debased the currency of political controversy.

I share none of these feelings. I thought Neil Kinnock's speech to be a fairly creditable example of a long and honourable tradition of personal vituperation in British politics.

After all, what was its most offensive ingredient? Apparently, the reference to Dr. Owen's 'ego' as 'fat on arrogance and drunk on ambition'. There is nothing particularly new or horrifying about calling a politician 'ambitious'. As for the 'fat' bit, this might have caused offence if Dr. Owen were in fact fat; even that, however, would have argued undue sensitivity. I, for example, have always relished metaphoric allusions to my own infirmity – in such phrases as 'our blind guide'. What is more, it is surely an accepted convention of British political life that insults spoken or written in the course of political argument are not to be taken literally or quite seriously.

I still remember with affection a reviewer's comment on a political address which I had given extempore and arrogantly omitted to correct before publication: 'the poverty of Mr. Utley's mind is equalled only by the incoherence of his style.' Only scruples about plagiarism have prevented me from applying the description to several other authors since. It is such descents into poor taste alone which keep politics from degenerating into an interminably tedious seminar about such concepts as 'gross national product' and the 'inflationary spiral'.

We British remain free essentially because we are a 'political people'. We are sceptical of politicians but we value their gladiatorial contests as a spectator sport. We would rapidly lose interest if the referee's rules became too strict.

Moreover, politics is about men as well as measures and the two are far more closely connected than is often supposed. In 1970, Mr. Heath held all the economic views of Mrs. Thatcher and presented them straightforwardly to the electorate. Had we given a closer and more critical attention to his complex character, we would have known for sure that he would abandon them at the first sign of difficulty. How could a man with such a pronounced taste for rationality and authority, endowed with all the best bureaucratic virtues, reconcile himself to surrendering the nation's fate to the arbitrament of a free economy?

Similarly with Dr. Owen: he is a great and formidable man but he stands, in terms of public personality, in the Gladstonian tradition of moral self-confidence bordering on the pompous. If he ever got to power, his vice would be to fall in love with a style of politics, in which 'moderation' (the most elusive of all political ideas) would be the dominant element, soon raised to the status of a panacea.

No, personal abuse, like the talent of the cartoonist, has a crucial role in democratic politics. What is not to be endured, on the other hand, is the irresponsible denigration of whole classes or groups, whether ethnically defined or not – e.g. Nye Bevan's 'lower than vermin' speech. This really does poison the atmosphere.

What also is not to be endured is the kind of destructive hyperbole in which many more ostentatiously moderate socialists than Mr. Kinnock habitually indulge about the state of the nation today – e.g. the assertion that we are drifting towards fascism and that such modest proposals for improvements in the law about public order as Mr. Brittan has presented herald the totalitarian state. That sort of thing not only discredits us abroad, it also makes nonsense of the political debate.

So my message to Mr. Kinnock is this: stick to personal insults and, if you do, more power to your larynx.

*   *   *

I am much disturbed by a symposium recently brought out by the Centre for Contemporary Studies. Its main burden seems to be that a body of historians, often inspired by evil political motives, is trying to prove that the Holocaust never took place, or was not as bad as supposed or that the Germans were not really to blame for it.

What shocks me is not the revelation that theories of this kind are being put about (some of them plain malicious trash, others with better scholarly credentials) but that the centre should feel it proper to demand a highly orchestrated response to them, including a new law of 'group libel' as a deterrent to their propagation. It is precisely from this kind of attitude to intellectual freedom that the Holocaust arose. No accepted account of historical events, however emotive, should be protected against critical challenge, however dishonestly inspired.

This does not mean that historians and publicists should be discouraged from giving these theories the drubbing they often deserve. It does mean that the best weapon against error is not suppression but the unfettered pursuit of truth.

And, by the way, I will not brook any suggestion that these words imply tenderness on my part for Nazism and fascism. My generation of Englishmen has every cause for hating both.

Commentary

The Daily Telegraph, 23 September 1985

I am prepared (I think) to offer a prize of £5 to the first regular reader of this column who can cite an occasion on which I have used the word 'democracy', or any of its derivatives, in a favourable sense. The bet can be safely placed since the boredom involved in winning this competition is quite incommensurate with the reward offered.

My objection to the word derives from several causes. In my lifetime it has come to be used as a synonym for everything remotely admirable – kindness, compassion, respect for freedom, the lot. It is therefore redundant; 'good' would do just as well and takes up less space.

But there are more serious objections. 'Democracy' is not necessarily, or even probably, consistent with these virtues. In its essential sense – government by the majority – it can be and is extremely tyrannical. The majority in most countries at most times has very little abstract love of freedom. It feels itself threatened by eccentricity and excellence. Its main desire is to get its hands on the fleshpots.

None of this matters, however, compared with the most devastating objection to democracy – it is fraudulent. The idea that policies for the government of a country can ever spring from the people is absurd.

Consider the democratic festival which we are now enjoying in this country, the annual party conferences. All of them have essentially the same theme – the attempt of roughly (in some cases very roughly) sane members of the political establishment to prevent their rank-and-file supporters from going mad.

Those who voluntarily go to party conferences are quite the most unrepresentative sections of the community: they either want political office, or just like the sound of their own voices, or are the representatives of vested interests who are seeking to capture the State; sensible representatives of vested interests know that they must conceal, not parade this purpose.

Anyway, in so far as the 'grass roots' prevail on these occasions, the result is a most unrepresentative party manifesto – simple, ideological, often cracked. It has nothing to do with the hopes and fears of ordinary people. Ordinary people are then obliged to choose between one or other of these documents. They do so with misery, scepticism and reluctance, but it is assumed thereafter that they have agreed whole heartedly to every item in the programme. That simply adds insult to injury.

This is quite different from the traditional British system of government by discussion and consent. Under that system, there is a political establishment divided into two; each side meets behind closed doors and decides what to offer to the people. Then the people have a choice between two evils, one of which they sadly and sceptically accept. The merit of the system is that they can get rid of anything intolerable without violence. That is the way in which things should be run.

Such were the thoughts which occupied me during a recent holiday in Portugal. We went to the Douro Valley – a place much to be commended for its scenic beauty and acceptable to me because of its associations with the Duke of Wellington and the Peninsular War. The food is more congenial to xenophobic taste than that offered in Spain, Greece or Italy, though not of course comparable with that offered in France. The weather was far too hot, and I have to say that the interval between ordering and receiving a drink in that country is greater than in any part of the world of which I have knowledge.

My wife spares me those elaborate and unevocative descriptions of the landscape which are among the chief burdens of blindness (her most succinct description was that of St. Peter's in Rome: 'it is very big indeed'). I must therefore abandon my role as a travel writer.

So what can I do on a holiday except think about politics, and what better place for doing that than Portugal? While I was there, they started a general election (not, I think, out of respect, but from sheer habit). Since, 11 years ago, they got their freedom, they have had nine national elections; after this, they are going to have a presidential election, and that will almost certainly be followed by another general election. They are at it full time. They have a wonderful system of proportional representation (German model), a rather bad compromise between the American and the British constitutions and a great zeal for politics. But where is it getting them?

We spent a very pleasant evening in a manor house in the Douro, entertained by a delightful young man who was about to go off to do his military service. I asked him whether he regretted Salazar – the man who said: 'the people have less need of being sovereign than of being governed': 'We need ten Salazars', my host replied.

I suspect he is right. Not that there is any immediate or remote prospect of a coup in Portugal; its admission to the Common Market and what is quaintly conceived as 'the civilised society of Europe' will condemn it to going on with this lark. But do beware of the SDP and the Liberals!

Commentary

The Daily Telegraph, 23 December 1985

Is there not something intensely odd about last week's decisions in the Commons on the question of registering Members' interests? The House continues to resist the idea that MPs should be obliged to specify in detail all their sources of income.

It accepts Mr. Biffen's view that a certain amount of confidence should be reposed in the honour and trustworthiness of those who are chosen by their constituents to offer counsel to the Queen. That is a view which I have always taken myself – and for a very practical reason. If you encumber a reasonably decent man with all sorts of rules and regulations, and threaten him with dire consequences if he breaks them, he is likely to feel entirely free to work out methods of evading the code without literally breaking it. If, on the other hand, you simply put him on his honour to behave like an officer and a gentleman, he is likely to take a far more stringent view of his duties, not least because of the public opprobrium which he will suffer if he is discovered not behaving himself.

Now all this presupposes, of course, the existence of some sort of consensus between MPs about what constitutes good behaviour. It is arguable that no such consensus now exists. For my part, however, I think that if that is so the chances of re-establishing a consensus will be much increased by pretending that it still does exist.

At least, one should try to do this as long as possible; and I still believe that if you are looking for common honesty in the face of great temptation, you are likely to find more of it among politicians than among businessmen, clergy, university lecturers, nowadays doctors – in short among any other section of the working community. I do not mention trade unionists because I think that manifestly and unquestionably they do have a code of honour, though one from which we have suffered grievously. I do not mention journalists because I am not qualified to judge them.

But why, if MPs are to be thus trusted, should their secretaries and research assistants be required to reveal the intimate details of their extra-mural employment (which apparently is what the House has in mind)?

Well, I am told (though, of course, I do not believe it) that the device is aimed against MPs, some of whom receive the aid and companionship of beautiful young women (or, no doubt, in some cases, beautiful young men) from important business concerns in return for an implicit understanding that the interests of these concerns will be promoted. If that is indeed the case (perish the thought!) the MPs should be obliged to declare their interests, including the young women or young men. If it is not, surely officers and gentlemen can be trusted to control the activities of their subordinates, and the subordinates spared the humiliation of inquiries into their private financial affairs.

I really wonder how much serious corruption can conceivably arise from the activities of secretaries and research assistants. My own layman's impression is that great nuisance springs from those activities. Zealous young men and women (sometimes working for virtually nothing, while the allowances which they ought to enjoy are distributed, no doubt legitimately, to hard working MPs' wives in their secretarial rather than their conjugal capacities), occupy themselves in formulating endless and costly questions for their masters to ask, or composing those often ridiculous early day motions. A secretary or two is tolerable, but let us get rid of these research assistants. MPs are not meant to go in for research; they must be amateurs if they are to continue to be representatives.

         *   *   *

The fashion is in favour of modern versions of Biblical stories.

Here is such a version of the parable of the good Samaritan; I received it the other day from the highest possible source.

An old lady was severely mugged and left in the gutter – couple of ribs broken, her face severely cut, there she lay bleeding profusely.

A social worker came by (not on the other side of the road) and paused to look at the victim. 'My God!' she exclaimed, 'whoever did that to you must really be in need of help!'

This is the season of goodwill. You must love the mugged as well as the mugger, not hate the Russians nor even those who hate the Russians, suffer in your own souls the cruel predicament of mankind. In the end, however, you must keep some sense of proportion, which is what the whole exercise is about. By all means contemplate the sins of your own political friends, but without fraudulently forgetting those of your political enemies. It is a tall order, but so was the crucifixion.

And, the sermon now being over, above all, have another drink and an extremely happy Christmas. By the way, please stop complaining about the Christmas rush and the commercialisation of the event. These are practically the only tributes which this secularised society now pays to its Redeemer; they should at all costs be preserved.

Time to cut through the sanctions sanctimony

The Daily Telegraph, 21 July 1986

How are we to estimate Mrs. Thatcher's political skill in handling the South African crisis? According to her critics, she has presented us with an example of tactical blundering unprecedented in the annals of political ineptitude. She has, they say, 'boxed herself in'.

Finding herself at variance with the views of other Commonwealth and EEC statesmen, she has trumpeted her own case to the world, denouncing their views as foolish and immoral and leaving herself no room for manoeuvre. Yet, they add, manoeuvre is inevitable. Britain cannot risk the disintegration of the Commonwealth and total or almost total isolation in the civilised world. So she will be obliged to retreat and, they contend, she is already making the first moves in that direction.

A good many of the assumptions of this indictment are to my mind wrong. I am not at all sure that she is contemplating retreat, and I myself question the belief that the abolition of the Commonwealth (if that, indeed, is conceivable) would be any great disaster. However, for the purposes of argument, let us swallow the assumptions. It still does not follow that Mrs. Thatcher has been uniquely foolish.

What this whole affair illustrates is not her stupidity or bossiness but the inherent defects of public diplomacy, one of the greatest evils of modern times. Consider how this matter would have been handled under ideal laboratory conditions of secret diplomacy.

The Commonwealth countries and the EEC countries would have conducted all their discussions in private. The public would not have been regaled with colourful extracts from their conversations at the conference table. They would have bargained in camera.

No 'eminent persons group' (it is hard to believe that this name was invented by anyone other than Peter Simple or the editor of *Private Eye*) would have been dispatched to patronise and irritate the South Africans and Sir Geoffrey Howe would have been allowed a much needed rest. Instead, Britain's ambassador in South Africa would have been sent round to President Botha to say roughly this:

'Look here Mr. President, we don't go along with all this twaddle about sanctions; we fully understand your necessity to appear to be in charge of your own affairs; we loathe your apartheid system, but we fully sympathise with your difficulties in dismantling it. However, we have this pack of assorted hounds at our heels who are howling for your blood. Unless you do something pretty dramatic of your own free will fairly soon, we shall not be able to call them off. Indeed, we shall have to go along with them in spite of our own better judgement. For Heaven's sake, do something obliging – and make it snappy.'

This approach might conceivably have done some good. Negotiation without the threat of force in some form or other is, as the Thatcher critics maintain, useless. Negotiation accompanied by a public threat of force is absolutely bound to defeat its own ends. The whole exercise, as it is being conducted, is ludicrous beyond the dreams of comedy.

If Sir Geoffrey were to succeed in browbeating President Botha into making some important concession, like the release of Mandela, how would the President defend this to his special party conference which is meeting in mid-August? 'Comrades,' he might say, 'I can tell you that I will never tolerate foreign interference in our affairs and that I have given this Howe fellow a piece of my mind. It just so happens that I think the time is ripe to release Mandela. I was never kicked downstairs; I just happened to be nudged at the top by this dead sheep and then freely decided to fall.' Strange as life has become, I think that nothing quite so strange as that is likely to happen.

We have to live with public diplomacy and Mrs. Thatcher has been right to fall in with its requirements. Provided she does not concede too much, she will cut a better figure with the electorate by appearing to have failed in a sensible course than by appearing to have gone along with spontaneous enthusiasm on a thoroughly misconceived course.

Above all, her bluntness may have helped to address the minds of the British people to an important truth which vanity and nostalgia conceals from them. British foreign policy now must rest first on the Anglo-American Alliance and, second, on reasonably close relations with our Western European allies. The Commonwealth comes a poor third, for it is now merely the anachronistic embodiment of a sentimental memory. If that lesson is not learned now, it will have to be learned sometime.

I look forward to hearing it spelt out in Mrs. Thatcher's strident tones with as much clarity as it has been spelt out for years by Mr. Powell.

Why PR might be worth a try

The Daily Telegraph, 25 August 1986

So the Alliance is going slightly tepid over proportional representation. That, of course, is a somewhat unfair statement, but no more unfair than is tolerable in polemical commentary.

All that has happened is that Mr. Des Wilson, President-Elect of the Liberal Party, has made the surprisingly mature observation that the Alliance cannot commit itself in advance to refuse to co-operate in the next Parliament with anyone who will not swallow PR.

The great and pure Dr. Owen has also said that it would be unfair to impose PR on a reluctant House of Commons without the authority provided by direct consultation of the people in a referendum. I think, in fact, that this is a sound point and that, on constitutional matters, referendums should be used.

But, I will not deny myself the luxury of suggesting (in a really rather beastly way) that Dr. Owen has convinced himself that the Alliance might win an overall majority at the next election or the one after and that, naturally, therefore, there would be no point in its banging on about the rights of minorities. It would not, of course, abandon the cause; its line would be that followed by St. Augustine's famous prayer: 'Give me chastity and continence, but not just now.'

But now let me make a shock-horror revelation to my small band of loyal admirers. If it is true that the Alliance is moving away from PR, I rather regret it because my opinions on this subject are heterodox.

Consider the broad and familiar arguments for retaining the present electoral system. I do not believe, for a start, that if that system were changed the British would instantly start behaving (as the vulgar would put it) as though they were a whole lot of hysterical foreigners who could not live with a Government for more than five minutes. There is quite a lot to be said for not being too tolerant of governments but, apart from that, the factors which make for stability in the British political system are numerous and do not consist solely of 'first past the post' elections.

What is more, the stability of the British political system can be easily exaggerated. Under our present electoral arrangements, we had two minority Labour Governments (by which I mean Governments with no overall majority in the Commons) before the 1939–45 War, in 1923 and 1929. In February 1974, we had another Labour Government without an overall Commons majority. We have had Governments with only minute overall Commons majorities in 1950, 1964 and, as a result of the October election, in 1974. If the electorate now gets into the habit of 'tactical voting', we may be saddled with this kind of arrangement for years to come, so perhaps we had better formalise it.

Then, again, it is said that under PR we would be governed perpetually by coalitions. But what happens to us now? Political commentators seldom put pen to paper without sagely asserting that all governments are in their nature coalitions. Mrs. Thatcher herself has presided over a coalition, a very creaky and uneasy one, between what used to be called 'wets' and 'drys' and what are now called 'consolidationists' and 'Thatcherites'.

Her madder friends deny this because they like to regard her as a strong, idealistic woman with no gift for the mean arts of party management. But, thank God, they are wrong; her enemies deny it because they like to regard her as a bossy woman and also something of a fanatic, but they are just as wrong.

Labour Governments are also coalitions. In this case, however, the system is different: the terms of the coalition are worked out in acrimonious public debate, not just leaked to the press. It is a settled principle that the 'moderates' shall in the end always appear to win but that, in return for suffering occasional ostentatious humiliations the 'militants' shall get most of their own way, though in a manner disguised by semantics, e.g. the substitution of phrases like 'social ownership' for nasty, brutal words like 'nationalisation'.

There is also the other quite different argument that under

PR extremist minorities, like the Front Nationale in France, get a look in which otherwise would be denied them. But is it thoroughly unhealthy to pretend that such minorities do not exist?

I am no fascist, but I represent a brand of Toryism, at once traditionalist and populist, which holds sway in every public bar in the kingdom and is almost entirely denied parliamentary expression by the Establishment.

Above all, PR would increase the independence of MPs both from their constituency associations and their party machines. I would give it a try. I am off on holiday, so any of you who hate these sentiments, can attribute them to my obvious need for a rest.

It was the implication of the European Communities (Amendment) Bill which would contribute, two years later, to Mrs. Thatcher's 'watershed' speech in Bruges on the EEC – with such devastating results.

Duped by a European smoke-screen

The Daily Telegraph, 10 November 1986

Last week the European Communities (Amendment) Bill received the Royal Assent and is now, accordingly, part of the law of this country. Are you rejoicing at this leap into the future or are you sunk in gloom at the thought of having lost your national independence? I suspect neither. You have not noticed the event at all.

Yet it should be noticed. Select Committees of both Houses of Parliament have declared that this Act diminishes the authority of Parliament. Lord Denning, who is not to be despised in such matters, has put it plainly: 'Gone is the concept of national sovereignty – to be replaced by European unity.'

What the Act does may be briefly summarised. It removes the British Government's veto on a whole host of issues which come under the consideration of the European Council of

Ministers. That means that we shall be outvoted on many matters which seriously concern the domestic affairs of this country by other member states of the Common Market. Their decisions will prevail and be automatically embodied in British law. What is more, the European Assembly (now to be called the European Parliament) will have its influence greatly increased, so that when it and the European Commission (the civil servants who run the show) agree about anything, that thing will in practice be very likely to happen.

Now what interests me about all this is how it happened. Had the British electorate ever been asked plainly whether it wanted to belong to a European state or to remain British, it would have said, with unmistakable emphasis, that it was in favour of an independent Britain. What is more, it would have consigned to perdition any political party which proposed the opposite. Yet, under the conditions of parliamentary democracy, the opposite is plainly coming about. A political élite has so far imposed its views on the people. How did it do it?

To start with, it told us that the economic arguments for joining the EEC were indestructible. This was a good idea because nobody understands economic arguments and, if they are advanced in calm and well-bred voices, everybody is prepared to accept them. However, this theme was not fruitful for long: we entered the Common Market and did not seem to be economically much better afterwards. So the next ploy was to tell us that, however temporarily unfortunate the economic consequences of joining the EEC might be (or might seem to be) the political arguments for doing so were invulnerable. What we did for one reason was eventually commended to us for quite another.

The task of accomplishing this transition was facilitated by another dishonest political technique which can best be described as that of 'false antithesis'. It was embodied in the phrase 'Britain cannot go it alone'. The implication was that if we did not join the EEC or become part of the USA, we would be totally isolated. Britain is a partly-European and a partly-Oceanic power: that has been the tradition of her foreign policy, and it remains the only reasonable basis for her national existence. What this means in practice today is that we must be free sometimes to side with President Reagan and sometimes to go along with the EEC. Apart from specific, limited treaty obligations, we must be free to conduct our own foreign policy. We must be flexible, which is a totally different matter from being isolated.

The other technique which has been employed is, of course, to make the whole issue as complicated and boring as possible. In this respect the Government has had vast resources at its disposal – the top Tory anaesthetist, Sir Geoffrey Howe, and the bland Foreign Office automaton, the Baroness Young.

But, above all, the Government has had going for it the obscurity which surrounds the word sovereignty. Those who believe in sovereignty think, to put it crudely, that it is convenient to have, in any country, a lawful authority which is entitled to have the last word about everything, and which, in terms of law, can do, undo or amend anything. This, of course, does not mean that in practice the sovereign authority can do anything, or that it is not severely limited by practical constraints. As soldiers used to say about King's Regulations, 'What it all means is that they can do anything except put you in the family way.' Nevertheless, we as a nation have found it convenient to assume that the Parliament at Westminster has, within these practical limits, the right to govern us. What we now know is that, in very many respects, it is in practice being deprived of that right.

I do not accept defeat, as Lord Denning does: what Parliament has given it can take back. Any party which will commit itself to doing so will stand a fair chance of getting my vote.

Myths and the monarchy

The Times, 2 November 1987

Is it not time that there should be some clear thinking, as distinct from interminable writing, about the role of popular monarchy in the governance of the country?

The chief element in that role, surely, is mythological and

ritualistic. The function of the Queen – and, by derivation, of her family – is to represent to perfection the national ethos. They are there to supply a perennial pageant of virtue – the virtues of family life, of civic obedience, of respect for the arts, of care for the poor and afflicted.

Since human beings, even if royal, are in their nature imperfect, there is an element of what the vulgar would describe as 'fraud' in this role. The imperfections of the actors must not be publicly displayed. What is more the 'fraud' cannot be kept up without a degree of co-operation from the public. Popular monarchy is a national pageant which demands audience co-operation.

This last requirement is hard to achieve in an irreverent age. Yet it was achieved to perfection in the years immediately preceding the abdication crisis. At that time, the fact that the royal family was human, as well as theoretically perfect, was conveyed not by the press but by 'the grapevine'. There was always somebody who knew somebody who had heard on good authority that some member of the royal family was capable of a minor human failing. This information was conveyed at dinner parties and even in the four-ale bar. It was spoken in whispers and conferred prestige on whoever supplied it. There was always a girl who had danced with a man who had danced with a girl who had danced with the Prince of Wales.

I remember one such story from my own childhood told by a delightful old clergyman in Westmorland *ad nauseam*. King George V, he used to say (in the deepest confidence), had once been out on some occasion with Queen Mary and had put his foot in a puddle. Having got mud on his trousers, he had said in a loud voice: 'Damn!' The Queen had instantly reprimanded him: 'George, wait till you get home!' With passing years, my clerical friend abbreviated the story in a rather confusing manner which embarrassed his family. The King went out with Queen Mary, 'messed his trousers', and the Queen said: 'George, wait till you get home!' This made the royal family look even more human.

However, in the early 1930s, this was about all we got in the way of scandal. It satisfied us all and reconciled us to the task of maintaining the royal and national pageant. How different things are now! Somebody has decided that the monarchy should be popular in the sense that all its doings should be publicly displayed and investigated. It must not only be required to represent perfection, it must be required to be perfect. Members of the royal family must conform at every point to what the popular press chooses to regard as 'decency'.

It is as though all the royal personages were constantly up for election, like American presidents and British prime ministers. They are not. That is precisely why we have a hereditary monarchy. There will be no point in having such a monarchy if the present ridiculous exercise continues. What is happening to us is that republicanism is being introduced by the back door.

There is a principle of liberty and a principle of authority in our affairs. The monarchy represents the principle of authority. Do we want to get rid of it altogether? Virtually nobody in this country does. Republicanism is not just an attack on hereditary monarchy; it is an attack on deference, on a system of national manners.

There are two principles of republicanism – in the broadest sense – which are at issue in this matter: the first is that all men start life as equals and must be regarded no more highly than their talents and performances permit. This is called 'equality of opportunity'. The second is that we should all be absolutely frank with each other and free to ask each other publicly about all matters, however intimate. This, in its application to public life, is called 'freedom of information'.

Against this, there is an English tradition – the tradition of a fundamentally hierarchic society – which asserts that everyone, high and low, should be treated with honour and respect, but that the form in which the honour and respect are expressed should be determined by such considerations as his age and position in society. Added to this, there is still a deep-rooted British belief that, in principle, a man's private life should be his private property.

What, then, should be done about this? The suggestion that the royal family should mount a vast campaign to restore its reputation is ridiculous. Royalty must proceed on Elizabeth I's principle that she could not accept the applause of her subjects without accepting their censure. It is the press which must consider its own position.

What the press has to recognise, if it wishes to survive, is that it is addressing a country which is fundamentally opposed to its manners and its morals. Everybody, of course, will read what it writes about the royal family, but everybody feels ashamed of doing so. The press has many powerful enemies, notably the Labour party, which also, in its own way, believes in the principle of authority in politics. Many of those who enjoy (with shame) reading about the private life of the royal family would heartily support a government which prevented the press from publishing such reports.

A bill to control the ownership of the press with this in view would, alas, not outrage the public; nor would some scheme for giving the Press Council power to behead certain impertinent editors. Both these proposals would be appalling, but they might well appear on the agenda. If Mr. Kinnock's sword (supposing he has one) leapt from its scabbard in defence of the monarchy he would be doing himself a lot of good. If I owned a newspaper I think I would now see the red light.

In praise of inequality

The Times, 26 April 1988

Commons question time: 'Is the Prime Minister aware of Mrs. Brown of 'artlepool? Is she aware that Mrs. Brown 'as been for years a martyr to arthritis, that she nevertheless provides constant nursing for her bedridden mother, that she has no 'ome 'elp because of cuts in council expenditure and that her income of £12 a week is now to be reduced to £5 in order to ease the income tax burden of the richest people in this country?'

How familiar that sort of outburst has become, though the terms of this one are of course imaginary. How familiar also are the replies which these outbursts receive. 'During this Government's term of office, expenditure on health and social security has expanded by x per cent. This compares

with Labour's miserable performance in the years 1975 to
1979 (or in any other selected period); adequate provision is
made for hard cases' – and so on in the same vein.

Who gets the better of these exchanges? Intellectually, of
course, the Prime Minister and her colleagues. Even if you do
not pause to check the accuracy of what she is claiming, you
get the clear impression that she is appealing to reason and
her opponents to emotion. But is this altogether a long-term
advantage in political terms? There are some subjects in the
discussion of which emotion has a built-in and overwhelming
advantage over reason. I suspect that as time goes on more
and more of the public will come to the conclusion that this
Government consists of hard-faced businessmen with whom
it is not seemly to be seen associating.

This is even more likely to prove so because of the cold,
bureaucratic, jargon-ridden language in which most of Her
Majesty's Ministers now habitually talk. It gives reason, and
even compassion, when that quality rears its head in government advocacy, a bad name.

Do not suppose, however, that when the public reacts
against Tory hard-heartedness it is being sincere. In Britain,
'stinking hypocrisy' is not confined to bishops and the media
or to those who attack apartheid. It is widespread among the
general citizenry. My impression based on observation and
anecdotal evidence (i.e. real evidence) is that a lot of people
are heartily sick of do-gooding politicians, regarding them as
frauds and opportunists.

I sometimes even suspect that a lot of people are tired of
Mrs. Brown of Hartlepool, either because they think that she
does not exist in quite the form in which she is portrayed or
because they have a deep conviction, of which of course they
are ashamed, that no human society will ever succeed in
eliminating all human ills and a suspicion that any human
society that seriously tries to do so will merely succeed in
creating more human ills. To announce these reservations,
however, would be to court social ostracism and, where
relevant, political annihilation.

If any of you belong to this category of closet Gradgrinds, I
have comfort for you in the shape of a pamphlet which can no
doubt be supplied under plain cover by The Institute of

Economic Affairs Health Unit. It is not, of course, wholly readable, containing much economic jargon and many contorted sentences. However, if all you need is a quick 'kiss of life', having been nearly drowned in a sea of compassionate rhetoric, you could confine yourself to the press release.

To begin with, take the pamphlet's title, *Acceptable Inequalities?* Well, even allowing for the question mark, that is a breeze of fresh air for a start. But read on. According to the authors, 'you can have too much equality' (and this, remember, in relation to the most emotive of all matters, the provision of health and medical care). The press summary, warming to its theme, then offers this stimulating headline: 'Inequality of health services is, in general, desirable.' You are feeling better already.

The pamphlet's broad thesis is an excellent one which, to my mind, applies to everything, not merely health. There are, it argues, three kinds of inequality: acceptable (indeed desirable), unavoidable and intolerable. Pursue equality as an end in itself and you will damage national health. Medicine does not operate with equal effect and at equal cost in all parts of the country: dividing subsidies equally between the regions (or even in a way that seems suitably equitable) may lead to the loss of life. Is the object to maximise health or simply to ensure that those living in certain areas which are more favourable to health than others shall not be allowed to enjoy that advantage even though depriving them of it will benefit nobody else?

Anyway, when distributing a scarce resource, endless cruel decisions have to be taken (either by doctors or by bureaucrats) about how it should be distributed. Such decisions, which are sometimes about life and death, are taken every day, though naturally they are not spelt out in public. If we want to reduce the need for them, as far as humanly possible, the only thing to do is to increase the amount of money avai lable for expenditure on medicine.

But since health and sheer physical survival are not the only objects of individual and social existence, the State's expenditure on doctors, nurses and hospitals has to be reconciled with its expenditure on defence, education and the rest and is limited, as every Government in practice recognises, by the community's willingness to put up with high taxation.

To all this (much of it, I admit, familiar though generally excluded from political debate, at least in the stark form of the IEA's authors) I would myself add but one general observation. The most effective impulses making for better health provision are the natural instincts of self-preservation and family affection.

If these are stultified, no one, rich or poor, will benefit, and allowing them scope does not make it impossible, but rather easier, to raise adequate funds for those who cannot provide medical care for themselves. Prohibiting or discouraging private expenditure on health even when this expenditure cannot be diverted by the State to public health is mad and wicked.

Incidentally, I rather hope Mrs. Thatcher does not read this excellent IEA pamphlet. Otherwise, unspeakably honest woman that she is, she will repeat its contents in the Commons on Tuesdays and Thursdays for several weeks to come, and without necessary adaptations of style. That would be premature.

Incidentally also, I am about to go into a public ward for a short operation, having failed to get a private bed in the hospital of my choice. Whether this is intolerable inequality, acceptable inequality or, as I suspect, just an infernal unavoidable nuisance, I do not know. Anyway, it will involve my absence from or only intermittent appearance in this space for a little while.

3 · Liberty and licence

Fourteen-day misrule

The Daily Telegraph, 14 November 1955

The profound if familiar observation that British institutions grow, they are not made, is well illustrated by the history of the notorious 14-day rule. It is an illuminating story of slow but steady progress from a necessary expedient to an absurd and rigid doctrine. Here it is:

The war-time Coalition was quick to realise the importance of home broadcasting as a means of stimulating the war effort. Since, in theory, there was no party politics at the time, no one could object to Ministers coming to the microphone from time to time to encourage resentment of the enemy or to commend the merits of Woolton pie.

Towards the end of the war, however, enlightened men in all political parties had decided that the demands of the war effort included an advanced programme of domestic reform for after the war. At the same time, politicians, even inside the great Coalition, were finding it increasingly hard to agree with each other, and the process of angling for advantage at the first post-war General Election had begun.

The trouble, as far as the BBC was concerned, started with Mr. Butler's Education Act. On the night before the second reading of that historic Bill, Mr. Butler came to the microphone in the normal way to explain and defend it as though it had been another rule about when to go to the shelters.

The Govenors of the BBC, however, took the view that it might be construed as a controversial piece of legislation. In the absence of normal party politics, it would scarcely have been possible to put any representative person up to attack it.

Accordingly, the BBC decided itself that Ministers must not be allowed to go on like this, and an instruction was privately issued by the Governors to the effect that Ministerial or other ex-parte pronouncements which did not concern the war effort as properly defined should not be broadcast while parliamentary discussion on the subjects they dealt with was either pending or actually in progress.

Observe that this rule was made by the BBC to protect its charter against abuse by a Coalition Government at a time when properly organised controversy was impossible. Nevertheless, the impersonal genius of the British Constitution, well known to be superior to reason, had been set in motion. An idea had been sown.

When the war was over the BBC decided to break away from its pre-war tradition of avoiding unpleasantness at all costs and to try to organise a balanced expression of controversial views about politics. In the negotiations with the political parties which ensued, the commonsense rule introduced for the BBC's convenience in 1944 was transmuted (I suspect by the literary talent of Sir Winston Churchill) into a grand, abstract principle: the BBC should not be 'an alternative simultaneous debating forum to Parliament'.

The parties were each to have a fair share of time allotted to them, and, when the BBC arranged a talk or discussion for itself, it was (according to agreements reached in February 1947) to see that it did not concern a 'subject of discussion in either House'.

Literally interpreted, this might have excluded all discussion on the air of a parliamentary bill from the moment of its publication to the moment of its receiving the Royal Assent. Accordingly, a further definition was issued in July 1948:

'(a) That the BBC will not have discussions or ex-parte statements on any issues for a period of a fortnight before they are debated in either House and
'(b) That while matters are subjects of legislation MP's will not be used in such discussions.'

This is the fourteen-day rule which the Postmaster-General has now officially imposed on an unwilling BBC and the ITA.

Whether it affects outside broadcasts or broadcasts on budgets is still a matter of dispute; why 14 days must be something to do with the impersonal genius of the British Constitution or a mere instance of mental association between the idea of censorship and the normal period of confinement imposed on petty criminals. It is certainly an indefensible period, since parliamentary business is announced only a week before it happens.

What started as a protection of the BBC against abuse by the Coalition is now a cherished safeguard for the front benches of both political parties against two dangers: first, the danger that good television stars, who are almost always bad party men, may debate controversial subjects in terms not approved by the party leaders, and, secondly, that backbench MPs may let off steam before they have had a proper respect for the party line instilled into them in the Whips' office.

It is not the dignity of Parliament or the BBC which is at stake, but the authority of the front benches, even if the majority of non-broadcasting back benchers are willing to acquiesce in this authority.

To do it justice, the BBC has always weighed responsibility against talent in choosing its speakers; but, in any case, even bad speakers are a small price to pay for free speech. Whatever happens the Government really ought to stop using the word 'dignity' to describe what it is trying to preserve by this ludicrous piece of obstinate stupidity.

The real challenge to liberty

The Daily Telegraph, 10 July 1957

In every age, freedom has its natural foes. The place to look for them is in the ranks of those who have put themselves beyond the range of criticism.

This maxim occurred to me when the storm over tapped telephones blew up. I am no friend of snoopers or official key-hole audiences, but I do not believe that it is in the Home

Office or the police force that we should look for our potential tyrants.

To begin with, I have never doubted that all telephone conversations were listened to by someone other than the person to whom they were directed. An elderly aunt of mine kept a tea cosy permanently over the telephone because she did not trust the instrument, even when the receiver was on, or the village post-mistress at any time.

Her mechanical information was wrong; her precautions unnecessary – since I am prepared to swear that she never had converse with anyone who might have called himself 'King of the Underworld', but her instinct was sound. In their nature, telephones are not private.

On the evidence available, I deplore the late Home Secretary's action and am sorry that his successor, who would be no better at tapping telephones than running a concentration camp, should have had to bear the brunt of it. Yet, I repeat, this is a side issue, for Home Secretaries, whoever they are, are not among those who are immune from public criticism.

Where then should we look for the foe within the citadel? The traditional candidates for the role of villain are all out. Monarchs are rubber stamps; generals are meek members of the legions of the disinherited middle classes; landlords have been virtually legislated out of existence, and priests are allowed to survive in a secularised society only on sufferance.

No, the enemies of freedom are today to be found among all those whose claim the sanction of the popular will for their actions and within all those vested interests which surround themselves with that aura of semi-religious respect that used to belong to royalty and its immediate appendages.

This is to say that they are to be found among all who act in the sacred name of democracy and among the trade unions whose claim to be above reproach is only now beginning to be timorously challenged.

Take the unions first: they claim not only the right to withhold their labour, which might be thought to be inherent in a free man, but the right to force others to join them on pain of unemployment, the right to commit any minority, however large, to whatever course of public policy is approved by a union majority however slight, and the right to trick any member who has not troubled to learn the rules into automatically subscribing to a political party of which he may disapprove.

What would you say if the British Medical Association allotted a proportion of every doctor's subscription to Mr. Oliver Poole's funds unless the doctor took the trouble to specify that he was not a Conservative?

Viewed in the abstract, the pretensions of the trade union movement in Britain are almost beyond belief – as witness Mr. Frank Cousins's speech yesterday.

What is revealing is the way this has happened: if you want to be a bully, take care to have it generally understood that you are an underdog.

The unions built up their claims at a time when the economic scales were weighted against them and when strong organisation was the only way of keeping the wage earner above the starvation line. In a siege, the case for abolishing liberty is always sound.

Now, the economic scales are permanently weighted in favour of the unions and the State committed to pursue inflation rather than suffer a suspicion of unemployment.

But these vast privileged corporations, heirs to the tradition of feudal resistance to the State and feudal domination of the people, still wear the armour of righteousness which they put on in the time of their tribulation.

Of course, it is a great mistake to suppose that the Government can do anything about this, and an even greater mistake to suppose that subjects should be suppressed outright because they have grown over-mighty.

If the unions are bent on kicking us about and we cannot stop them, that is that; but let us tell the truth about what is happening. It is sensible to give way to superior force; it is senseless and even wicked to describe surrenders as victories and routs as compromises. Tyranny is built on such hypocrisy; the best defence against it is telling the truth.

When the State was first identified with the people we entered a new phase in which the subject ceased to be able to think of himself as the natural enemy of government. After all, how could he be this, since, according to the theory, he was governing himself? Whatever mischief his rulers now wreak upon him is done by the fiction of his consent. Here is another fruitful source of hypocrisy and tyranny.

Soon, the sober Sir Oliver Franks will be telling us at length how administrative tribunals work, how Crichel Downs can be prevented, and informing us, I have no doubt, that a good deal of regulation is necessary because of the complexity of modern life. We shall have his report by August; I predict that it will be extremely dull and immensely useful, but will not touch the heart of the matter, which is a question of morals, not public law.

Self-government is a contradiction in terms. There are, there always have been and there always will be two ends to the stick of government and it is profoundly important to know clearly at which end of it we are standing at any given moment.

Now, there are spheres of life in which I wish to command as opposed to obeying, and the same goes for everyone else: our business is to keep these spheres outside the range of government. Yes, I am preaching the Victorian gospel of consumer's choice. Here is a present to the 'This England' column of the *New Statesman*: the defence of freedom in a commercial civilisation depends on the habit of servility among tradesmen.

Put production and distribution in the hands of the State and you reverse the proper relationship of producer and consumer; it is the producer's place to serve, not to govern the consumer.

That is the central issue in British politics and the essence of the argument against Socialism.

And what, above all things, is necessary to a free society is candour, the habit of calling things by their proper names, of calling government government, and exploitation exploitation, and seeing them for what they are. If we have these habits, it will not matter over much if the switchboard girl talks.

Is hanging necessary?

The Daily Telegraph, 10 January 1958

Soon after Members return to Westminster the House of Commons will debate capital punishment again. The ground is being prepared now by a campaign in the country of unusual vigour in favour of abolition.

This campaign has attracted support from many unsuspected quarters. They have included recently some eminent ecclesiastics and an impressive band of those professional leaders of opinion whose names tend to appear together in collective signatures to the letters printed by serious newspapers.

It must be said at once that the campaign is doing very little to illuminate the question. It is distinguished, as the campaigns of reformers often are, by the arrogant assumption that no rational or benevolent person could dissent from its aims, and sometimes even by a tasteless exploitation of the irrelevant sentiments produced by sensational murder cases. The time is therefore ripe for an attempt to weigh carefully the arguments presented on both sides.

I suggest that the starting-point must be the recognition that there is no tolerable halfway between retention and abolition. The Royal Commission which reported in September 1953 was prevented by its terms of reference from discussing the proposal to abolish the death sentence; the various modifications which it suggested as an alternative have nothing whatever to commend them.

To abolish 'the doctrine of constructive malice' – by which a man may be hanged for murder if in the process of committing certain felonies, he kills someone without the intention of doing so – is to attack the present law at its strongest point, that is, the protection which it claims to give against murder committed by professional criminals in the course of burglary.

To suggest that juries should be practically free to improvise their own definition of insanity is to make the administration of the law intolerably capricious. To propose that juries, having pronounced the verdict, should then themselves award the punishment is to give them a function for which they are always unsuited, and for which they are particularly unsuited when the matter is one about which public opinion is so deeply divided as it is about the death penalty.

Other suggestions for modification are no more convincing. For the Home Secretary to be made to publish his reasons for deciding whether or not to advise the exercise of the prerogative of mercy would merely be to strengthen the dangerous tendency of every case of hanging to become a matter of public debate.

Equally, there is clearly no rational or moral ground for discrimination between the sexes in the administration of the penalty.

Unless anyone can suggest (no one has) a less defective definition of insanity than that provided by the McNaghten Rules, it is, I suggest, evident that the choice is between total abolition of hanging and its retention precisely as now.

It should be noticed here that the evidence for hanging being the quickest and most humane form of the death penalty at present available is overwhelming.

In approaching this choice between retention and abolition, the first consideration is whether there is any intrinsic moral connection between murder and the death sentence. It is fashionable to regard retribution as a motive for punishment as primitive and sub-Christian. But the notion of retribution, the idea that punishment should bear some relation to guilt, is deeply rooted and no one doubts that it is healthy when it is used to justify the reduction of a sentence on grounds of mitigating circumstances.

What can be said is that it is a very primitive conception of the idea of retribution which suggests that the criminal should always have done to him precisely what he has done to his victim. The principle of retribution demands that society shall solemnly and dramatically express its abhorrence of murder by imposing a grave punishment on murderers; it does not necessarily mean that society must kill murderers.

A closely related consideration is whether public opinion is so wedded to the death penalty as to make its abolition dangerous. It is true that nearly all reforms in the criminal code have been brought about in the face of public opinion; in the matter of hanging, however, the danger has always to be reckoned with that, denied satisfaction by the State, the passion for retribution would find its outlet in lynching.

I suggest, however, that in a law-abiding community like ours that danger can be discounted. Whether the death sentence was abolished or suspended for a period of years, public opinion, if sufficiently outraged by some murder or series of murders, could effectively agitate to have it put back. In Britain the desire to avenge some particular wrong would almost certainly stop short of popular violence.

It is clear that the decisive question is whether hanging is a necessary deterrent to murder. The strongest argument for retention is the common-sense conviction that nothing can have so great an effect on the mind of an intending murderer as the prospect of death.

It is true that the majority of murders at present arise from such causes as personal quarrels, drink and sex, and in such cases there is not likely to be much calculation of any sort. Inevitably, the cases which occur, however, are those in which the death penalty has not proved a deterrent; this does not prove that many potential murderers are not every year deterred by the fear of hanging.

Judges and the police are almost unanimously convinced that professional criminals would be tempted to carry firearms and to use them but for the fear of the gallows. In a country where the police do not carry arms this is a paramount consideration.

On the other hand, the statistics which the Royal Commission examined from countries which have abolished the death penalty gave absolutely no evidence for supposing that there was a connection between this penalty and the murder rate. They showed no connection either between the abolition of the penalty and the number of murders committed by professional criminals.

They certainly did not prove that the death penalty deters no one. But, the abolitionists will argue, if it had the deterrent effect attributed to it, this would have been apparent in the figures.

On the common-sense plane, the abolitionists say that to

the adventurous gangster life imprisonment is worse than death. Retentionists point out that at present life sentences are substantially reduced for good behaviour, and that if they were to become real life sentences the pressure on prison space would be increased and the difficulty of containing such dangerous criminals would be very great.

Retentionists point out that there has lately been an immense increase in violent crime committed by the young, and that this class of criminal might commit murder but for the death penalty. Abolitionists suggest that, on analysis, it will be found that this sort of crime consists mainly of malicious woundings arising from such causes as street brawls and is not likely to lead directly to murder.

Retentionists reply that these crimes are significant of the habit of violence which is growing and which most abolitionists are not prepared to see checked by the re-introduction of flogging.

All agree that the present judicial system is as fair as possible. But abolitionists point out that, being human, it is liable to err and that the death penalty is irrevocable.

If capital punishment is a necessary deterrent this risk must be taken. The decisive test therefore remains: on the available evidence, which is at many points conflicting, is capital punishment necessary?

Critics of criticism

From 'Letters to the Editor'
The Daily Telegraph, 7 May 1959

Sir – A series of recent news items raises the perennial question: what are the proper limits of free speech?

It has been suggested that Field-Marshal Montgomery ought not publicly to criticise the Americans, (a) because he is a Field-Marshal and as such unfit to express political opinions, and (b) because his words are likely to injure the Anglo-American alliance. Mr. Gaitskell has taken exception to an article in the *Christian Science Monitor* which implied that the result of the next British General Election was a legitimate factor to be taken into account in shaping American foreign policy.

Sir Patrick Spens has condemned Sir Oswald Mosley's advocacy of colour discrimination as likely to cause civil disturbance. Miss Siobhan McKenna has been reprimanded for criticising Mr. de Valera, and the point has been emphasised by the suppression of a second and apparently innocent instalment of her broadcast.

No one will deny that the right of free speech within the limits of the law ought to be exercised with reasonable discretion, and that it may therefore be legitimate to censure a man for the use which he makes of a liberty which it would be wrong to deny him. In general, when freedom of discussion is used not for the purpose of forming opinion but for that of obstructing government, it is badly used.

A good instance of this would be the gratuitous insulting of a foreign Power with which the Government was anxious to preserve good relations. Another instance would be the deliberate inflaming of a religious or racial minority to the point at which it was tempted to resort to violence. It would be possible to commit both these errors without infringing the law, but both of them would be worthy of censure.

The point which in all these discussions tends to be overlooked, however, is that one of the worst enemies of free speech is excessive sensitivity to criticism. To encourage this sensitivity by trying to protect everyone against the danger of having his prejudices affronted is to defeat the ends of freedom.

It would be a very bad thing for Anglo-American relations if Mr. Herter were to try to influence the result of the British General Election; it is a great disservice to Anglo-American relations for Mr. Gaitskell to warn him of the danger of doing so on the assumption, derived from an American newspaper article, that it might occur to him to make the attempt. This is to encourage the British to be sensitive about a grievance which is still hypothetical.

What is most surprising, however, is the behaviour of that ponderous guardian of liberty of expression, the BBC. It is quite impossible to believe that Miss McKenna's silly irrelevance could have caused more than temporary irritation to the loyal hearts of such Ulstermen as watched her broadcast.

It is fantastic to pretend that any serious harm to the Commonwealth or even the BBC could have followed from exposing Northern Irishmen to the pain of seeing and hearing somebody who recently offended them engaging in a conversation which, to judge from the published extracts from the second script, could not have offended anyone. Ulstermen are known to be brave and self-controlled; it would surely have been safe to presume a little further on their patience.

Free speech will not flourish in a society in which politicians and public corporations are continually occupied in protecting people against having their sensibilities offended. Those who take offence easily, or encourage others to do so, are at least as dangerous as those who gratuitously give it.

Is capitalism immoral?

The Daily Telegraph, 16 September 1971

'There are few ways in which a man can be more innocently employed,' remarked Dr. Samuel Johnson, 'than in getting money.' 'The old freewheeling concept of liberal capitalism,' affirmed the Pope [Paul VI] in his encyclical last week, 'led to considering profit as the key motive for economic progress, competition as the supreme law of economics and private ownership of the means of production as an absolute right that has no limits and carries no corresponding obligations. . . . One cannot condemn such abuses too strongly.'

I have myself no doubt that Dr. Johnson was as good a Christian as the Pope, and that his interpretation of a Christian's duty in matters connected with the production and distribution of wealth was as strict and conscientious as anything which has emanated from the Papacy in the last 50 years. The fact remains, however, that the capitalist system is far easier to attack on Christian grounds than it is to defend.

Last week's Papal encyclical was notable in applying the familiar Catholic social doctrine, for the first time in such a document, to the contrast between the rich and the poor nations. Past concepts of capitalism, it declared, had become outmoded in the face of this imbalance.

The Pope commends such devices as a world fund to combat hunger and international schemes to support the prices of primary products. What he wants, in fact, is a species of world welfare state.

On the face of it, at least, it is an affront to justice that some nations should luxuriate in riches while others starve. On the face of it, also, the solution to this problem is for the rich to bestow their surplus wealth on the poor.

Nearly all the known systems of morality rest on the premise that co-operation is good and conflict bad; how can it be that in respect of the production of wealth the opposite should be true? A Christian must surely acknowledge that the aim of all legitimate labour is the glory of God and the improvement of man's estate, and this should surely point to a society in which men work together for the attainment of an ideal of social justice rather than to one in which they scramble for personal advantage. Such a society may not be Socialist – since Socialism rests on the premise that everything should be organised from one centre – but it must surely be co-operative rather than competitive, a society in which every unit (family, profession, factory) has its appointed function and its corresponding rights and duties.

It must in fact be the kind of society which Papal political theory has consistently commended over the last half-century.

This attractive scheme of things, however, is built on one cardinal fallacy, which would appear also to be a Papal fallacy. A co-operative society presupposes an authority morally and intellectually competent to define the ends of co-operation and the responsibilities and privileges of all who take part in it. Where, under the régime of original sin, is such an authority to be found?

As a collection of essays under the title *The Case for Capitalism* just published by Michael Joseph in association with Aims of Industry shows, the argument for the capitalist system is in the last analysis an argument against the concentration of power, against the intrusion into economic affairs of professedly infallible authorities. If the proper aim of production is the satisfaction of human wants and if, as Christians believe, men are infinitely various, the first condition of a sound economy is an objective and reliable means of finding what these wants are. Is any more dependable method to hand or even imaginable than that supplied by the Free Market – the method under which all men are free to offer their services to all others and all are equally free to reject the services thus offered? Co-operative production will be of little use if it is not directed towards producing what is genuinely wanted.

Capitalism, like all known systems of social organisation, produces inequalities. The difference is that these inequalities are, in so far as the system works, automatic rewards and penalties for success or failure in satisfying known human wants. They do not spring from the arbitrary judgements of politicians and bureaucrats about what different people deserve.

Christ condemned not the rich but those who put their trust in riches.

Souls no doubt may be destroyed by avarice, as they may just as easily be destroyed by the pursuit of power and prestige. Under capitalism, however, it is open to anyone to opt out of the rat-race. Personal wealth is not necessarily personally consumed, and again capitalist philanthropy and patronage of the arts have the merit of not being concentrated in the control of a single authority.

No doubt a just society does not automatically result from the operation of a competitive economy. No doubt the State must be ever alert to intervene in the process of competition in order to secure fundamental human rights. It is part of the duty of the head of Christendom to instruct rulers in that obligation, but is it his duty to choose or appear to choose between opposing economic systems, to invoke, by implication, the authority of the Holy Ghost for the highly contentious view that the prosperity of India can be more efficiently promoted by public than private investment?

Capitalism, like most things, needs Christianising, but the social system recommended by the Pope would be at least equally vulnerable to human frailties of a different kind – the arrogance, for instance, of the professional do-gooder.

Can there be any doubt that at this moment in history more and graver crimes are committed in the name of disinterested service of humanity than result from the indulgence of private affections and ambitions? Between Dr. Johnson and the Pope, I at any rate opt for the Doctor.

No neutrality in morals

The Daily Telegraph, 16 September 1971

Why has the debate about the permissive society become so inexpressibly boring? Because, I think, it has for so long been bedevilled by intellectual dishonesty as distinct from mere intellectual confusion. This imparts to the arguments used on both sides an atmosphere of almost total unreality. It also makes them extremely predictable.

Take, for example, the view now being advanced, with varying degrees of wit (though most of the jokes must by now be exhausted) in defence of pornography. It is that relaxing the restraints on the publication of pornographic literature will promote purity by making imaginative lust tedious and commonplace. A few uncritical people (mostly drawn from those who attach high importance to good literature as an ennobling influence on character) may sincerely believe this to be true. The majority of those who put forward this defence, however, manifestly do not believe it. They are simply resorting to one of the oldest weapons in the progressive armoury – the dogma (contradicted by all experience) that prohibition is the source of all vice.

A friend of mine, acting under the influence of that penitential spirit which often afflicts members of the privileged classes in late middle age, and to which the rich in Britain were particularly vulnerable during the war, decided to send his son to a little known progressive, co-educational school which used to boast of its enlightened attitude towards sex. After two years the boy was sacked, allegedly for having seduced his housemaster's wife.

My friend, a rational man, was understandably horrified.

The boy, he contended, had merely reacted like any normal healthy young Englishman to the opportunities presented to him by a community which had renounced sexual inhibitions. Should he not have been complimented on the rapidity with which he had learnt and the assiduity with which he had set out to practise the principles in which he was being educated? The same sort of disappointment awaits all those who are credulous enough to swallow the hackneyed proposition that enlarging freedom is the most efficient way of encouraging restraint.

The other side in the controversy, however, is equally destitute of candour. It shrinks, in shame, from confessing any direct concern for the moral welfare of society at large. It has recourse to vague abstractions about the need for preserving the cohesion of society. It represents every invasion of liberty which it proposes as a defence of someone else's liberty, and as a result gets submerged in a fathomless bog of casuistry. No doubt there is truth in the argument about social cohesion, but it is a truth too subtle for most of those who invoke that argument. It is simply not possible to reconcile the view that the State should be neutral about morals with a view that it should uphold morality. Far too much intellectual effort is wasted on thinking up sophisticated utilitarian arguments for doing what conscience dictates.

It is refreshing, therefore, to find a book as free from these dishonesties as is John Selwyn Gummer's *The Permissive Society: Fact or Fantasy?** The theme is indeed well worn and there is nothing particularly provocative in the manner of its treatment. The arguments for and against permissive legislation are competently and lucidly rehearsed and subjected to an analysis which is almost always revealing. Anyone who wants to clear his own mind on the subject (and indeed anyone who wants to document his own prejudices) would do well to read this study.

The conclusions are predictable enough from such a mind. Permissiveness should neither be accepted nor rejected *in toto*. Society is right to be afraid of drugs and obscene literature; it has evaded the moral issues presented by suicide and abortion; it is, on the other hand, right to be humane
*Published by Cassell.

towards discreet homosexuals and to provide realistic sex instruction for the young on the premise that they will increasingly fall short of the ideal of chastity. Above all, it should see the rebellion of youth as springing largely from the defects of present-day social organisation, and should respond to that rebellion positively and not just by repression.

I would myself have like to see Mr. Gummer's thesis reduced in the end to a few rather harshly defined propositions, most of which are implicit in his book. The first is that this is not an argument about liberty at all. While the State has been withdrawing in the field of morals, it has been expanding in every other direction. What is more, this expansion has been particularly promoted by the advocates of moral permissiveness. The society into which we are moving, therefore, is one in which virtually everything outside a limited range of mainly sexual activities is subjected to unprecedented control.

The principle which underlies this society is that man's obligations to his fellows are strictly material. He must exert himself as never before to bring comfort and security to his neighbours, but he must at the same time adopt an attitude of total neutrality towards all aspects of their welfare which are not materially measurable.

Now there is no reason in the world for supposing that it is possible to maintain this strict dichotomy between material and moral concern. To take the most sensitive of all areas of human relationship – that between parents and children: the kind of affection which makes men slave to feed and educate their offspring is totally incompatible with an attitude of complete detachment as to whether their offspring shall or shall not become drug addicts or hippies. Permissive society, in fact, becomes practicable only when what are properly defined as the economic functions of the family are delegated to the State.

But the State itself cannot fulfil these functions unless it can saddle to its own service the devotion which used to be spent on the service of the family. That kind of devotion itself springs from a moral consensus about the ends of human life usually expressed in some sort of myth about national character. Socialism has only become effective when it has developed into national socialism.

All this high-flown philosophising is only another way of expressing the immemorial truth that man is by nature a meddlesome animal who needs to have his prejudices confirmed by those of his fellows and who shows his love by seeking to influence the conduct of those fellows. The need for a measure of consensus about the objects of existence is inescapable either in a liberal or in an authoritarian society.

The nature of that consensus will of course, continually change. We are not to set out to preserve it as though it represented an absolute and immutable morality. Its preservation, however, does require not only a rational determination to distinguish between good and bad innovations, but also an instinctive revulsion from novelty. That revulsion has been just as important a factor in the development of civilisation as the zeal for enterprise to which we now constantly do homage.

If consensus is necessary, what becomes of a society such as ours is said to be in which consensus has been destroyed? The question is a large one but happily it is not necessary to answer it, since the assumption on which it rests is largely false.

The victories of the 'Lilac Establishment' had been the victories of an oligarchy not of a popular revolt. They have been made possible partly by the success with which progressives have conned their adversaries into accepting that power and influence are evils whenever they are exercised in defence of society and are morally tolerable only when employed for its reform or disruption. They are also due to the strange convention of British political life which excludes almost all law-making about private morals from the effective decision of the people, vesting it in those members of the House of Commons who happen to have an interest in such 'trivia'.

I would hazard a guess that there is only one respect in which the convictions of most Englishmen about sexual morality have changed fundamentally in the past 30 years. The improvement of contraception has rendered female chastity practically less important and its violation or renunciation less sinful than it used to be. Many parents now wish their daughters to be brought up as boys have been brought up for generations – to embrace chastity as a rule, and to recognise that it is peculiarly hard to observe and that it should be broken only with taste and prudence. For the rest, the popular consensus remains for anyone who has the courage to reveal it.

Why we still need the rich

The Daily Telegraph, 26 March 1974

Are the rich really necessary? To that question most people in the civilised world 50 years ago would have answered with an unequivocal and unashamed 'Yes'. What is more, right up to 1945 politicians had at their disposal an impressive stock of perfectly respectable arguments for the justification of economic inequality. The burden of proof rested on those who held that so manifestly just and inevitable an institution ought not to exist.

Today, all this has been reversed: all arguments about the distribution of wealth are conducted on the implicit assumption that equality represents the natural and just order of things and that deviation from it must either be specially justified or discreetly accepted as an unavoidable concession to the weakness of fallen man.

How did this revolution come about and what are its implications?

Justifications for inequalities of wealth fall, historically, into two broad categories – those which relate to societies based on status and the aristocratic principle; and those which relate to societies based on contract and the liberal principle of individual competition.

The first type of argument depends on attributing to some class a special kind of excellence in leadership and specific functions the proper discharge of which is held to require exceptional wealth and financial security. Naturally, this kind of argument is most convincing when addressed to the privileged themselves. It flourishes, therefore, in societies where political power is vested mainly or entirely in those who enjoy wealth.

For this reason, it has become almost extinct under

democracy. Lately, however, it has acquired a new though frail lease of life by virtue of the Government's attempt to establish an incomes policy. The whole doctrine of relativities, for example, postulates some kind of pre-ordained 'pecking order' between different sections of the working class.

Being human, every section of that class is favourably inclined to the view that its services have an intrinsic value and importance which justifies it in demanding a greater reward than can properly be given to some other lot of workers.

Since, however, in a democratic electorate, the number of those who would have to pay for these privileges necessarily exceeds the number of those who in any particular case are demanding them, the relativities argument tends to be a bad political weapon. It is for this simple reason that any kind of incomes policy is foredoomed to failure so long as democracy survives.

It is, therefore, to the classic liberal arguments for inequality that we must turn if we are to have any hope of justifying the institution at all. The chief of these arguments is an application to economics of a simple principle which is recognised as valid throughout the rest of life – the principle that whereas ordinary services may be successfully commanded under threat, exceptional services (which it is in the power of only a few to perform) can be elicited only by reward.

For example, soldiers may be induced to remain in the line by being threatened with a firing squad should they desert. By contrast, it is impossible to increase the supply of VCs by threatening to shoot everyone who does not display courage and resource on the scale which earns that reward.

Similarly, exceptional managerial talent (the power to direct the manual activities of others so intelligently as vastly to increase the sum total of their value) will remain hidden unless it is deliberately tempted into the open by the offer of unusual rewards. There is no doubt an intrinsic satisfaction and a congenial degree of prestige to be derived from managerial activity; but no one in practice assumes that this will suffice as a substitute for the incentive of high financial rewards.

So far the liberal argument for inequality, though it

increasingly affronts modern taste, is not considered so obscene as to make it impossible to use it in public. Politicians still talk about 'incentives', which is a dead enough word not completely to outrage egalitarian prudery. As so far stated, however, this argument does nothing to justify the existence of a rentier class – those who live not by the immediate reward of their own exertions but on the past fruits of their own or other people's exertions. The liberal case for the existence of this class is just as impressive and topical as the case for paying high salaries to expert managers.

In order to survive and progress, society must always set aside from its current production large amounts of wealth for investment in future production. Now, the poor, and even the relatively poor, are under a strong temptation to consume immediately everything they can lay their hands on.

Given a system under which the distribution of wealth is determined by majority vote, a system under which, in the simile of the great Marquis of Salisbury, the cat is put in charge of the cream jug, nothing would ever be saved for the future. Worse still, as experience has shown, having eaten up everything which is to hand, Demos, still unsated, will oblige the Government to give it the illusion of still greater prosperity by debasing the currency.

Accordingly, so the classic argument runs, investment in future production can only be secure in a society in which there are large (or fairly large) concentrations of private wealth. Those in possession of this wealth will not be subject to the demonic impulse to spend it immediately if they are offered judicious rewards for lending it – rewards which will bring privilege and security to them and their children. The cost of these rewards would be repaid a thousandfold by the increase in the nation's wealth which will result from them.

The trouble with all this, of course, is that the system cannot work unless either political power is vested chiefly in those who enjoy economic privilege or the political majority (which inevitably consist of those who do not) is willing to refrain from using political power as a means of seizing wealth. Long after the achievement of democracy, the convention survived that it was generally speaking immoral to confiscate private wealth. That convention has now disappeared.

Demos is therefore required to exercise that very foresight and restraint from the need for which the existence of a rentier class is supposed to exempt it. Popular envy, armed with political power, spells death to capitalism.

Where then can we look for hope? I suggest, in the fact that the current egalitarian passion springs not merely from envy (a sentiment which can be controlled up to a point by morality) but from foolishness and a corrupt ethic. Even those who admit the force of the practical arguments for capitalism feel shame in stating those arguments because they appear to rest on a low view of human nature. If this were true, it would not of course invalidate the arguments.

In reality, belief in the moral need for inequality and in the legitimacy, within reason, of pursuing private interest in open competition with others are among the most deeply and widely held of human convictions. They determine a large part of day to day human behaviour. Those who habitually sacrifice the welfare of their own families, for instance, to some abstract kind of social idealism, arouse contempt not respect.

The instinct to which capitalism appeals – respect for the individual as such, regard for privacy and the sanctity of private affection and careful thought for the interests of posterity – are noble as well as useful instincts. When the only alternative to capitalism is seen to be authoritarian economy both removed from popular control and unresponsive to individual need and when the current clamour for equality is rightly identified, not as a religion but as a blind appeal to popular greed, the case for liberal capitalism will be found still to have an irresistible appeal to common sense.

Human rights are wrong

The Daily Telegraph, 16 March 1981

Twenty-one judges of the European Court of Human Rights are currently engaged in determining the case of three employees of British Rail who in 1976 were sacked without compensation for refusing to join one of three specified trade unions. Mr. Prior's critics are awaiting the outcome of the action with bated breath and in high hope that it will go against the British Government and make a further reform of trade union law unavoidable.

It is possible that some of them are exaggerating the significance of the case. The Government stoutly maintains, for instance, that the Employment Act of 1980 has already made it unlawful to dismiss workers for refusing to observe the terms of a closed shop agreement negotiated without their individual consent and when they were already in their jobs. Such workers, it is said, will in future enjoy the same formidable protection (including words of encouragement from the Employment Secretary himself) which has just failed to keep Miss Joanna Harris in her job as a poultry inspectress.

Be this as it may, a defeat for the Government on this issue at Strasbourg would undoubtedly be a powerful blow against all those members of the Cabinet here who are still flinching from the task of effective trade union reform, which they were chiefly elected to perform.

Why is it, then, that I devoutly hope that the admirable Sir Ian Percival, who has the Government's brief at Strasbourg, will win his case? Certainly not because I have any tenderness for the closed shop or anything but the minimum of Christian charity requisite during Lent towards Mr. Prior. I believe that his Employment Act was a disaster which may yet prove irretrievable. I am convinced that if, in the end, Mrs. Thatcher fails (with all the horrible consequences which that would entail) the cause of her failure will be seen to be her refusal to act firmly on trade union law as soon as she got to office.

If the recession ever ends, the country could well be deprived of all the advantages of that relief if the unions are still in a position to extort extravagant wages from employers. What is more, the objections to Mr. Prior's inept, provocative and ineffectual legislation are not purely economic. He missed a unique opportunity to restore a just balance between the rights of the individual worker and the rights of unions. This failure was a blow against civil liberty.

What is at stake at Strasbourg, however, is something even more fundamental than that. It is the right of the British Parliament to create and sustain the laws by which the British people are governed. That right is being challenged from many quarters but one of its most formidable adversaries is undoubtedly the doctrine of human rights, an alien and intellectually contemptible theory which has infected nearly all British politicians and has even acquired a regrettable influence over the robust mind of the Prime Minister. Mr. Prior is wrong because he has misread the economic needs of the country, the nature of its legal traditions, the temper of public opinion and many other things which a politician should understand. If the Strasbourg court decides against him, however, it will not be these faults which it is censuring.

On the contrary, it will be asserting that the closed shop (or one particular manifestation of that phenomenon) is contrary to the universal human conscience, an evil thing never to be endured in any circumstances or at any time and to be instantly abolished wherever it exists without thought to the political consequences. This, clearly, is absurd in several ways.

There are, I have no doubt, permanently and universally valid goals towards which politicians everywhere should strive; there are things, like torture, in which no one should ever engage even on the pretext of saving the State; but to define these ethical absolutes in concrete terms which are applicable to all times and places is an impossible task.

What is more, it is sheer hysteria to suggest that a particular method of organising labour which has existed for a long time in this relatively free country of ours, and which has become a source of major trouble only in recent years, comes in the same category as slavery (an institution, incidentally, which is itself difficult to define in concrete terms).

Mr. Prior and (let it be added, in overdue deference to the now threadbare principle of collective responsibility) Mrs. Thatcher and the rest of her colleagues have got the trade union thing wrong not because they are tyrants, latter-day King Bombas, and certainly not because they are efficient, old-fashioned Tory empiricists. They have quite simply made a major political misjudgement.

What is reasonably certain, however, is that in general this country is more likely to be justly and efficiently governed by its responsible representatives in Parliament than by assemblies of foreign jurists. By the same token, the Tynwald is better qualified to settle the merits of birching in the Isle of Man than is the European Court, and British school teachers are more likely to be right about the value of the cane in British comprehensives than is that august body.

Incidentally, on this last point, it seems likely that the court will decide that in future children can be caned only if their parents approve. Is it easy to imagine a more degrading lot for an English schoolboy than the knowledge that he is exempt from being beaten because mummy won't allow it?

So let us resolve to get our own trade union law right before the European judges tell us to, and let us proclaim, with Disraeli: 'To the liberalism they profess, I prefer the liberties we enjoy; and to the Rights of Man, the rights of Englishmen.'

Commentary

The Daily Telegraph, 18 March 1985

On telephone tapping, the following generalities have to be stated: it is a necessary and legitimate practice when undertaken for the detection of serious crime and in particular for the preservation of the State against sedition and treason.

It is also a dangerous practice, in that it may put into the hands of malicious people information which they would use for purposes other than those for which it had been properly acquired. It is dangerous also because there is a certain intrinsic virtue in privacy. Tapping should therefore be controlled as far as it can be (which is not awfully far) and the control should be independent and judicial in character rather than political.

These platitudes out of the way, I want to address your minds to the possibility that, as a nation, we tend to keep ourselves to ourselves rather too much, to assume that there are whole areas of our lives (really public in their consequences and significance), which should, nevertheless, as a matter of sacred duty, be protected against all intrusion. This

I believe to be a deepset defect in the English character, and one which is on the increase.

That there are properly private areas I do not doubt – for instance, the bedroom and, within reason, the private dining-room and drawing-room. I also value the protection tradition-ally accorded to the Royal Mail. Families and friends separated from each other by long distances should be able to communicate freely without fear of prying eyes.

I wonder, however, whether the same privileges should be extended to telephoning. This is partly because I belong to a generation which has never for a moment supposed that they were. In the old, pre-war days, all telephone calls passed through the post-mistress, who invariably listened to them. This enabled her to perform a useful social function, that of telling you where the man or woman you wanted to speak to actually was and when he or she would be back.

A typical call to the operator in the thirties in rural England would run something like this: 'Windermere 233 please.' 'Well, if it's the Brigadier you want, Master Peter, you'll not get him till after midday; he's gone to the bank manager to discuss the overdraft.'

I recall from my childhood a bevy of ageing aunts who lived unsullied lives in the recesses of North Wales, making few concessions to modernity and defending with something approaching fanaticism what they would never have de-scribed as their 'life-styles'. They were eventually persuaded to have a telephone put in their drawing-room. However, with remarkable prescience, they foresaw the potentialities of this instrument and insisted that whenever it was not in use, it should be covered by a tea-cosy.

In Northern Ireland today, it is a matter of assumption that every telephone call you make will be tapped by at least three people who will assess its contents from different doctrinal points of view. This has not greatly (if at all) reduced telephoning or interrupted legitimate business, though it has led to an interesting form of codified speech: 'I was talking to our friend the other day about what we were talking about last Wednesday in relation to what J. said the Friday before, and I can tell you it isn't on.' (J. of course being the pseudonym of a man whose name begins with M.) Such communications often require a pause for interpretation, but this only stimulates the intellect.

My point is simply this: why does not the Government now say that anyone making a telephone call must from henceforth assume that he is making a public pronouncement? This would cause a measure of public inconvenience, but to my mind nothing excessive, and it would greatly discourage crime.

It would also discourage the hasty and ill-considered transaction of business orally, and (provided the Royal Mail continues to enjoy what I hope is its relative immunity from interference) it would provide an incentive even to the criminal classes to regain the art of literacy. 'Selling the pass to Big Brother' you will say, but if we err too far on the side of privacy with things as they are today, I can tell you who the beneficiary will be – none other than 'Big Brother' himself.

Mrs. Victoria Gillick, a devout Roman Catholic and mother of ten, fought unsuccessfully in the courts to prevent doctors prescribing contraceptives to underage girls.

Commentary

The Daily Telegraph, 28 October 1985

'Yet proposals to extend birth-control facilities to these classes of people, particularly the young unmarried girls, the potential young unmarried mothers, evoke entirely understandable moral opposition. Is it not condoning immorality? I suppose it is. But which is the lesser evil?'

What more persuasive, moving and balanced statement could be made of the case against Mrs. Gillick? Surely these prescient words must have won for their author the same sort of unanimous applause which has been lavished on the sensible, humane and enlightened judges who have sent this bossy, reactionary lady about her business. The man who

uttered these words must surely be a hero of the enlightenment.

But who was he? The extract comes from a famous political
speech by Sir Keith Joseph delivered at Edgbaston on 19
October 1974. When Sir Keith arose, he was the front runner
for the succession to Edward Heath; when he sat down, his
hopes of ever becoming Prime Minister were wholly extin-
guished. The sentences I have quoted had killed them. Why?

No doubt, you will say, because the Tory party at that time
was dominated by horrible reactionaries and Puritans like Mrs.
Gillick. They would not have their sacred 'families' eroded by
sensible people who realised that girls would do it anyway and
that it is better that they should not have babies, unless they are
equipped financially and psychologically to bring them up.

But you will be wrong. Sir Keith was blackballed from the
premiership not by the reactionaries, but by the progressives –
the same people who are now exulting over Mrs. Gillick. He
did himself in and condemned himself to his present lugubrious
role in British politics, as other statesmen have done by one,
single, crucial slip. The Left said that this concern about giving
little girls contraceptives, particularly when they came from
the impoverished classes, showed arrogance and fascism. They
implied (knowing, of course, that he was a Jew) that he
espoused Nazi theories of eugenic control, that he had
retrospectively justified the Holocaust.

Now, of course, one must be fair. He did use some phrases
which are a red rag to a bull to the Left. He spoke about the
nation's 'human' stock, implying that it was a national interest
that one should not have too many one parent families presided
over by eleven-year-old mothers. It is a very wicked thing
nowadays to invoke the national interest in favour of anything,
except, naturally, stopping people smoking in order to reduce
the costs of the Health Service. Although he took the
precaution of quoting from a publication of the Child Poverty
Action Group he should have stuck to the vocabulary of
compassion, animadverting on how difficult it is to bring up a
child when you are still in the nursery yourself, particularly in a
society in which illegitimacy is still treated with some reserve.
Perhaps the language was bad, but the argument was
essentially the same as that advanced by Mrs. Gillick's critics.

This strange comparison seems to show not so much that it isn't what you say but the way you say it, as that it isn't what you say but quite simply who you are.

But hold it! There is another paradox yet to come. Before he made his speech, I was 100 per cent in favour of Sir Keith for Prime Minister; after it, my doubts grew until they developed into certainties. Why? Precisely because he had shown himself to be not a fascist but a social engineer of dangerous proportions. Institutions like the family, which are centres of independent power in the community, are in their nature capable of producing evil as well as good. There is no way in such cases of removing the possibility of evil without also diminishing the capacity for good. A Tory's bias is in favour of preserving the institution until it is manifestly doing more harm than good. Sir Keith's bias was the other way.

That is why Mrs. Gillick is right and Sir Keith and the progressive establishment (for once united) are wrong. That is also why the Government should now decide to end the absurd contradictions proposed by the Lords' decision and make the law what Mrs. Gillick wants it to be.

Suffering along with Samuel Smiles

The Daily Telegraph, 7 April 1986

Few books in the English language have been more persistently misunderstood than Samuel Smiles's *Self-Help*. Originally published in 1859, it was a *succès fou*, rapidly becoming a family bible for the Victorian middle classes and being translated into many strange languages. It was mid-Victorian England's message to the world. Now we are offered it again by Sidgwick and Jackson at a price of £12.95 and with an admirable introduction by Sir Keith Joseph.

The misunderstandings began in Smiles's own time. He complains in his own preface: 'In one respect the title of the book . . . has proved unfortunate, as it has led some, who have judged it merely by the title, to suppose that it consists of a eulogy of selfishness.' The same mistake has been made by later generations. Peter Walker, who has probably heard of it, has no doubt identified it as an ominous anticipation of Thatcherism; Sir Ian Gilmour, who will certainly have acquainted himself with its contents, probably regards it as the antithesis of the Tory ideal of 'Merry England'. Both would be right.

Samuel Smiles's thesis was simple: he believed that the greatness of nations depended on the moral qualities of the people who composed them; he believed that virtue resided in the individual; he held that legislative and administrative reform could do very little to improve people.

But what he emphatically did not believe was that the making of money was an end in itself, or that there was no place in the arrangements of a healthy society for help to others as well as to oneself. He lauded judicious generosity, provided that it was not distributed in a patronising manner and was not calculated to enfeeble the efforts of those to whom it was directed. He was a real Thatcherite.

He also thought that England had always been a mobile society. Great fortunes and great status had been achieved quickly and lost quickly. He understood that England, thoughout the centuries, has been based on class, not caste. There was nothing of the inverted snob about him. His preference was for tailors, cobblers or potters who had studied metaphysics in their spare time and eventually became peers; but he was quite gentle towards hereditary wealth accompanied by virtuous self-denial. One suspects that he even tended to suppose that great success was itself evidence of such past denial.

Now, Sir Keith Joseph is quite right to think that all this is very relevant to our own age; but there is another side of the picture which I think he somewhat underestimates. Old Samuel had a passionate belief in mediocrity. He thought, or half-thought, that there was not much difference between one man's talent and another's. All depended on effort, the more painful the better. It was a good thing for Thomas Carlyle that the first volume of his *French Revolution* had been used to light the fire. It was character-forming.

The British, who are dedicated to constipation, enjoy

saying that everything should be done the hard way; but is this not a supreme error, indeed a gross immorality?

If one was at all malicious (which, particularly in the context of Sir Keith, one is not), one might be disposed to ask whether the Secretary of State's admiration for Samuel Smiles does not at last supply the rationale for the Government's education policy? What could be better, on Samuel's principles, than to arrange that children should be taught for examinations which will never take place, and then made to take examinations for which they have not been taught? Surely, the recipe for a generation of intellectual heroes.

But, more seriously the truth surely is that although we are suffering from everything Samuel Smiles disliked – idleness, licentiousness, dishonesty (mostly in relatively low places), trades unions and the rest – we are also suffering from an extravagant faith in mediocrity and a ludicrous belief in doing things 'the hard way'. I seem to have a memory of a comment by Enoch Powell on that maxim, the maxim having been uttered, if my memory serves me, by no less a moralist than Mr. Heath: I seem to remember that Mr. Powell said that anyone who did anything in a harder way than was necessary must be a fool – or some politer equivalent.

Anyway, *Self-Help* is an immensely good read, written with a vigour which puts present-day journalism to shame. You should buy it for your teenage children and observe their reactions. You would learn much, and it is even possible that they would learn something. I am a Merry England man who, towards the close of his career, rather wishes he had been more of a Samuel Smiles man; but how many Samuel Smiles men, in the same state, wish they had been more of Merry England men?

No mercy for Myra

The Daily Telegraph, 22 November 1986

What is the essential moral issue presented by the campaign for the release of Myra Hindley, which Lord Longford has thought it prudent to resume at the very moment when police are searching for the bodies of two more child victims of the ghastly holocaust known as the Moors Murders?

Consider the protagonists: Lord Longford is an eccentric nobleman of strong religious convictions and humanitarian instincts; Hindley is a woman convicted of two unspeakably sadistic murders, now serving a life sentence in Cookham Wood jail. Lord Longford wants her to be released from prison. To understand why, it is now necessary to attend briefly to serious intellectual issues.

Emphatically, Lord Longford is not simply following the line most fashionable among progressive figures about crime and punishment. That line is, to put it simply, that the criminal is not responsible for his offences; he or she is the victim of social circumstances or congenital deficiencies. In the moral sense, therefore, he is not a suitable object of punishment at all. He is not to be exposed to reprobation or revenge. Equally, he is not to be 'forgiven', for, since he was not responsible for his deed, there is no occasion for forgiving him.

On this view, all society has to decide (and to do so in as calm and clinical a manner as possible) is what it is most expedient to do to the criminal. Logically this might range from shooting him down, without malice, like a mad dog or sending him for a prolonged and pleasant holiday in some super modern establishment for the care of such victims of social or biological misfortune. The softer option is usually preferred.

This attitude empties punishment altogether of its moral content. No normal human being accepts it, because it runs counter to deeply-implanted moral instincts. It also suffers from an internal contradiction: if the general good of society was all we had to consider in deciding how to treat the members of society, there would be no reason for drawing any distinction between guilt and innocence when awarding punishments. There are times when it would be politically convenient to expose an innocent man to a fudged judicial process and then proceed to hang him. This procedure would horrify enlightened penologists – but why? Only because they have not in fact expelled the notion of retribution from their thinking, much as they would like to do so. They still take the plebeian view that the innocent should not be punished.

Lord Longford, I repeat, is not in this contemptible category of enlightened thinkers. What he says about Myra Hindley is this: 'she may have done evil things but which ones of us hasn't?' Well, in the light of the available evidence, 'may' seems to be a curious word to employ. However, Lord Longford's case rests not on the assertion that Hindley never was evil, but that she has ceased to be so. This has been brought about, so he maintains, by an act of religious conversion. To all intents and purposes, she is no longer the woman who indulged her lust by participating in the murder of children.

As Christians, he continues, we should all accept her new personality, let bygones be bygones and admit the erring sheep back to the fold. Did not Christ himself forgive those who crucified him? Are we not told that our own prospects of salvation depend on our willingness to forgive those who have injured us, and that there is no limit to the mercy which in this respect is expected of us?

Now all this is sound theology and, as far as it goes, entirely true, and I never enjoy the spectacle of Lord Longford being bully-ragged by the popular press as though he were almost a conspirator in murder. But, underlying his position in this matter, there is a huge moral and theological fallacy. It is best indicated in an admirable article by Joanna North in the July issue of the Conservative philosophical quarterly *The Salisbury Review*. Miss North writes: 'nor must we suppose that forgiveness requires the forgoing of retribution . . . And though it is possible for forgiveness to occur without retribution it is more likely that forgiveness can occur if the wrongdoer has faced the fact of his crime and recognised the justice of his punishment.'

It is penitence alone which makes forgiveness possible, but even penitence and religious conversion do not obliterate sins. What would you expect to be the attitude of a sadistic murderer who had genuinely repented? Not, of course, to try and escape from prison, or even to seek release on parole; rather to demand and expect nothing; not indeed to wallow in aimless remorse, but rather to live out the rest of his or her life as usefully as possible within the restraints imposed by society's reactions to his or her crime.

I am not in the business of deciding whether Hindley has or has not repented. On this the evidence is contradictory, and the testimony supplied by Lord Longford seems to me to be facile. But, even if she has, there remains the duty of restoration, her duty to repair as far as possible the damage she has done.

How ludicrous and even cynical that last phrase seems; what restoration can she make other than revealing to bereaved families, if she knows it, where the bodies of their mangled children lie? There is, however, another act of restoration which she can make – it is to co-operate with the rest of us in affirming the moral awfulness of her crimes – and that by perpetual penance. Only thus can she be forgiven.

Society must affirm its reprobation of those crimes by punishing her. There is a practical as well as a moral reason for doing so; the appalling truth is that the sons of Adam generally lack the discrimination of Lord Longford. They have to be reminded of the horrible character of crimes like murder by seeing those crimes conspicuously punished. If the State does not impose such conspicuous punishments, the ever-present danger is that the mob will do its own justice. For Hindley's safety and also, I suspect, for her salvation, she must be in prison for the rest of her life. I hope the régime will be humanely conducted, and I am glad to learn that she is doing an Open University course.

As for Lord Longford, I think that, in the interests of his protégée, he should now stop. His approach is sincere but sub-Christian. When he describes Hindley as 'a nice person', he seem to me to be trivialising a grave matter. He may well be right, but the phrase is not only tactless, it argues a degree of moral insensitivity so great as to come close to moral imbecility.

This was Utley's last piece for The Daily Telegraph.

In God's name do we moralise too much?

The Daily Telegraph, 22 December 1986

My Christmas thought for 1986 is that one thing which is wrong with this country is that there is altogether too much moralising.

Let me explain myself; the Scriptures teach us (if I have interpreted them rightly) that we live under a strict moral law which from time to time is most vigorously and even brutally asserted by the power of God. They also teach us that we have become largely incapable of observing this law by our own moral exertions. Nothing but the grace of God will save us. What is more, the grace of God is to be achieved only by applying our minds principally to the examination and repentance of our own sins and by showing charity and forgiveness to others.

These are very difficult precepts to define, let alone to observe. They do not command us, in my opinion, to refrain from punishing very wicked acts which are subversive of the social order, or to refrain from defending ourselves and our friends from the aggression of others. They do command us, on the other hand, not to have minds which are obsessed with seeking out evil in others, and to be more concerned with our own beams than with other people's motes. They do enjoin us to put the best credible interpretation on the behaviour of our neighbours. They do exhort us, principally, not to think that everything in the world is a moral issue and that we ourselves are always possessed of the moral answer. All this is what has been implied throughout the ages by the old-fashioned concept of a Christian gentleman. I think this concept is going out.

One glaring example of its departure seems to me to be the words of Chief Constable Anderton about the victims of Aids 'swirling around in a human cesspit of their own making'. Again do not misunderstand me: if all Mr. Anderton is saying is that sexual promiscuity is a principal cause of this terrible disease, he is entirely right. What is more, I am not much impressed by those theologians who blandly announce that Aids has nothing to do with 'the judgement of God'. God created the laws by which the universe works and He cannot escape responsibility for their consequences, He punishes the just and the unjust in what, by ordinary human standards, is a most arbitrary and disgusting manner. Nobody who cannot accept this arbitrariness has a right to call himself a Christian. God is not bound by human standards of morality.

From time to time, it would appear, He takes the most extreme and liberal steps to draw our attention to the wickedness of the human race. But He knows well and has told us that, meritorious as these remonstrances may be, we shall be saved not by fear but by love. We should listen to His voice in history but we should recognise that its purpose is to bring us, not in trepidation but in affection, to His feet.

So what should we do about it? Not be over-given to moralising about the faults of others or to rejoicing in the miseries which attend their offences. Above all, we should not be given to searching out sin. Consider this quotation from the prospectus of a comprehensive school in Wolverhampton which is currently trying to force its English pupils to learn Punjabi: 'It is positive policy to develop among staff and pupils awareness of attitude and behaviour which reflect racism . . . Anyone who persisted in racist behaviour, whether pupil, member of staff or visitor of any kind, would be asked to leave the premises.' Substitute 'unchastity' for 'racism', and would anyone regard this as a recommendation to Christian behaviour, let alone enlightened behaviour?

I wish you, therefore, a Happy Christmas. My pastoral advice is to abandon moralising for the season, and just wallow in the mercy of God.

Mrs. Currie was to survive Utley's column by a mere 14 months.

Lighting up for liberty

The Times, 3 August 1987

Last week's news that the Health Education Authority had drawn the Government's attention to the fact that under existing law it will be possible to prosecute employers who permit smoking in their offices and factories; and that those employees dismissed for persisting in the practice would have no legal redress, aroused in me the sentiment which those familiar with my writing could have predicted.

Maurice Green, the late lamented editor of the *Daily Telegraph*, once remarked that the right to smoke was the only subject, except Ulster, on which 'Utley writes with a small semblance of sincere feeling.' So, with last week's rash attack, all the familiar phrases sprang to my lips: 'the nanny state', 'monstrous interference with' etc., 'back to Calvin's Geneva'.

I have to confess, however, that there has always been at the back of my mind a lingering doubt about this rhetoric. Our ancestors, like boring old John Stuart Mill, applied themselves fairly rigorously to the question of what were the proper limits of State authority. We are all libertarians now, in the sense that we all prattle on about liberty. But we all agree that liberty must have some limits, and we are quite arbitrary in our judgement of what those limits should be.

I, for example, am a libertarian about smoking. I am not a libertarian about hard pornography (particularly child pornography), about the drug traffic as it is normally understood, about the publication of official secrets by people who have earned large sums of money on condition that they would not reveal them.

I am, by contrast, a libertarian in the matter of 'race relations'. I stoutly defend the right of people to express their views about the virtues and vices to which particular ethnic groups are prone in particular circumstances, so long, of course, as those expressions of opinion are not calculated to cause instant public disorder.

Others have different criteria. They think that publishing secrets is all right, suppressing child pornography is a curtailment of artistic freedom, that smokers should be persecuted in order to prevent the spread of cancer but that nothing should be done to embarrass or otherwise discomfort homosexuals in order to prevent the spread of Aids.

We must get back to the abstract discussion of what the State should and should not do about serious social evils. To this noble end, I advance a few principles upon which I invite you to meditate during the summer. I shall not thoroughly defend them, because space and my current resources of intellectual energy do not permit such defence. But here they are.

• It is not enough to prove that a practice in which someone is engaging (smoking for example) is bad for his health in order to justify suppressing it by law. A smoker might well feel that the consequences for himself and society of abruptly abandoning the habit would be worse than those of maintaining it. In the case of introverts, these consequences might include suicide; in the case of extroverts, murder.
• It is not enough to prove that the practices engaged in do harm to other people. The distinction between 'self-regarding' and 'other-regarding' action, promoted by J. S. Mill, is fraudulent for reasons too obvious to be described. If we accepted it, we would, for example, abolish motoring, not only drunken driving but all driving. We would conclude that, if motor cars are permitted, there are bound to be some 'innocent deaths', and we would chuck the whole thing. We all live in society and are, therefore, bound to accept the risks which arise from that necessity.
• There are times when the State should intervene to suppress great evil. But the decision to do so should be taken by the people, in the process of developing a consensus, not by 'experts'. There are two reasons for this. The first is that 'expert opinion' is not infallible. Science changes its mind, particularly medical science. It is not concerned about

absolute truth, but with useful hypotheses. I remember the time when it was thought that no one should have his tonsils out and the time when it was believed that everybody should have his tonsils out. I do not for a minute doubt (as a layman) that there is some sort of connection between smoking and lung cancer; but I am impressed by the evidence that, in many countries (Japan for instance), people smoke inordinately from early on without getting the disease. Other factors plainly intrude. The unqualified statement 'smoking causes lung cancer' is a lie.

• It is a bad thing to give scientists the impression that they have to reach a common opinion on all contentious subjects and then proceed to impose those opinions on society with the aid of government. They are there to reveal the facts as they see them and to leave others to draw inferences. History reveals many cases in which scientists, less concerned with the integrity of their own operation than with the betterment of mankind, have fudged the evidence. I do not know whether this is happening now, but I do not know that it is not.

I leave you to think over these propositions, and to consider whether the Prime Minister would not be well advised to sack Mrs. Edwina Currie.

Imbeciles of the moral world

The Times, 7 December 1987

Many years ago I was introduced (I forget by whom) to a new phenomenon or, to be exact, a phenomenon with which I was already familiar was given (for the first time in my experience) a precise definition. That phenomenon was 'moral imbecility'. It is the total suspension of normal critical faculties and the normal capacity to distinguish facts which afflicts a great many highly sophisticated people when confronted with 'moral issues' involving their prejudices.

It is being handsomely displayed at present in the chorus of *bien-pensant* opposition to David Alton's abortion bill. To name but a few manifestations of this phenomenon – there is the tiresome but extremely able Miss Polly Toynbee, the delightful and more than averagely intelligent Miss Julia Langdon and the 'prestigious' Mr. Simon Jenkins. There are many more whom I shall forbear to name. Mr. Alton has put their collective 'knickers in a twist'.

Let us consider, then, what Mr. Alton's bill is about. He is not concerned with the criteria which are held to make abortion legitimate. I myself regret that fact, but I record it. He is concerned solely with the stage of pregnancy at which an abortion can properly take place. Here, we all start from a common premise. It would be wrong to kill a child who had already been born just because his continued existence would be a nuisance to society. It would be wrong to kill a perfectly formed foetus on the verge of birth for the same reason. The law says it should not be done after 28 weeks. Most of the opponents of Mr. Alton's bill are content with that definition. Mr. Alton thinks it should not be done after 18 weeks: he has powerful evidence on his side, and evidence which would be seriously considered and debated by anyone who was not a 'moral imbecile'.

But what happens? A chorus of abuse is directed against him for having given to the press a picture of an 18-week-old foetus. He is appealing, it is said, to 'emotion' and 'sentimentality'. Why emotion should be a bad thing to appeal to I do not know. But reason, surely, is a good thing to appeal to; it should temper emotion. Do these smart people object to the publishing of lurid descriptions of operations for lung cancer in order to discourage us from smoking? I do not object to that either; I simply claim the right to dispute the intended inferences from those pictures. In this matter I am rational, they are not.

Other worse arguments are invoked. It is said, for instance (I cannot remember by which of them), that the matter of an abortion should be determined solely between a woman and her doctor. In the terms of the argument, that is 'moral imbecility' *par excellence*. It is almost the precise moral equivalent of saying that if a man (I include woman) is to be murdered, the matter should be decided between the prospective murderer and his (I include her) accomplice. We are all agreed that some abortions are wrong; on that basis we cannot possibly maintain that they should be authorised simply by the fiat of a woman and her medical adviser.

The husband or lover surely has something to do with it. The law imposes on him some obligations to support a living child. It must therefore give him a say in whether the child should live. The tiresome Miss Toynbee seems to be congratulating herself on the fact that she extracted from Mr. Alton a somewhat ambivalent reply about whether he was homosexually inclined. She in fact got a very honest answer. What is odd, however, is that she seems to have thought that a male homosexual would be automatically opposed to a 'woman's right' to kill her children. In my experience, this is not so. Most male homosexuals whom I have known are quite excessively protective of women and regard the measures that are necessary to the procreation of children to be an unpleasantly brutal assault. That appears to me to be *au fond* Miss Toynbee's view, though I would never dream of describing her as a 'lesbian', which I suspect, with no experience to guide me, is not the fact. Might she then not have attacked David Alton's bill on its merits? Well, I suppose not – she had to write a sparkling article.

Yet there are warnings which I will give to Mr. Alton. The plain truth of the matter is that the majority of people do not regard abortion as 'murder'. Of the numerous admirable secretaries I have employed in the past 30 years, I would say that, at a rough estimate, 50 per cent of them have told me, in the course of discussing this subject, that they have had abortions (in this matter there is no causal connection). I do not regard them as murderesses, but simply as the victims of 'moral imbecility'. If Mr. Alton decides to go in for arranging demonstrations and pickets he will do his bill grave damage. Moreover, if he attacks private hospitals about the amount of money they make from abortions (making money is not a bad thing in itself) he will be desperately confusing the issue. After all, he has a strong intellectual case; his opponents – the 'moral imbeciles' – have nothing to offer but an incoherent repetition of the clichés of the 1960s.

4 · 'Forgive our foolish ways'

Bishops without God

Sunday Telegraph, 24 March 1963

What should happen to an Anglican bishop who does not believe in God? This, I hold, is the condition of the Bishop of Woolwich, as revealed in his paperback *Honest to God*,* and it raises, I maintain, a question of Church discipline which cannot be shirked without the gravest repercussions on the whole Anglican Communion.

The Bishop, of course, says that he is not trying to dethrone God but to re-define Him in a manner acceptable to those who will not adopt the premises of the Christian religion. He sets about the task in the familiar manner of liberal theology: there is a great deal of ruthless analysis appearing to lead to atheism but always stopped short at the last minute by the invocation of that dependable *deus ex machina*, the inscrutable mystery of the Christian faith.

In the end God pops up again – as a principle of harmony at work in the universe, as 'Love', or as 'What we take seriously without reservation'. As a person, however, He is simply abolished.

Now, whatever this religion is, it is not the Christianity of the Nicene Creed, which consists of a number of crude and precise historical statements about the respective activities of the three members of the Holy Trinity. What the Bishop requires of a Christian is not that he should believe that Jesus was born of a virgin, crucified under Pontius Pilate and rose again from the dead, but simply that he should believe that there is something 'sacred' at the bottom of human existence,

*'Honest to God' by the Bishop of Woolwich, Dr. John Robinson (SCM Press).

that he should love his neighbour and that he should be indisposed to make absolute moral judgements such as are implied in the orthodox view that fornication is always wrong though often difficult to avoid.

The avowed object of the exercise is to make religion acceptable to the irreligious, to prove that it is possible to be in reality a Christian without believing in the teachings of the Church, and to accept God without using the word.

The Bishop writes with the authority not only of the Apostolic Succession but also with that of a witness for Penguin Publications in the case of *Lady Chatterley's Lover*. To that extent, what he says is liable to cause a degree of scandal which must raise the question of whether he can properly retain his office.

When Bishop Colenso of Natal in the last century denied the existence of Hell and suggested that a charitable Deity might take a lenient view of polygamy among the natives, the Archbishop of Cape Town tried to sack him, with only partial success; the erring bishop lost his ministry but retained his episcopal income.

In our own day, two eminent clerics persistently defied the conventions: Bishop Barnes and Dr. Hewlett Johnson, the lately retired Dean of Canterbury. Both were allowed to end their ecclesiastical careers honourably, although they were frequently denounced by their brethren as heretics.

A comparison of these two cases shows the difficulties confronting those who are concerned to root out heresy in the Church of England. By secular standards, Dr. Hewlett Johnson was far the more serious offender of the two; by theological standards, he was unexceptionable. The Doctor, who was appointed to his Deanery not, as is commonly believed, by the express personal wish of Mr. Ramsay MacDonald but by that of a deeply conservative Archbishop of Canterbury, had no difficulty in accepting every article of the Christian faith as traditionally defined; he suffered not from heresy but from an extreme ineptitude of political judgement, a frequent failing among Christians. It is easy to conceive circumstances in which it would have been the duty of Government to hang him as a traitor, but quite impossible to defend the view that he should have been burnt as a heretic.

Dr. Barnes was in an extremely different case: he denied the virgin birth as a literal historical fact, but as the debates in Convocation showed, he did so with so much subtlety, erudition, and respect for orthodoxy as to make it quite impossible to prove that in a fundamental sense he had done it at all.

Where, one must ask, will the ravages of liberal theology end? The Devil and Hell went long ago; the position of the Blessed Virgin has been seriously undermined; God, who until last week was invulnerable, is now distinctly on the defensive. What will ultimately be left except a belief in the need for bishops, if only to give evidence in trials about obscenity and to talk to pop singers on television?

It is hard to give an account of Anglican opinion on the Bishop of Woolwich's latest contribution to this process, since most of those best qualified to judge have not yet read the book. Bishop Wand has already expressed charitable dissent and the Dean of Salisbury, who has just reached the last chapter, confines himself to saying that he has no doubt that the Bishop is 'a profoundly orthodox liberal and a sincere believer.'

The Church of England has always had a horror of heresy-hunting, stoutly holding that conformity in morals and worship is more important than the acceptance of agreed definitions of doctrine. Added to this is a new obsession, which appears to afflict the entire Episcopal Bench, with the importance of not appearing to be old-fashioned.

Furthermore, there is really no way of getting rid of the Bishop of Woolwich except by prosecuting him for heresy, with an ultimate appeal to the Judicial Committee of the Privy Council where hard-bitten lawyers would sit in judgement on the Fathers of the Church. The Bishops' Retirement Measure recently passed relates only to incompetence, senility and misbehaviour and expressly excludes from its purview the preaching of heresy.

No one in the Church of England wants a new Inquisition. Yet there must surely be a vast number of simple parsons, for whom no deanery or bishopric beckons, whose work is rendered more difficult by the activities of the Bishop of Woolwich.

To teach men the simple lessons that they were created by a
personal God to whom they will ultimately be accountable,
that they are commanded by Him to do their best to live in
chastity and charity, that by diligently seeking His aid in
prayer and faithfully receiving His Sacrament they can find
the power to obey His Will and eventually earn His Eternal
Companionship – these traditionally are the Church's practical tasks. The aim of this teaching is to induce men to follow a
particular discipline of life which clearly depends on the
acceptance of certain historical assumptions about the truth
of the Scriptures; these assumptions are now either denied or
treated as irrelevant by the Bishop of Woolwich.

It is one thing to restate the eternal truths of religion in
contemporary language and quite another expressly to repudi-
ate fundamental doctrines which were believed by those who
learnt Christianity from the lips of Christ. It is not always clear,
indeed, whether the Bishop's aim is to convince agnostics that
they can conscientiously go to church or to persuade Christians
that there is no real need to do so. At the lowest, he seems to me
to be violating the principles of honest commerce by trying to
sell as Christian a commodity that bears no relation to the
historical and accepted meaning of that word.

Can the Church of England, in the name of intellectual
liberty, be content to allow its bishops to use the authority of
their office, and by implication that of the Gospel, to support
any trend of opinion they happen to favour? I cannot see how,
on this occasion, the Church can avoid the duty of facing the
question squarely – yes, even at the cost of being thought
'square'.

South Bank religion: where is it leading?

The Spectator, 27 March 1964

There have lately been some signs that both sides in the South
Bank controversy are beginning to feel that the time has come
to ring the bell.

This is, indeed, the natural climax to any dispute in the

Church of England, and this dispute, in all its phases, has been nothing if not Anglican in quality – Anglican in its ferocity, in the forensic over-simplification in which both parties have freely indulged, in the recurring hint from the orthodox that the time may have come to invoke the blunt instrument of authority, and in the often ill-concealed determination of both contestants that the row shall end in reconciliation.

What holds the Church of England together as a temporal institution is the unshakable conviction of its members that a profound identity of belief underlies every patent contradiction of opinion. I remember recommending a Cambridge don, of quintessentially Anglican character, for the delicate task of writing for a great national newspaper the commemorative article on the occasion of the third centenary of the execution of Charles the Martyr. 'What will he say?' the editor asked. 'He will say,' I predicted, as it proved correctly, 'that Charles I and Cromwell were both fighting for the same thing.' 'How annoyed they would have been,' commented the editor, 'if they had realised it.'

To what extent can the same claim be made for the exponents of the South Bank religion and their critics?

So large a variety of phenomena are comprised under this heading that it is very hard to attempt a general answer to the question. There is, for instance, no necessary connection between liberal theology, on the one hand, and jazz Masses or dramatic representations, in a contemporary idiom, of traditional Bible stories. The pastoral effectiveness of these devices may be debated, but the debate does not involve any issue of principle. The Church has always sought to express its teaching and its worship intelligibly, and this has necessarily involved, from time to time, changing the forms in which they are expressed. It is not in these fields that the real challenge of the modernists, if it is a real challenge, is being made.

This challenge may best be considered under three heads: there is the insistence on the need for changing the symbols in which religious truths are conveyed, the campaign against the withdrawn, sectarian exclusiveness which is alleged to distinguish Christians in their relations with the rest of society and, most contentious of all, the demand for a change in the form, and in some respects also in the content, of Christian moral teaching, particularly about sex.

In the first of these phenomena there is certainly nothing new. It is one of the recurring features of liberal theology, which at times is preoccupied with explaining the miraculous elements in Christian belief as symbolic devices legitimately used to give poetic expression to rationally understandable truths, and is at times concerned to attack traditional symbols as impediments to the apprehension of these truths. It cannot be doubted that the Christian religion has benefited infinitely from the exercise of both these activities, that, but for liberal theology, it would be virtually impossible for a rational man to be a professing Christian today. Among the burdens which the Christian faith imposes is the knowledge that at any moment the formulae in which it is expressed will contain at least some statements, apparently purporting to be of historical fact, which cannot by the ordinary processes of historical science be proved, and which, if past experience is any guide, are open to the hazard of refutation. What part of the Christian profession is permanent and inviolable, and what part may be subject to necessary revision is a question which can never with certainty be answered; if it could, there would, indeed, be no need to ask it, for the Church would undoubtedly exclude from its creeds what could not be counted on as permanently valid truth. I do not believe that, if conclusive historical evidence incompatible with the view that Christ was born of a virgin could be adduced tomorrow, my faith in the essentials of the doctrine of the Incarnation would be gravely affected. It is a meagre and puerile kind of Christian apologetic which looks to history for the validating of theology, rather than to theology for the validating of history, which tries to convince us that the evidence of the grave clothes is incontestable proof of the fact of the Resurrection, and that from this fact the whole duties of a Christian can be simply and authoritatively inferred. At times, the cause of orthodoxy has suffered grievously from this sort of advocacy, and the damage it has done has, I have no doubt, been more serious than any wrought by Dr. Barnes or the Bishop of Woolwich. The historical statements in the Creed are relegated to subordinate clauses and by this means we are instructed that they are to be believed by virtue of our belief in Christ, not that our belief in Christ is an inference to be drawn from history. If science requires us to change either the status or the content of some traditional formulation of faith, we must surely obey it, for there is a sense in which a Christian's loyalty to truth must take precedence over his obedience to Christ.

All this the temperate orthodox will be disposed to admit. Yet, confronted with any such proposal of change, a Christian must ask whether science really obliges him to accept it, or whether his scepticism may not derive less from respect for evidence than from a fundamental doubt about the truths of belief which can neither be sustained nor refuted by evidence in the scientific sense. Is it the idea of the Virgin birth that is making the theology of the Incarnation unacceptable, or is it our doubt about the theology of the Incarnation which is making it impossible for us to believe in the Virgin birth? After all, the scientific truth that people are not usually born of virgins, far from being an impediment to the belief that Christ was so born, is the only thing which lends significance to the assertion that He was.

Strong as these doubts are, however, the fact remains that Christian mythology is from time to time altered, and that a proposal to alter it in the interests of pastoral efficiency is not in itself horrifying.

Similarly, the South Bank warning to Christians against the danger of sectarian exclusiveness and detachment is neither new nor, in itself, cause of scandal. A 'peculiar people' is always open to the temptation to arrogance; we should remember that this temptation afflicts the heirs of the New Jerusalem as powerfully as those of the old. We should also remember, of course, that the notion of the Christian Church as inheriting the special divinely-appointed mission originally entrusted to the Jews, is essential to our faith, and that to this extent it is as a 'peculiar people' that Christians must demean themselves. Here again it is a question of keeping the balance.

Even in respect of the new morality, as the Bishop of Woolwich has lately displayed in his generally admirable pamphlet *Christian Morals Today*, the differences between the orthodox and the innovators are not so deep as it behoves sprightly journalists to pretend. It is not to liberal theologians, but to conservative theology that we owe the 20th-century insistence, from which the understanding of Christ's teaching has so much benefited, that He was nothing of a moralist, that His specific contributions to ethical theory were almost negligible, that the New Testament is about the nature of forgiveness rather than about the nature of sin. Certainly, there is nothing new (on the contrary, it is the traditional preoccupation of casuistry) in the Bishop's insistence that even the most seemingly inviolable positive laws of Church and State may be subject to amendment, or in his emphasis on the fact that when Christ spoke of human duty He generally expressed it in terms of the obligations inherent in particular personal situations, rather than in terms of abstract, definable and absolute law. Whether His observations on adultery and fornication are the only exception to this rule may be a subject of intelligent and dispassionate discussion, but the Bishop, who holds that pre-marital sexual intercourse is wrong in nine cases out of ten, cannot be fairly accused of deliberately fostering sexual licence.

Surely, the real test of the Bishop's orthodoxy is to be sought, not in what he tells us we need not believe, but what he tells us we ought to believe, and it is this test which, I maintain, reveals the true weakness of his position.

We are to believe in God, Who has all the attributes of personality, but we are to do so without the aid of a visual image. We are to believe in the positive, perennial and effective intervention of Christ in human history, though we may do so without accepting as valid any of the most striking instances of that intervention reported to us by tradition. We are to be absolutely chaste and charitable, but we are to be so without the aid of those generalised rules of behaviour in which the duties comprised in chastity and charity have been customarily expressed.

What really keeps the young out of church today is surely the honest difficulty they have in reconciling with their own somewhat superficial idea of the evidence supplied by the natural sciences the Christian belief that the processes of nature and history, so full of apparent waste and pain, are a sacrament of the Divine Love. What puts them off Christian morality in matters of sex is surely not the feeling that one in every ten engaged couples really ought to be sleeping with each other without incurring the censure of society, but rather the honest conviction that there can be nothing wrong in sexual activities which can be rendered socially harmless by the use of contraceptives, and which are as pleasurable as they used to be in the days when there were practical objections to indulging in them.

To all this the South Bank Movement is utterly insensitive and wholly irrelevant. All it has done is unwittingly to suggest to the muddled, the lax and the sceptical that the comforts of religion may somehow be rendered compatible with those of muddle, laxity and scepticism.

State as the Church's umpire

Sunday Telegraph, 13 June 1976

When the rest of Britain's links with her past have been severed, one, it would seem, is destined to survive – the traditional, wholly anachronistic and (to judge by the arguments by which it is generally supported) totally indefensible relationship between Church and State.

Last Tuesday Mr. Callaghan took one timid step towards modifying that relationship. He proposed that in future the Church should be formally consulted about the appointment of archbishops, bishops and deans.

For years it has had a decisive say in all these matters. Now it has practically complete authority over the contents of its liturgy and the discipline of its clergy. Yet, for some obscure reason, the State stops short of recognising it as a wholly independent and private body.

Parliament retains the right to veto ecclesiastical measures and Mr. Callaghan gravely assures the Commons that there would be serious objections to his abandoning the ultimate duty of recommending to the Queen who should get the senior ecclesiastical jobs.

What does the Church of England get out of this arrangement? Certainly nothing in terms of hard cash.

There is the theory, of course, that its occasional involvement in major public spectacles like the Coronation jolts its multitude of effectually lapsed members into a salutary awareness of their dereliction. If so, the normal size of Anglican congregations suggests that this spiritual experience is of only brief duration.

The one solid benefit which survives is the right of certain bishops to sit in the Lords and the extent to which that contributes to the reconversion of Britain is, to put it respectfully, a matter for speculation. However, the price exacted for these doubtful boons is negligible. Only those Anglicans who not only want to be free, but are determined that they should be seen to be free, resent it all.

Parliament will never again attempt the assertion of power which it made in 1928 by rejecting the revised prayer book. Yet the advantages of the State (or at any rate the Government) preserving the established Church are even more elusive. There was a time when the function of the Church in relation to temporal power was clear and beneficial.

Its teachings conduced to public order, not, let it be observed, by enlisting positive enthusiasm for the commands of government, but by fostering the belief that government was a necessary evil, a thing to be endured and accepted like sickness and death, with a fortitude which would receive an eternal reward.

When the primary purpose of government was to maintain the stable order of society this discouragement of secular enthusiasm and Utopian dreams plainly served the purposes of the State. But what of a State like ours which has set itself up as a constant agent of social reformation, which positively encourages expectations of endless material progress and which, in its relationships with other States, often appears frankly in the role of a harbinger of social and political revolution?

It is easy to see how, by a ruthless use of the power of ecclesiastical appointment, the Church might be bent to serve these ends, as it sometimes has been in Iron Curtain countries. What could be more congenial to Mr. Callaghan, for example, than a bench of bishops prepared to invoke the Holy Spirit in support of 4½ per cent wage rises. Why, then, has this device never occurred to our Socialist rulers?

For one simple reason which goes to the whole heart of the matter and is instantly apparent to anyone who cares to study the proceedings of the Church of England's General Synod.

At this juncture in history the State has absolutely no need to bribe or bully the clergy to give this kind of assistance; they are already falling over backwards to provide it. The upper reaches of the Church of England have been swept by a wave of egalitarian sentiment which has transformed it practically into the Socialist party at prayer.

Its gospel is now a social gospel, compounded of racial and sexual equality, collectivism and concern for the environment. Its anathemas are reserved for profiteers.

No wonder a Labour Government is content to restrict itself to purely formal authority over the clergy. No wonder it still wishes to bolster up the Church's prestige by preserving the theory of the establishment.

In its nature the Church of England, for all its countless virtues, is prone to internal strife, susceptible to the influence of fashion, vulnerable to the temptations of temporal power and liable to fall under the dominion of unrepresentative cliques.

There is a sense in which its genius flourishes best in a straitjacket. In the past it has been preserved from these perils mainly by the moderating influence supplied by its special relationship with the State.

Its leaders have not been chosen by popular ballot or by an established clerical junta, but by detached Prime Ministers and patronage secretaries. At their best they have been bent only on preserving its unity, giving a balanced representation to its diversities and prepared above all to search for pious, scholarly and independent-minded men content to get on with the business of redeeming mankind. This has given Anglican culture its unique quality.

It has also made the Church of England one of the few continuous elements in national life.

Perhaps there are dangers in allowing Church patronage

to remain even formally in the hands of one so deeply engaged in fleeting controversy as a Prime Minister necessarily is.

But unless some other lay national figure (perhaps the Lord Chancellor) can be found to fill the Trollopian role to which Mr. Macmillan applied himself with such diligence, the Church of England will have lost the chief stabilising factor in its turbulent life and the nation will have lost one of the few surviving institutions which express its continuity.

There is indeed still a case for an established Church, but only if the State discharges, in fact as well as in form, its traditional role (essentially that of the umpire) in Church government.

Learning to live with Rome

Sunday Telegraph, 23 January 1977

Nothing, including the ascent to the moon, it may be confidently suspected, would have surprised our Victorian ancestors more about the history of the past 75 years than last week's report by a joint commission of Anglican and Roman Catholic theologians on the relations between Canterbury and Rome. In one brief, though tightly and at times obscurely reasoned paper, the commission seems to have swept away the whole *raison d'être* of modern English history.

By proposing that the Church of England should prepare to acknowledge the primacy of Rome, (though not Papal infallibility), it has, on the face of it, removed the foundation on which not only that Church but its historic companion, the English State, was built. By the same token, it must have made many English Roman Catholics wonder why their forefathers allowed themselves to be conveyed to Tyburn.

Moreover, this revolution has been accomplished in less than a quarter of a century; 25 years ago, I, a straightforward if somewhat pedantic Anglican brought up in neither the Anglo-Catholic nor the evangelical tradition, married an English Roman Catholic girl. It is now almost impossible to credit the elaborate paraphernalia of examination and consent and the semi-penitential ritual with which that operation was attended.

The rules required that I should be examined on three separate occasions by a Roman Catholic priest in order to establish beyond peradventure that my conception of the nature of marriage was consistent with the teaching of the Roman Church. I was required, of course, to sign a document pledging me to ensure that the children of the marriage were brought up in the Roman Catholic faith.

The ceremony itself was designed to emphasise the exceptional and mildly regrettable character of the occasion. There were to be no hymns, though an organ voluntary was permitted as a daring concession to ecumenism, and my wife was debarred from taking a vow of obedience to me.

What, of course, made these humiliations tolerable was that this majestic display of ecclesiastical arrogance was a façade, a bureaucratic flourish bearing little relation to the beliefs and practices of civilised Roman Catholics like my wife and, be it added, the majority of her pastoral advisers.

Even on the theological plane, I knew and she knew that, as a baptised Christian, the Roman Church was bound to recognise me, albeit somewhat surreptitiously, as a member of the universal Catholic Church; that her obligation to pursue my conversion by all available prudent means was wholly reconcilable with not pursuing it at all, and that my duty to educate our children in the Roman Catholic faith did not, contrary to the sustained propaganda of the Church's publicity machine, involve any obligation to send them to Roman Catholic schools.

In the event, my three preliminary examinations were reduced to two glasses of sherry and a conversation about the current state of politics with a well-bred Jesuit, and even the omission of the vow of obedience was more than compensated for by a sermon of unusual length and theological distinction by Father Michael Hollings, including the imperishable dictum that 'while the husband must think of his wife's virtues when he is tempted to dwell upon her faults, the wife must remember that he is in every respect superior to her.'

Now what these personal reminiscences illustrate is the settled policy of the Church of Rome a quarter of a century ago, a policy based on the maxim that in a hostile world the prudent

course was not to waver or concede but to present, at least to
the imperfectly instructed, an unassailable front of uniformity
and unyielding authority.

There seemed, indeed, to be many sound arguments for
this policy; not least of them, indeed, was the contemporary
state of the Church of England which, from its reverence for
intellectual freedom, had already degenerated into something resembling a debating society from whose agenda
nothing, however ludicrous, blasphemous and morally offensive, was excluded. But the arguments for papal intransigence
were fundamentally political and as such represented the
wisdom of men and not – what is required of the Church – that
of God.

Rome has paid a heavy price for its pre-Council exercise in
worldly prudence. What began under Pope John as a long
overdue scrutiny of inherited practice, not a species of hair-
brained radicalism but a diligent and scholarly appeal to the
teaching of the Gospels and the discipline of the early Church,
and a triumph for what was best in Reformation theology, has
developed into a storm of miscellaneous and ill-regulated
innovation.

That storm, which has convinced many pious Papists that
God has deserted His Church, has produced an extraordinary
consequence. The most extreme exponents of the principle of
papal supremacy find themselves deserted by a reformist
Vatican and are themselves driven into rebellion. This
development is significant: by inducing those who have so far
taken the loftiest view of the role of the Papacy to adopt a
more liberal attitude it could help to reunify Christendom.

Meanwhile, the Church of England's anarchy has also
progressed. Bishops who do not believe in God, canons who
applaud homosexuality, synods which appear to equate
Christianity with support for overseas aid have become the
order of the day. Just as the Roman contribution to last week's
synthesis shows a new apprehension of the pastoral character
of authority within the Church, of the dangers of a blunt and
naïve authoritarianism, so the Anglican contribution shows at
last some awareness of the need for a measure of Church order,
a belief fundamental to traditional Anglicanism but one which
has become almost extinct in the past half century.

If, as a result of all this, the reunited Church emerges as something between a debating society and an army, one apostle of the *via media* at least will be well satisfied.

My wife and I continue to go to our separate churches; she, to what sounds to the uninitiated rather like a non-conformist prayer meeting into which is normally inserted a sermon on the housing shortage, and I to a dignified and orderly version of the Mass accompanied by a brief and competent exposition of the Church's doctrine with few overtones of contemporary sociological significance. In all this must there not be some message about the way in which God performs his wonders?

Advent

The Daily Telegraph 19 December 1973

If we took Advent seriously (instead of simply regarding it as the run up to Christmas), we should all now be going about, with quiet concentration, preparing 'for the coming of the Kingdom'. The pubs would be hushed (in Fleet Street they are not), we should be fasting (I proudly record the existence of one colleague who has given up biscuits), and busily but unhurriedly laying in the champagne, the smoked salmon and the turkeys for the great day. Then we should have 12 days (public holidays I suggest) of sheer abandon. Bad for the economy? I think not. The present arrangement which permits only a semblance of work in the weeks until Christmas and leaves us exhausted and petulant when the supreme moment arrives is worse both for our souls and our bodies.

Being, mostly, reared in the vile heresies of liberalism, you will tell me that this happy change in our customs cannot be brought about by the authority of government. I think you are wrong, and I look to the Prime Minister.

Commentary

The Daily Telegraph, 10 February 1986

I would almost have signed a petition against Sunday trading presented to me after Holy Communion last Sunday, but for one fact: in commending it, my vicar stated that under the new law it would be compulsory for people to work on Sunday, regardless of their convictions.

This is, of course, not the case, and vicars should be at least as careful about such statements as politicians are required to be. As I understood it, the proposed Bill, now going through the Lords, protects any shop assistant currently employed from being dismissed for refusing to work on the Sabbath; it does not, I admit, extend the same protection to shop assistants who may be employed in future – any more than it extends such protection to such as me, who have often to work on Sundays in order to adorn your breakfast table on Mondays.

My vicar (John Foster), I should point out, is an admirable man – as honest as the day; he presides over a beautiful church (St. Mary's on Paddington Green), which presents a decent liturgy and an admirable sermon every Sunday. But, like most other Christians, he is capable of becoming over-zealous and of accidentally distorting the truth in the process.

I have another clerical friend, the Rev. Basil Watson, of St. Lawrence Jewry. He is a robust figure – a 100 per cent in favour of Mrs. Thatcher, the nuclear bomb and, needless to say, the Shops Bill. He takes the line that it is not the business of the State to impose standards of Sabbath observance, much as he wishes to preserve the traditional English Sunday. But he has some curious arguments for his position. One of these, expressed in his news letter, goes thus: 'Christians in the first century had to get up early on the first day of the week to carry out their religious devotions: often at the cost of their lives for doing so.'

Now this particular piece of nonsense continually recurs in current discussions. The argument is that if you make things very difficult for Christians you give them an opportunity of displaying their heroic qualities, and thereby you serve the faith. By the same token, you should support a bill in favour of throwing Christians to the lions. It simply will not do.

You can see that I am ambivalent on the subject. I certainly do not accept the ordinary libertarian arguments for Sunday trading any more than I accept the ordinary libertarian arguments for anything else. If I were allowed to buy motor cars on Sunday, I would probably do so; but I much prefer not to be allowed that liberty. One has to judge these things by their probable consequences for the quality of life, and I think the removal of all restraints on Sunday trading will produce very bad consequences which almost all of us will bitterly regret. If there were huge demand for this act of emancipation, there would be much to be said for it; one should not fly in the face of such demands, but manifestly there is not.

It is this which makes the Bill so ludicrous. Politicians always act unwisely unless they are acting under pressure. It is not their business to go about thinking how they should reform us; it is their business to respond to our needs and aspirations. Generally speaking, they should not move until they are kicked.

On Sunday trading, they have not been kicked (in spite of the polls which constitute no evidence at all); they have acted, I understand, for two reasons. The first is the view that the present law is often defied and is not easily enforceable, and that the contempt for it brings the law into disrepute. That is an old and frightfully silly cliché. In bygone times, the law firmly condemned homosexual acts and made them punishable in a most onerous manner, but the police did not go round looking for homosexuals, but contented themselves with punishing grievous and ostentatious examples of the vice. It is often a great part of wisdom to turn a blind eye to breachers of the law until they become socially offensive. In my judgement, we get on very well as we are about Sunday trading. Nobody will be much put out if we go on as we are; quite a lot of people will be put out if we change the arrangements.

The second reason for the Government's action is that it is one of their principles to deregulate trade. Well, that is pure doctrine, and as such wholly contemptible. In politics, going round doing things on pure grounds of theory makes you either ineffectual or tyrannical.

Why on earth the Government, with everything else it has on its hands, should have taken up this gratuitous burden, I cannot imagine. Perhaps, they are a bunch of ideologues after all, though until now I never thought so.

*　　*　　*

There are, nevertheless, occasions when the Government should be strong and radical. When some established institution has manifestly broken down, it should be abolished and superseded. That, on the anniversary of the teachers' strike is surely the case of the education system.

The Bishop of Durham – oh so reasonable

The Daily Telegraph, 14 July 1986

I am not among those who think the Bishop of Durham to be the devil incarnate. For his part, as his speech to the General Synod last week showed, he does not believe God to be the devil. This should provide the basis for what is currently described as 'a fruitful dialogue'.

There is, in my view, a great deal to be said for the Bishop. He has, for example, the conspicuous merit of being in no way original. There have been Anglican bishops and deans like him in plenty, and they are all an essential part of the great tradition.

What is more, a good deal of what he says is incontestably true. All the physical miracles attributed to God in the Bible have spiritual significance, and it is their spiritual significance that matters. This does not mean that they did not happen (the Bishop, if I interpret him rightly, thinks that they could easily have happened); it simply means that whether they happened or not the spiritual significance would remain. Believe in the miracles (the Virgin birth, the empty tomb and the like) but do not believe in what they imply and are meant to signify, and you do, indeed, convert God into a 'cultic idol' at the best, or even 'the very devil'.

Moreover, it is not right that our beliefs should depend on the conviction that these physical miracles occurred. The historical evidence for them is fairly meagre. A man's faith should not depend on anything so fragile as historical evidence. If I could be convinced with absolute certainty tomorrow that the tomb was not in fact empty on Easter Day, I would continue to believe in the Resurrection.

I would not either wish to have suppressed any historical investigation which might lead to the conclusion that the tomb was empty. At Cambridge I was taught history by a great Anglican historian, Charles Smyth, and I have never forgotten his precept that, as a Christian historian, my first duty was to the truth and only my second to Christ. I believe that that is the principle on which the Bishop of Durham acts, and I admire him for it.

What then is wrong with Dr. Jenkins? Quite a good deal I think. I discern him to be obsessed with the view that a great many potential Christians are at present being put off by the intrinsic incredibility of much which the Church requires them to believe. Now the Bishop himself requires them to believe an immense amount which does not come naturally to the secular, scientific mind. He wants them to accept God as the creator of the universe and the redeemer of mankind. That takes a lot of swallowing, rather more, I would have thought, than the empty tomb and the Virgin birth.

In short, Christianity, by the standards of the secular, scientific mind, is in its nature intrinsically incredible. Those who can take the first leap can quite easily take the rest. If some of them are worried about the Virgin birth and the empty tomb, simply on grounds of historical evidence, they should certainly not be excommunicated; but the idea that there are many people who will swallow the Creation but feel obliged to expectorate the empty tomb seems to me ridiculous. The Bishop, in fact, is making a great deal of fuss about very little. Let us recite the creeds and, within reason, put our own interpretations upon them.

It is when the Bishop comes to the problem of pain, of how we have a good and omnipotent God who can nevertheless allow Hiroshima to happen, that he is at his most vulnerable. There is no wholly and rationally satisfactory answer to that problem, and what I suspect to be the Bishop's answer, that if we were all very good Hiroshima could never have happened, does not seem to be an answer at all. In any case, there is a vast amount of suffering in the universe which is not directly due to human sin. What, for instance, about the 'natural disasters', the earthquakes and so on? For years I used to write pious leading articles about those, until eventually I told the Almighty that, though I would continue to be PRO to the Metropolitan Police, the RUC and the British Army, He must make His own arrangements for natural disasters.

We all of us have the choice; is the universe an accident (itself not an easily credible hypothesis) or has it a purpose and, if so, is the purpose benign? For many people the analysis ends in a question mark; but for some this does not preclude a leap in faith. That act of acceptance, however, is not facilitated by the speculations of intellectually buzzing bishops. There the Christian case must rest.

The drift towards a secular church
The Times, 2 March 1987

'The Church which is married to the Spirit of the Age will be a widow in the next.' So said Dean Inge, in words which have been firmly implanted in my mind since I first read them and which have been evoked again by a collection of essays on the secularisation of the Church to be published this week. It is called *After the Deluge*, published by the SPCK and edited by William Oddie, one of the few rising stars in the Anglican intellectual firmament.

Its thesis, crudely summarised, is that the western churches are rapidly abandoning their interest both in biblical theology and in the universal Christian tradition. Instead they have swallowed, more or less hook, line and sinker, secularised and humanistic concepts. Their thought on matters of theology and ethics starts not from an earnest attempt to discern the will of God for his Creation, but from an attempt to calculate where lies the benefit of mankind interpreted in terms of human happiness. This is, however, a book not to be summarised but to be read.

There is, surely, no time at which it could have appeared more appositely. We had last week the *cause celèbre* of the Oxford undergraduate who wanted his child to be born. That has produced yards of inconclusive and, with rare exceptions, intellectually inept argument. Why does the debate appear to be so sterile? Largely because it does not proceed from any agreed premise. Talking to many of one's dearly loved friends and colleagues about it is a painful and fruitless exercise.

There is an unbridgeable divide between those who believe that the act of human procreation is part of God's purpose for mankind and those who think that it is a mostly convenient device, to be interrupted when it seems likely to prove inconvenient. Not that the acceptance of traditional Christian premises will relieve us of all the dilemmas presented by this subject. Christian theology cannot precisely determine the point at which an embryo acquires a soul, or relieve us of the difficulty of determining what should be done when childbirth would gravely endanger the life of a mother, or when she has become pregnant as a result of physical coercion. On those issues Christians will differ; but in debating them they will at least be talking the same language.

It will not be the language of their humanist friends. They will adopt the hedonistic calculus, trying to establish whether it is a good thing for a child to be born to a mother who does not want it, or a socially desirable thing that an unwanted child should run the risk of becoming dependent on the Welfare State. These speculations are as barren and unprovable as any in which the theologians engage. Yet they are advanced as though, by this means, the argument had been raised to a level of scientific integrity and rationality. The issue really depends on where the argument begins. Christians can talk about it to each other; humanists can discuss it with each other; but the profit from conversation across the battle-lines is minimal.

So it is with woman priests. I do not deny that a serious theological debate has taken place on that subject. In so far as that debate is conducted in terms of theology, that is to say of the purposes of God as revealed to mankind, I have no doubt myself that it is overwhelmingly biased in favour of the traditional position. After all, since Jesus conspicuously appointed no woman apostles and Himself consented to be born as a man, the dice are pretty heavily loaded from the start. Translate the argument into secular terms – if Mrs. Thatcher, why not woman priests? – the discussion becomes different. It is in this second way that most laymen now approach the matter, and it is largely in deference to that fashion that the Church is proceeding with such alacrity in its present direction.

A further example of secularisation, dredged up from my recent memory: an eminent South African churchman (whose name and colour I will not mention, since I have not the precise text of his words before me), recently said that if Jesus were to come to South Africa He would undoubtedly be arrested by President Botha. Can you think of anything more improbable?

When Jesus came to Palestine, He was expected to be the leader of a movement of national liberation. Instead He announced that His kingdom was not of this world, cured a centurion's son (equivalent of a South African policeman's servant) of a mortal disease, and replied to a question about the propriety of paying taxes to the imperial power with calculated Foreign Office ambiguity, and refused to arbitrate in the matter of inheritance on the ground that He was not in the least concerned with distributive justice.

President Botha would regard Him as, in the idiomatic sense, an 'absolute godsend' and, I think, would do his best to make Him a bishop. Jesus, of course, would refuse.

So my sad conclusion is this: I shall have to become a ghetto Christian. This is a tragic thing for a man who is, not only by intellectual conviction but to the marrow of his being, an Anglican, one who loathes the idea of belonging to a sect which separates itself from English life and closes its mind to the changing fashions of English culture. If the Bishop of London leads us out of the Church of England into some Uniate church in communion with Rome I hope that I shall find the courage to follow him.

Still waiting in Willesden

The Times, 27 April 1987

The Blessed Virgin Mary was scheduled to appear on Easter Day outside a Roman Catholic church in the north London suburb of Willesden. She had appeared several times to a pious lady and had revealed to her this intention. The Blessed Virgin's aim, as is usual in such cases, was to convey an important message on matters of both eternal and contemporary interest such as Aids.

However, strings were attached to the engagement. 'Our Lady' (as the Roman Catholics call her) demanded an audience of at least 500 and, furthermore, required that all its members should be praying with sincere hearts. These conditions were not fulfilled; the audience fell short of the required number and, I have no doubt, contained at least some journalists and cameramen whose capacity for cordial sincerity is notoriously questionable. Accordingly, the apparition was postponed, and a further attempt will be made at Whitsuntide.

Such is the language in which my professional colleagues (and, no doubt, most rational people) describe this engaging non-event. Such is the language in which they always describe such things. It is good fun and makes excellent holiday reading. But to some of us it presents an intellectual dilemma.

Let us consider first those to whom it does not present any dilemma at all. These are scientific rationalists who hold that the universe is governed by constant laws and that any suspension of those laws is intrinsically incredible. If there is an apparent suspension, it must arise simply from the fact that some little qualifying law has not yet been discovered and formulated. No dilemma is presented either to those liberal theologians, popularly symbolised by the Bishop of Durham, who (though with more sophistication) think roughly the same. Such people are morally entitled to deride.

But what about that large section of Christian opinion (in which I include myself) which finds no difficulty in accepting the miraculous events recorded in the New Testament, ranging from the bodily resurrection of Christ to the conversion of water into wine? We laugh with the rest over these alleged manifestations of the Blessed Virgin (which have now come to be almost a persistent nuisance to the ecclesiastical authorities) – in Egypt, Yugoslavia, Ireland and now Willesden. Are we committed to the view that miracles could take place 2,000 years ago but are now to be dismissed *ab initio* as nonsense? We are in a considerable difficulty.

Of course, we are absolutely right to say that the assertion that a miracle has taken place does not constitute proof that it has. We are equally right to say that it is intellectually dishonest to take the view that because belief in miracles fosters the Christian faith, it must be indiscriminately encouraged. We are equally right to maintain that any alleged extraordinary event must be subjected to the closest scrutiny before it is accepted as true. There are a lot of maniacs and frauds about.

My own view is that belief in the Resurrection and other extraordinary phenomena recorded in the Gospel does not wholly rest on historical evidence. It rests chiefly on personal spiritual experience fortified by the historic testimony of the Church. If it were otherwise, no one who was not a competent historian would have much hope of salvation. I do not know that my position, in this respect, is much different from that of the Bishop of Durham, though I think that he has expressed his with a lamentable and, indeed, unpastoral record for the sensibilities of his unacademic public.

Anyway, back to the point: why are we so reluctant even to envisage the possibility that Christ who rose from the dead and turned water into wine has authorised his mother to appear to the people of Willesden and conduct the propaganda against Aids rather more efficiently than it has been conducted by the State? Our objection, I think, is principally aesthetic, normally a synonym for snobbish. When the Blessed Virgin appears, commercial consequences usually follow – like the tourist industry at Lourdes or the airport at Knock in County Mayo (what a future for Willesden!). Our objections are also political: was not our Lady of Fatima a most apposite propaganda response to the traumas of the First World War and the Russian Revolution?

But hold on! Would not God want to make quite a number of comments on such discontent, and, given His omnipotence, could He not well depute the task to Christ's blessed mother?

I am not arguing that the impresarios of miraculous appearances of the Blessed Virgin should be protected from ridicule. That is a matter to be dictated by manners. A tough Irish priest who is capable of setting up an international air service to bring pilgrims to a shrine can take a bit of rough treatment; it is the fire through which the righteous must pass.

Yugoslav children, unless they are manifest frauds, should be treated with tender scepticism, and pious suburban ladies with gentle consideration. Above all, if we want to be intellectually honest we should treat scepticism itself with a degree of scepticism.

Thatcher's new crusade

The Times, 16 February 1988

I am very glad that Mrs. Thatcher took the extraordinary decision to summon a number of bishops to Chequers (about the same number, if my failing memory serves me, as are necessary for the exorcism of a ghost) to discuss the nettled question of Church and State. It cannot be said that the encounter has produced instant amity, but it has cleared the air and, in particular, brought out one or two distinctions of crucial importance to the debate.

The first of these is the difference between the proposition that the Church should not meddle in politics and the proposition that the Church should proclaim courageously and without equivocation the Christian message on personal morality.

The first statement, presented starkly and without qualification, is not defensible. In reality, Mrs. Thatcher, Mr.

Gummer and all the more respectable critics of the episcopate have never made it. Mrs. Thatcher knows well and has often, at least by implication, asserted that every political judgement has some moral ingredient. The complaint of these sophisticated Tory critics has been that churchmen, instead of isolating this moral ingredient, have allowed themselves to be betrayed into making judgements about political expediency in a manner which suggests that they are moral judgements made with the full authority of the Christian tradition and that their acceptance is incumbent on all faithful people.

Bishops are also citizens (and, indeed, some of them have a secure place in our constitutional arrangements). They are entitled to make observations about politics, but they must not make such observations *ex cathedra*. This calls for a measure of tact, in which some of them seem to be conspicuously deficient.

What is more, even the most sophisticated Tory critics of the Anglican contribution to the current political debate have got visibly tired of the unanimity which now marks episcopal advice on such matters. This is a consequence of synodical government. The Synod makes no claims to infallibility, but when it solemnly resolves, for example, that the poll tax is intrinsically unjust and, therefore, contrary to the will of God, it is not surprising that much of the media should infer that this highly contentious, not to say ridiculous, view has been added to the Thirty-nine Articles.

None of this means that the grand tradition of radical clergy (such as the 'Red Dean' of Canterbury) should be ended. In the days when the Prime Minister had a greater degree of influence on top ecclesiastical appointments, the guideline was that some sort of balance should be maintained between the various ecclesiastical parties into which the Church of England, by its nature, is divided. A 'High Church' Archbishop of Canterbury could be countered by an evangelical Archbishop of York.

Today these traditional divisions have been largely superseded by the division between exponents of the social gospel, which has now acquired liberal ingredients in both the political and the theological sense, and traditionalists. The complaint is that the traditionalists no longer get a look in.

Should Mrs. Thatcher ever recover some of the former powers of her office over church appointments, I suspect she would not abuse those powers to pack the bench of bishops with fully paid-up Tories, but merely to re-establish some equilibrium in the Church's leadership.

The controversy, however, has now moved on to rather new ground. We are no longer debating what bishops should and should not be allowed to say about politics and how and where they should say it; we are discussing what the Church's hierarchy should say about private morals, and the initiative in that discussion is being taken by Tory politicians. Is this intrinsically unseemly?

I think not. It is true that politicians run a grave risk when they turn themselves into full-time moral leaders; in such circumstances, morality also runs a grave risk. It is also true that the Church of England is not a 'state' church but an established church; it is not there simply to do what the State tells it to do. However, the ancient partnership (from which the Church still derives considerable advantages) can hardly survive if the nature of one of the partners changes completely. To reduce the question to the absurd: if the Synod decided to transfer its allegiance from Christ to Mohammed, the Archbishop of Canterbury could hardly expect to continue to preside at the Coronation.

Moreover, just as the Church should not be indifferent to politics, neither can the State be indifferent to religion. It must foster certain moral sentiments in its subjects. If Church leaders abandon those sentiments, or start preaching them in obscure and equivocal terms (this last is the chief complaint against current practice), politicians have a perfect right to protest.

So far Mrs. Thatcher has handled the matter not only with characteristic firmness but also with a commendable delicacy of touch. The position seems to be roughly established that when churchmen enter the political arena blatantly they must expect to be answered back; equally, there is no doubt that when politicians enter the religious arena they will be answered back as well. This, if it continues, will make for mutual candour, which is better than unilateral abuse, but is not a recipe for peace.

In the long run, I believe, Government and Parliament must try to recapture some of the ground which they have lost in the management of ecclesiastical affairs. There is no reason why the Callaghan convention on the appointment of bishops should be sacrosanct forever and no reason why the power of the Synod should remain as great as it is. I am, I agree, inviting the Prime Minister to tread a minefield, but that is a task at which she is adept. What is more, in treading it, she could, I think, count on a large measure of support from the lower clergy, the laity and the general public.

I have another doubt: it is all very well for Mr. Hurd to say that there is a limit to what the Government can do, without the aid of the Church, parents, and teachers, to restore good order in this country. That is so, but it is also true that the Government can do *something*, and even more strikingly true that the State has done much to destroy good order in the last few decades. Permissive legislation about divorce encourages divorce, ill-thought-out legislation about homosexuality encourages the public advocacy of that aberration. If there are some vestiges of a traditional moral consensus in this country they must be discreetly encouraged by legislation.

All I am arguing is that Mrs. Thatcher's healthy and apparently civil confrontation with the bishops must not be allowed to be a 'one-off' affair. She must give to this aspect of her programme the same vigilant and continuous attention that she has successfully given to other aspects. Above all, she must not be frightened off by clichés like the 'moral majority'. This does indeed signify something very horrible, in its American context, but it does not signify anything which she is likely to be tempted to embrace.

Mrs. Thatcher's address to the General Assembly of the Church of Scotland was perhaps her most notable attempt to relate her religious and political convictions.

Hidden dynamite in that sermon

The Times, 27 May 1988

It is a curious, but I think explicable, fact that the passage in Mrs. Thatcher's Edinburgh address which on the face of it gives most pabulum to her critics is the one that they all seem to have ignored. You must wait for a while, before I tell you which the passage is. They have preferred to concentrate on what was familiar to them – her well-known beliefs about the relationship between Christian morality and economic policy. She has explored this theme often before, notably when lecturing at St. Lawrence Jewry.

Its contents can be briefly summarised. Christianity undoubtedly has something to do with politics in that it is the business of Christian politicians to look for the best ways of embodying in their policies the ethical concepts of Christianity. They will differ in their conclusions, and all that is required from them in respect of these differences is that they should express them with mutual charity and courtesy. They must all of them accept the principle of individual responsibility, for even when that responsibility is exercised by collective action it remains *au fond* individual; voters who believe in high expenditure on social services, for instance, must be prepared to vote for high taxes or high inflation, which, incidentally, very often they are not.

So much for the general rules. Mrs. Thatcher then usually goes on to explain what particular interpretation she puts on her own Christian duties as a politician. She believes that the poor must be cared for, but she also believes that in order to care for them wealth must be created. She believes that it will not be created adequately unless our economic system gives reasonable scope for the pursuit of self-interest and, above all, for the exercise of those benign instincts, such as devotion to the family and the wish to engage in private effort to alleviate the lot of the miserable. She does not believe that the whole of welfare can be entrusted to the operation of those instincts, and she therefore thinks that the State must always be at hand to intervene when private effort would clearly be inadequate. If proof is needed of the genuineness of this last belief it is surely supplied by the vast sums of money which her administration spends on welfare and the extreme caution with which it approaches all proposals for really radical reform of the Welfare State.

Well, 'proof' is probably a strong word, because, like all other political actions, this deference to the concept of public welfare can of course be attributed to political expediency. However, if one gets involved in the speculation about the motives of politicians one does not always get very far; what matters is that Mrs. Thatcher's actions in relation to this aspect of policy are wholly in accordance with her declared philosophy.

Now, I would wager that the vast majority of people in Britain today would accept most of these abstract propositions about the relationship of economic policy to human benevolence. Many of them have grave reservations about their actual applications, but that is another matter. Many of them also are deeply embarrassed by politicians who moralise and quote the Bible; but this is mostly because they think that such politicians (and in our history they have been chiefly on the Left) are hypocrites. It is really very hard for a fair-minded person who listens to Mrs. Thatcher to suppose that she comes in that category. You might think her naïve, pompous and bossy, but you have to be very sophisticated indeed (i.e., so sophisticated as not to believe at all in the possibilities of sincerity in a politician) to think that she is fraudulent.

It would be a bad thing if the practice of making moralising speeches were to spread widely among her colleagues. Mr. Hurd, for example, has tried it with results which must surely have been as embarrassing to his audiences as to himself. No, it had better remain Mrs. Thatcher's prerogative.

The critics, of course, have found a so far relatively successful method of rebutting Mrs. Thatcher's moralising. It is quite simply and blatantly to misrepresent what she says – to accuse her of preaching 'a creed of greed', to ignore her admonitions about private philanthropy while asserting that she recommends the abolition of public welfare, to imply that she believes that no Christian can be anything but a believer in capitalism and to suggest that her strictures are addressed always to the poor and never to the rich.

These misrepresentations still have a fair amount of success and may continue to do so for a while. After all, prime ministerial statements are not read very closely by most people. Anyway, in the absence of any effective reply to her argument, common abuse and misrepresentation are probably the best line to take.

But you have waited long enough for my promised revelation about the buried dynamite in her speech.

Turning from the economy to the nation, Mrs. Thatcher said: 'The Christian religion – which, of course, embodies many of the great spiritual and moral truths of Judaism – is a fundamental part of our national heritage.' She went on to point out that you could not understand the British tradition without also understanding the parts which the Old and New Testaments had played in its creation. Without such knowledge you could not make sense of Shakespeare or of the constitutional conflicts of the 17th century. She reminded us in fact that we are a nation whose historical culture is largely biblical.

'Pleasant clichés' you may say; but what of their implications for those numerous British citizens from alien cultures practising alien religions?

The Prime Minister did not hesitate to address herself to the question. It was our well-established tradition to admit into the country the heirs of other religions and cultures; they must always be assured of full equality under the law and be shown open and generous friendship. But 'there is absolutely nothing incompatible between this and our desire to maintain the essence of our own identity.'

She was of course absolutely right in that claim; but it was a claim that implies that, culturally, not legally speaking, a practising Muslim from Pakistan who is (say) a second-generation immigrant is not wholly British in quite the same sense as a native Englishman.

Well, of course that is so; the British know it and the immigrants and their descendants know it. Immigrants into Britain have made a precious contribution to our culture in the past, but always by accepting that it was up to them to show a manly respect for and interest in the traditions of their fellow citizens, that it was more important for them to learn about those traditions than it was for the British to learn about the traditions of their guests, though that also is eminently desirable.

However, Mrs. Thatcher's critics, with their gift for slick misrepresentation could easily have converted these innocent words into a demand for the institution of second class citizenship. One can positively hear them at it: 'Now that the Prime Minister has made it clear that those of our fellow citizens who were not brought up in the Judaic-Christian tradition are not really part of the nation, what action does she propose to take to translate this principle into policy? What is it to be? – compulsory or so called voluntary repatriation or compulsory instruction in the Christian faith as interpreted by Mrs. Thatcher?' Why have the critics resisted the temptation to indulge in this blatant nonsense?

Because they know that a very large majority of the electorate is far more interested in maintaining our 'own identity' than in the preservation of capitalism as such. This Tory element in her speech was far less vulnerable to attack than were the classical liberal elements. There is a lesson for all of us in this, and particularly for the Prime Minister and such of her colleagues as profess purely counting house ethics.

5 · Lessons of Ulster

From – as he states in this first extract – a position of lack of interest in the problems of Ulster, Utley quickly established himself as the Unionists' most powerful advocate in the national press; and their cause was to occupy him from 1969 until his death.

Britain's interest

Extract from *Ulster: A General Background Analysis* published by the Unionist Research Department, 1972

Let me begin by 'declaring my interest': I am not an Ulsterman nor have I any family connections with Ulster. Indeed, before the middle 1960s when I started to visit the province frequently for professional reasons, I had only been there once in my life before, and the fact that this first visit occurred on the twelfth of July was purely fortuitous.

I have never been involved either in what may be described as specifically Irish religious controversies. I am myself a practising member of the Church of England, but I am married to a Papist (she prefers that traditional pejorative designation) and my children are Papists. I suppose, therefore, my approach to these matters could be considered to be rather more than averagely ecumenical.

I look at Ulster, then, with the eyes of an Englishman standing broadly in the tradition of Burkeian Conservatism. From that standpoint, and in the light of those prepossessions, the first point which strikes me is the simple, elementary one that the Six Counties of Northern Ireland are by law and custom an integral part of the United Kingdom. Now, it is part of the essence of a State (and one of the primary conditions of its survival) that it does not go about continually enquiring into the historical and metaphysical justifications for its existence, and the limits of its jurisdiction. I assume, for example, that I as a Londoner have an interest in and a duty towards the defence of Northumberland against foreign attack and internal rebellion. When the challenge comes, I do not immediately ask myself whether there might not in fact be something to be said for altering the limits of the United Kingdom in order to avoid the need to respond to that challenge. My response is, or ought to be, immediate and instinctive. Even if there were a strident demand for self-determination in Northumberland, there would be a very strong case for resisting that demand so long as it was promoted by rebellion. Rebellion against lawful authority may sometimes be justified, but the presumption is always against it, because, quite irrespective of the merits of the particular case, such a rebellion, if successful, weakens the whole principle of lawful authority everywhere. The first interest of an Englishman, therefore, in what is now going on in Northern Ireland, is precisely this: it is a threat to lawful authority, an invitation to men of violence to take up arms against lawful government, and that threat is being made and that invitation issued within the borders of this kingdom. Anyone who supposes that this can, at this moment in history, be a matter of indifference to the British Government and people must have a total lack of understanding of the age in which he is living.

But in the case of Northern Ireland there is another factor just as obvious and just as overwhelming. It is not a matter of dispute but a proposition that is universally admitted that two-thirds of the population of that province actively and stridently insist on continuing to belong to the United Kingdom and to enjoy the rights and discharge the duties which that status implies. If you put the question 'What is Britain's interest in the future of Ulster?' that in itself supplies the answer. Metaphysical disputes about whether there is or is not an Irish nation, and if so what it consists of, are barren. You can argue till the cows come home about what a nation is. When you come to consider what are the suitable foundations for a State, however, the acid test is the will of the people concerned. There is a settled conviction on the part of the vast majority of Ulstermen that Ulster should be part of the United Kingdom. That is the habitual allegiance of the majority of those people, and they have discharged its obligations in peace and in war. If that does not establish an indissoluble contract between Ulster and Great Britain, so long as their wishes remain unaltered, what morality is left in politics and what guarantee can any section of the people of the United Kingdom have of the loyalty of their fellow members?

I am labouring this point deliberately. I am doing so because it seems to me that this discussion is often befogged by a tendency to treat Britain's relations with Ulster as though they were relations with a foreign power or at any rate with a colonial dependency towards which Britain's obligations were custodial in character, and therefore limited in time. Britain's obligations to Ulster are not limited in time so long as Ulster remains what it now is in respect of the sentiments and loyalties of its people. As to what those obligations would become if the sentiments and loyalties of Ulster were to change, that is a remote and hypothetical question which need not, and indeed ought not to be considered unless and until it arises.

Nevertheless, the British have one curious characteristic which distinguishes them sharply from the Americans. Americans, it is often said, are always looking for moral reasons to justify policies in fact dictated by expediency. The British, being a less moralistic people, tend to reverse the process and look constantly for reasons of expediency to justify policies in fact dictated by morality. Britons will probably not be wholly satisfied about their duties to Ulster, unless these are firmly grounded on arguments of prudence. Suppose the British had no obligations to Ulster, they would still have, as they always have had, a cogent British interest in a peaceful, friendly and stable Ireland. Everyone who in modern times has sought the destruction of Britain has fished in the troubled waters of Ireland. Marx himself predicted that it was through Ireland that the Revolution would come to Britain. If you look at the revolutionary forces now at work in Ulster and the Republic, and at the known sources of support for some of them, you cannot suppose that this consideration has become irrelevant. Make no mistake: these forces are not limited in aim to the achievement of a United Ireland. They have revolutionary social and political objects going far beyond this. Some are explicitly working for a revolutionary Socialist state in the United Kingdom; others for some sort of dictatorial régime – national, radical and authoritarian, in Ireland – and both are willing to accept help from anyone willing to supply it. Britain has at least as much interest in the future of this territory as she has traditionally in the defence of the Netherlands.

I have started by running, as the Presbyterians say, 'oe'r the fundamentals', in order to establish, for the moment, only one proposition – that this question of Ulster is one which profoundly concerns what, in the old-fashioned phrase, is called 'the honour and the interest of Britain'.

The inevitability of O'Neill

The Daily Telegraph, 12 February 1969

By now the British public must be reasonably aware that Ulster's forthcoming General Election is, by all the standards of normal democratic behaviour, a pretty odd affair.

Its oddities include the following: it is not being fought to determine which party shall govern the province (the Unionists govern it almost by constitutional right); it is being fought to decide whether Capt. O'Neill shall continue to lead the Unionist party. He claims to be the true repository of Unionist doctrine, to belong to the same apostolic succession as Carson, Craigavon and Brookeborough, yet his chances of survival depend very largely on his ability to gain the votes (many of which he will certainly get) of Nationalists who are, of course, doctrinally committed to the dissolution of the Union.

Capt. O'Neill's critics (men like the tough Mr. Craig and the wily, Butlerian Mr. Faulkner) also claim to be the repositories of authentic Unionism, yet their language sometimes suggests that they favour (or are at least prepared to envisage) an Ulster wholly independent of Britain.

Both factions receive the official support of the Unionist organisation. Since the central party has no control whatever over the constituency parties, any Unionist candidate who has been adopted by his local association, whether he be pro- or anti-O'Neill, must be treated as bearing the party ticket. Independent Unionists (of which there will be several) will be technically the enemies of the party, whether they be anti- or pro-O'Neill.

As far as party political broadcasts go, however, the choice of Unionist speakers will rest with the party leadership, and all three Unionist broadcasts will almost certainly go to O'Neillites. The elaborate rules governing political impartiality on the air were plainly not devised to meet all the contingencies of Irish politics.

By common consent this will be the bitterest (indeed the first real) election which Ulster has ever had, yet both the contestants for supremacy passionately proclaim devotion to essentially the same policies, which they invariably designate as 'progressive'. Asked what they are striving for, and why they wish to get rid of the Prime Minister, Capt. O'Neill's critics without any exception make one instant answer: in order to restore the unity of the Unionist party. Some of them are inclined to increase the paradox by adding that they have no objection to the Prime Minister as a man.

What Capt. O'Neill hopes to get out of this election (which is of his devising) is a clear mandate for the policies of his Government, a decisive expression of the sovereign will of the people of Ulster. To suppose that from so complex a fray anything approaching the 'general will' will emerge would put a strain on the credulity of the most convinced of Hegelian political philosophers. Why then did the Captain do it?

He still had a majority in his Commons and in his parliamentary Unionist party. He is far too astute a politician to suppose that this extraordinary General Election will necessarily produce any change in the composition of the Stormont. If, after all this trouble, he gets much the same kind of following as he had before (and this is certainly on the cards), he will be exposed to the charge of having plunged the province into a useless and dangerous election purely in order to preserve his own personal ascendancy and to settle a domestic disagreement over personalities which should have been settled in the party meeting which he declined to hold.

Capt. O'Neill called this election, I believe, in the full knowledge that it was the final gamble of his career, but also in the full conviction that he had no alternative. Within one week he suffered three resignations from his Ministry, none of them based on any reason which would have seemed even remotely credible by the standards of British parliamentary life.

On 12 December the Prime Minister had received from his parliamentary party a vote of personal confidence with only four abstentions. By 30 January, 12 backbenchers led by Mr. Craig had demanded his resignation. On 26 January one of his Junior Ministers, Mr. Burns, publicly declared himself loyal to the leadership; by the 30th he had resigned. Few critics of Capt. O'Neill are now more vitriolic than Capt. Brooke, the son of the former Prime Minister – yet in December Brooke had voted for O'Neill, albeit somewhat sheepishly.

With one important Minister (Mr. Craig) sacked (for consistent defiance of Government policy) with three other resignations on his hands (Mr. Faulkner's, Mr. Morgan's and Mr. Burns's), with a substantial contingent of back benchers stridently telling him to go, and no doubt others waiting to see which way the cat jumped, how could even this gallant warrior soldier on? Northern Ireland, like Britain, has a Budget in the spring, and the Government of the day cannot risk being denied Supply. It was certainly in no spirit of bravado that the Captain decided to go to the polls.

If the critics could have been placated by concession, there might have been something to be said for placating them. The truth is, however, that apart from a few minimal disagreements about such matters as the establishment of a Commission to investigate the causes of civil disorder there is not a single issue which formally divides them from their leader. They just want him to go.

What they are doing is taking revenge on him for having dragged them (albeit by the most gentle tugs) away from the concept of an Ulster built expressly on permanent Protestant ascendancy. They have liked none of it – the moderate rapprochement with the Irish Republic, the reform of the

LESSONS OF ULSTER   223

parliamentary franchise, cautious promise of reform of the municipal franchise, the gentle importation into Irish government of Whitehall's pedantic standards of integrity. They have hated it all – and not much liked its author either.

An Etonian, a member of the Brigade and a man almost wholly English in his approach to people and to politics, Capt. O'Neill lacks the earthy, Irish qualities even of a Brookeborough. He employs a brilliant young man (Kenneth Bloomfield) to write intellectual speeches for him which, but for their extraordinary literacy, would recall the best young brains in the Conservative Research Department, but which are frequently a little above his audience. Altogether, in spite of that wonderful ancestry, he is not quite an indigenous plant. If he were, he would not have dared to attempt even the reforms which he has already accomplished.

As for the rebels, they are for the most part (and with the convivial exception of Mr. Craig) tea-drinking Presbyterians or Baptists of solid bourgeois stock. They have social as well as political reasons for disliking their amiable, witty and civilised leader. For years, they have been restive. With a British Parliament glaring at them and Ulster visibly moving, through the force of social and economic change, into an emancipated, secularised era, they have had to endure.

What gave them their chance, paradoxically, was the students' civil rights march which ended in Derry on 5 January. This, and the disgusting and ferocious reaction which it provoked from the Paisleyites, made it possible for avowedly moderate Protestants to vent on the Prime Minister the accumulated resentment of years. It is easy for the simple-minded to feel with sincerity that but for all O'Neill's interferences with the settled, cosy Protestant ascendancy none of this would have happened.

Ulster is not a society of fanatics, but a society peculiarly susceptible to manipulation by fanatics. Neither the extremist elements in the civil rights movement nor Mr. Paisley's followers represent substantial sections of the community. Together, however, they convince conservative Protestant opinion that nothing has really changed, and that the established Ulster policy of doing nothing whatsoever to alter what was accomplished nearly 50 years ago is the only recipe for peace. In reality, it is a recipe for civil war and the dissolution of the Union, or its maintenance by British military strength.

The knowledge that this is so is the basis of Capt. O'Neill's policy. That knowledge is shared by a vast and increasing number of Ulstermen, both Protestant and Roman Catholic, men who realise that Ulster's peace depends on the elimination of religious controversy as the governing factor in her politics.

If disaster is to be avoided, this simple conviction must somehow succeed in expressing itself in the result of this ludicrously complicated election. Since Capt. O'Neill is the only leading Ulster politician who has yet shown himself capable of making it really articulate, it is inevitable and proper that the election should be essentially about him.

His task is what it always has been – to impose change on a political hierarchy which is fundamentally conservative, and moderation on minorities which are traditionally fanatical. What other course had he than to appeal to the mass of the people in the hope that, in spite of the processes of democracy as understood in Ulster, it would make itself heard?

Exactly a week after the publication of the following article, the conflagration in Ulster began in earnest.

Ulster – how near the brink?

The Daily Telegraph, 8 August 1969

To understand what has happened in Belfast in the past week you must know the story of Skinny Lizzic. The bearer of that affectionate nickname, which is owed to her robust physique, is a Protestant lady in her seventies who kept a huckster's shop in Roman Catholic Hooker Street until it was razed to the ground by fire in a minor riot a few months ago.

For 363 days out of every year Skinny Lizzie enjoyed more cordial relations with her Roman Catholic neighbours than any decent Protestant in the province of Northern Ireland. She was famous for her genial character and her facilities for extended credit. Yet she remained a woman of conviction. Each year on 10 July she would put up the Union Jack in preparation for the celebrations of the Twelfth. The higher echelons of the Royal Ulster Constabulary would visit her with earnest petitions to remove the offending symbol and even to take a few days' holiday in another part of the city until the Twelfth was over and normal civil life resumed.

Once rumour had it that her pet dog had been strung up on a lamp post: an investigation personally conducted by the Minister of Home Affairs at midnight was required to establish that the animal had died a natural death and that Protestant reprisals would therefore be out of place.

In two ways Skinny Lizzie explains the paradoxes about Ulster life and politics which have so effectively eluded most British commentators. It is trite and true to say that the vast majority of respectable prosperous inhabitants of Belfast of whatever denomination loathe violence and despise agitators. What is not commonly understood is that those who, on ceremonial occasions, resort to violence, those who can be counted on to respond pathologically to the sight of a Union Jack or a tricolour, are for most of the time capable of conducting normal and even amicable relations with their sectarian enemies.

That is why, as the people of Shankill Road, Hooker Street and Unity Place survey the consequences and count the cost of their midsummer madness, they are today strongly inclined towards peace, so strongly indeed that they are at the moment hotly engaged in fixing up private amnesties and armistices to last until the next ritual feast.

The trouble is the abundance of ritual feasts which the rich history of this province provides. You can compile with precision a calendar of violence. On 12 August the Apprentice Boys of Derry will commemorate their successful defence of the Maiden City against James II. And so on.

What is worse, history goes on being made and the number of anniversaries demanding commemoration accordingly increases. So it is that civil rights marchers will seek to stage a demonstration on 5 October to mark the first anniversary of the Battle of Burntollet Bridge.

To impose a ban on any one of these demonstrations which can cite a respectable pedigree would be to court an open defiance of authority. What is more, it would be extremely bad police tactics; a crowd regularly assembled in a particular and predictable place is far easier to control than a series of sporadic outbursts of disorder throughout the country. The Prime Minister clings to the hope that he may be able to persuade responsible Protestant and Roman Catholic leaders to abandon some of these occasions voluntarily. If the sacred festivals could thus be disposed of, the minor demonstrations could be safely banned by Government decree for a cooling-off period of (say) six months.

In the meantime the main concern of the police must be the defence of life and property against the continuing activities of small bands of thugs who are threatening families with eviction from their houses, and factories employing preponderantly Roman Catholic or Protestant labour with destruction. The hard core of sheer criminality in the recent disturbances witnessed, for example, by the looting of Protestant-owned shops by Protestant rioters – must also not be underrated.

The Government's hopes of voluntary restraint are small. It was left therefore initially with the task of maintaining order in Northern Ireland with a police force no larger in proportion to that of the population than are the police forces in Britain. It should be clearly understood that, in the light of all the most probable contingencies, this task will prove impossible unless two conditions are fulfilled:

> The police must be free to use all reasonable instruments of coercion at their disposal (which in practice means tear smoke for the dispersal of crowds);
> and they must be able to count, on conditions acceptable to the majority of Ulstermen, on the ultimate support of the British Army.

Consider, then, the dilemmas of Mr. Robert Porter, the distinguished QC who is Minister for Home Affairs and constitutionally responsible for keeping the peace in Ulster. His police force, though excellent in quality, is inadequate in numbers; he is precluded, by radical prejudice on both sides of the Irish Sea, and by the very nature of the case, from any massive use of the voluntary Special Constabulary, historically a Protestant force (in the recent trouble the B Specials were successfully employed but only for the most carefully defined duties). If he were to use smoke to quell a disturbance even of the magnitude of that of last Saturday he would, I suspect, risk the gravest censure from Whitehall.

Can he, like any magistrate in a British village, count in the last resort on the support of the British Army to maintain the civil powers against odds which would otherwise be overwhelming?

The ostentatious movement of a hundred British soldiers to Belfast police headquarters in the course of the recent riots probably had the decisive effect in averting disaster. It has also raised a crucial problem. Lawyers cannot doubt that it is the common law duty of the soldiery (as indeed also of all civilians) to lend their aid in the maintenance of civil authority in any part of the United Kingdom. Equally, it is the duty of British forces everywhere to obey the orders of the British Government.

A massive and continuing deployment of British troops in the defence of law and order in Ulster (should that ever become necessary) would obviously require the consent of Whitehall, and Whitehall would properly wish to have a say in the manner in which those troops were used.

All this is common ground between the Government of Ulster and the British Government. Now, however, it is suggested that the British Government may also take the much more extreme view that any grant of military aid should be accompanied by the suspension of the Northern Irish Constitution and the assumption of direct control from Westminster.

It would be hard to imagine a more disastrous course for British policy at this juncture to take. If Protestant extremists were to believe that Ulster was on the verge of being wholly absorbed in the British political system they would react with no less vigour than Carson did to the proposal that she should be absorbed in a wholly Irish political system. Equally those elements in the civil rights movement whose conscious first aim is total authority for Westminster in Northern Ireland would infer that the high road to success was a campaign of disorder vigorous enough to necessitate the use of troops.

The story of Skinny Lizzie, which is the story of Ulster, has elements of hope as well as of misery. But if Mr. Wilson wishes to preside over an Irish civil war, with all the commitments which that would involve, he has the means ready to hand. What neither he nor anybody else can count on is an endless supply of honourable men willing to accept responsibility for maintaining order in a province of the United Kingdom while persistently denied the means of doing so.

Britain's role in Ulster

The Daily Telegraph, 15 July 1970

If there is now to be a breathing space in the affairs of Ulster (and this can be nothing more than a happy speculation) it should be used for calm reflection on the principles and aims of British policy in the Six Counties.

Let us begin by casting away some widespread illusions: the Irish settlement of 50 years ago did not come about as a result of a deliberate attempt by a Protestant Britain to preserve a haven of Protestant ascendancy in Northern Ireland. It did not come about either as a result of any determination on the part of the people of Ulster to achieve limited self-government and equip themselves with all the paraphernalia of semi-Statehood with which they have been invested. It was a compromise dictated by the wish of the British Government to maintain, as far as possible, the unity of the United Kingdom on terms compatible with peace and order in Ireland.

That problem remains essentially what it was in 1920. One simple way of escaping the dilemmas it presents would be for the British people to resolve here and now to renounce the ambition to maintain the United Kingdom, to renounce responsibility for a turbulent and costly province which has nothing to commend it save an embarrassing degree of loyalty to the Crown. There can be few precedents in history for a nation's deliberately cutting away a loyal member which passionately demands subordination to the whole.

Is it surprising that the people of Ulster, who see this suggestion made in presumably responsible quarters, recall that they have left their bodies on the battlefields of two great wars for the survival of Britain, that they have paid their taxes and generally performed with more than average zeal the duties of British citizenship? Is it conceivable, even as a fascinating intellectual speculation, that any British Government would deliberately abandon them either to anarchy or to enforced partnership with the Irish Republic?

Even assuming that the limits of the United Kingdom are a proper subject for debate, is it so crystal clear that the strategic importance of Ireland to the defence of Britain (if Britain is still willing to contemplate defending herself) has altogether ceased? A united Socialist Irish Republic, secularised and militant, may seem a remote dream, but it is a dream that has inspired the throwing of many a petrol bomb in Ulster during the last year. The outflanking of Britain by such a régime is not a possibility to be discounted by those who think beyond tomorrow. The solid fact is that Ulster is the one part of the United Kingdom in which largely successful revolutionary action has already been taken by professing Marxists, Trotskyites and anarchists. That this action has only been one ingredient in a revolutionary situation which has been produced mainly by more traditional conflicts does not deprive it of importance.

For better or for worse, therefore, Ulster remains, and will remain, a British commitment. To cast the least doubt on that proposition is to adopt the surest way of promoting an instant civil war. What remains to be asked is whether the constitutional settlement of 1922 is still the best available method of discharging that commitment.

Few solutions are more attractive to the British mind than the simple expedient of incorporating Ulster wholly within the United Kingdom by subjecting it to direct rule by Westminster. Are there not elements of absurdity, and dangerous absurdity, in the majestic trappings of illusory sovereignty with which the Parliament at Stormont has been decked? A spacious building, an elaborate procedure pedantically modelled on that of the mother of Parliaments, a Speaker, a Deputy Speaker, Privy Councillors – all conspire to conceal the truth that Ulster's Parliament is a subordinate legislature exercising comparatively small powers on sufferance over a community no larger than that over which many a county council presides.

If Ulster's representation at Westminster could be increased (not a course, incidentally, which would commend itself to most Socialists), would not this constitutional anachronism be eliminated? And would not the effect be to vest power in an inevitably divided province in clean and impartial hands?

The truth which this panacea flouts is embodied in the ancient maxim that all government is local government. Whoever exercises ultimate sovereignty over Northern Ireland, the physical duty of keeping the peace there, without a permanent and costly military occupation, must in the last resort devolve on the people of the province themselves. The streets must be patrolled by local policemen (could 3,000 British bobbies be recruited for the purpose and, if so, how efficiently would they carry it out?). It is not conceivable that the allocation of houses in Ballymuck could be effectively conducted from Whitehall. None of the animosities which have contributed to the disorder in the Six Counties would be diminished one jot by the introduction of direct rule.

One of them, at least, would be immediately and disastrously increased. Ulster was ultimately reconciled to her semi-independent status mainly by the fear that a British Parliament, in total control of her affairs, might be tempted once again to hand her over to the keeping of a Parliament in Dublin. That fear is as alive today as ever it was. It has, indeed, been fanned by the knowledge that many of those (Miss Devlin among them) who, from time to time, urge direct rule do so explicitly on the view that it is the best and quickest way to a united Ireland.

Only one policy could reconcile such men to the abandonment of Ulster's special constitutional status. It is the policy shrewdly recommended by Mr. Powell – a combination of government from Westminster with strong and unmistakable gestures of rejection, if not of actual hostility, towards the

Irish Republic. By this means, Britain might be seen to have committed herself irrevocably to the perpetual preservation of the Irish border. By it, she could dash at one blow the lingering hopes of the Roman Catholic minority in Ulster, thereby, incidentally, inviting yet another rebellion. By it, also, she would deny that unmentionable truth, subconsciously acknowledged by every Irishman, that the bonds of love and hate uniting North and South are too strong to be destroyed by any political act and might one day prove strong enough to be given permanent political expression.

So what is left for Britain but to maintain faithfully and unquestionably the compromise settlement of 50 years ago which is still the least of the innumerable possible evils which could befall Ireland today? Given a decade of relative peace, all the strongest forces in Irish life on both sides of the border (the slow abatement of religious fanaticism, the gradual advance of liberal thinking in two increasingly modern and industrialised societies) all tend, as O'Neill calculated, towards reconciliation.

What that process requires, however, is a prompt and sustained assurance that the authority of the Ulster Government (committed as it now irrevocably is to reform) is to be restored and fortified, not, as under Mr. Callaghan, systematically enfeebled. Given this, there is hope for Ulster, provided that politicians and pundits forswear the luxury of peering into the future in the hope of discerning a solution to the Irish problem.

The public's duty to Mr. Faulkner

The Daily Telegraph, 27 August 1971

Absurdly understated as the judgement seems, the crisis which now threatens Mr. Faulkner's Government and with it the whole communal existence of Northern Ireland is essentially a crisis in public relations.

Consider the spectacle presented to the outside world by Stormont today: here is a régime which to a greater extent than ever before now depends for its survival on the obtrusive and continuous exercise of force. It is to all appearances kept in being solely by the exertions of vast numbers of British troops; in order to maintain any semblance of order it is obliged to resort to imprisonment without trial. In spite of all this it is powerless to prevent shooting and bombings and largely incapable, so it would appear, of bringing their perpetrators to book.

Meanwhile a large section of the population (possibly at this moment a growing section) is engaged in a comprehensive campaign of passive resistance to public authority. Rents and rates are unpaid. Quite responsible and hitherto moderate Roman Catholics resign from public offices; the parliamentary Opposition withdraws from Parliament.

All this conspires to give the impression that Mr. Faulkner and his colleagues represent not the public will but the interests of a sectarian majority. That impression is constantly fostered by the propaganda activities of the Irish Republic, now officially committed to the peaceful destruction of Stormont, and actively co-operating with the Opposition here to bring that about. Little wonder that the journalists knowingly ask whether the institutions of Northern Ireland have not utterly lost their 'credibility'.

Every element in this picture, however, is distorted. To start with, the purely material dangers to which Stormont is exposed are continually overrated. It is simply not true that internment has proved to be a grotesque failure. In the first place its critics conveniently forget that the much advertised 'polarisation of opinion' was well on the way before internment had been introduced. The Opposition had already withdrawn from Parliament and already started civil disobedience. In the second place there is plenty of reliable evidence that in two ways internment has struck a formidable blow at the IRA: it has had a demoralising effect and it has put the police and the Army in possession of valuable intelligence which they would not otherwise have got.

It is this second, and most valuable, effect of internment, however, which could now be put in jeopardy by the British Government. No doubt an inquiry into allegations of brutality strictly restricted to the examination of what occurred during the first 48 hours of the operation is right and inevitable, but it would be the gravest possible error to conduct any public inquiry into the subsequent treatment of internees.

Imagine the effect on the process of interrogation, to which internees are properly exposed, of assuring them that any grievance, however fantastic, which they may care to think up against their captors will be given an instant public forum. It is also important that the Commission of Inquiry should not examine Army and police officers in the presence of internees. Such confrontation could easily expose the police, and their families in particular, to an unending danger of reprisals.

It is true, of course, that internment has not stopped urban guerrilla warfare. The difficulty of coping with this kind of assault, however, is not confined to Northern Ireland. If bombings are allowed to extract political concessions here, the effect on public order in Britain, and indeed in the West generally, could be disastrous. A battle has been joined and must be won.

What is more, all the available weapons of defence have not yet been used. Northern Ireland's 250 miles of border is at all times hard to defend adequately. It may well be necessary to take drastic action, such as the blowing up of roads, to stop the flood of men and arms from the South.

Border security in the past has always depended on the efforts of armed men with local knowledge. Members of the Ulster Defence Regt. today can be sent, like ordinary troops, to serve in any part of Northern Ireland. In my view far greater efficiency would result, and recruitment would be improved, if volunteers from the Border counties were assured that they would be employed as a home defence unit in their own areas.

For the first time Mr. Heath's intemperate telegram to Mr. Lynch has not only ranged the British Government clearly and unequivocally behind Stormont but has also opened the way for the application of long-overdue pressure to the Government of the Republic. It is fantastic that a technically friendly Power should be permitted to harbour within its borders the murderers of British soldiers and Northern Irish civilians and to permit training facilities for the terrorists who operate here. Is it too much to expect a marked intensification of diplomatic pressure on Mr. Lynch within the next few weeks?

Even the material effects of civil disobedience can be exaggerated. Many of those who fail to pay their rents receive rent allowances out of supplementary benefits; it should not be beyond the wit of Government to divert the funds from the pubs to the housing authorities and private landlords for whom they are intended. What is more, civil disobedience is itself largely the product of intimidation, and every successful blow struck against the terrorists will diminish the force of passive resistance.

Again, the real sting of civil disobedience is in the area of public relations. The point which Mr. Faulkner (possibly with the aid of a much strengthened information service in London) must drive home is that those who are striving for religious apartheid in Northern Ireland are not commonly the supporters of his Unionist party, but rather the official Lynch-sponsored Opposition. A minority which in order to preserve its grievance refuses to exercise its rights is not entitled to the kudos of an underdog.

The one thing which is certain is that civil disobedience can never achieve its vague, complex and divisive object – the introduction of some sort of separate political representation of the Catholic community in Northern Ireland. The best that it could hope to achieve is to force Britain to play the last card in her hand – the imposition of direct rule. This course, indeed, has nothing to commend it either to Britain or to Stormont, but has it much to commend it either to the long-term champions of Irish unity?

If direct rule were to be imposed now, it would be in the context of bitter hostility between Britain and the Irish Republic. Its object would be to intensify, not diminish, the effectiveness of military operations here. It could well set up a barrier to co-operation between the North and South of Ireland far more formidable than is supplied by Stormont, an institution, let it be remembered, which was widely regarded at its inception as a halfway house to a united Ireland.

Amid all these hazards Mr. Faulkner will keep his head. He will firmly maintain that any constructive development to take place here must do so within the context of the Union and of normal parliamentary democracy. If the official Opposition will not play, he will, I predict, find ways of inducing responsible people outside the ranks of Unionism (including constitutional-minded Catholics) to participate in government. Given time and constant and unwavering support from Britain, based on a properly informed public opinion in Britain, I believe he can still succeed.

The greatest danger to his position and to the future of Northern Ireland is the almost automatic response of ignorant opinion in Britain to every successive outrage and crisis – a claptrap demand for a 'political initiative', or in other words another concession to violence.

As the troubles worsened, Utley became a more frequent visitor to Ulster. This article is very much a view from the front, written in one of the province's bloodiest years.

Ulster: anarchy or law?

The Daily Telegraph, 14 July 1972

To say that Ulster is moving, at an ever-accelerating pace, towards anarchy is emphatically not to indulge in alarmism. It is to express a literal truth, the meaning of which, for all the diligent efforts of press and television, cannot be fully grasped by anyone who is not here. The outward physical facts – the nightly murders, the destruction by bombs of a large part of the centre of Londonderry, the appearance of new 'no go' areas, Catholic and Protestant – all these facts are familiar enough to the British reader. As stated, they may even give a somewhat extravagant impression of the kind of misery which the people of Ulster are now suffering. As in most situations of social disorder falling short of total civil war, most normal life goes on without interruption. Unless you happen to be in the wrong place at the wrong moment, you may go for weeks without encountering imminent physical danger, though the possibility of it is perpetually present.

But the current state of anarchy is something far deeper. It consists of a total state of uncertainty in which many of the ordinary assumptions and probabilities of social life have been destroyed.

It is basic to the concept of civil society, for example, that the authorities can be supposed to be at least trying to catch and convict those who break the law. But this is no longer true in Ulster, except in some remote and metaphysical sense; the State has not formally abandoned its existence but it is daily seen pampering, placidly recognising, now parleying with those who are publicly pledged to destroy it.

The notion of impartial law has not been abandoned, but there is scarcely any possible police action in current circumstances which does not appear to somebody to be grossly partial. If your fellow-citizens habitually get away with murder, and are permitted to flaunt their defiance of Government by enclosing themselves behind barricades, if a large part of the community is known to be regularly defaulting on its rates and electricity bills, why should you go on paying your parking fines?

These sentiments, of course, have been rampant for some time; but the knowledge that the chief agent of IRA murder and sabotage in Belfast, Twomey, was flown, under Mr. Whitelaw's protection, to London for negotiations with the Secretary of State, and that the proposals put by the IRA (amounting to the total acceptance of their programme) were to have been 'considered' by the British Government, has removed the last visible shred of Protestant confidence in Mr. Whitelaw. It has finally removed one more fixed point of reference – the assumption that British policy is aimed, not at compromising with the IRA but at detaching moderate Catholic opinion from the IRA.

It is no use pointing out that Mr. Whitelaw did not accept IRA demands. It is enough that he is seen to have promoted the IRA to the rank of a recognised belligerent, to have conferred on it the status of a negotiating body, with which at least he gives some sign of being willing to negotiate yet again.

Should the truce come back, trust in Mr. Whitelaw will not return with it. What was the last truce worth, after all? Seventeen people were killed while it was on and it was bought at the cost of a substantial relaxation of security. What better tactics for a revolutionary organisation than to prove repeatedly that it can make war and peace at will, that it has the initiative, that it can invariably succeed in at least blurring the responsibility for any breach of faith which it chooses to commit?

These questions are not being asked by Unionist hardliners alone. As a member of the moderate (Catholic and Protestant) Alliance party put it to me: 'British liberal opinion simply does not understand the meaning, to a moderate Irish Protestant, of dealing with the IRA.'

The horror which this decision has aroused is also shared by members of the Northern Irish Labour party, and is widely felt among politicians of both Government and Opposition in Eire. It may be thought in Britain to be unjust and extravagant, but it would be the sheerest and most culpable stupidity not to acknowledge it as the dominant political fact in Ulster today.

The anarchy created in the minds of everyone, whether Protestant or Catholic, is another of the most conspicuous features in life in Ulster today. Nothing now seems impossible; no questions remain unasked, no fears unstated. Will the British clear out if Mr. Whitelaw fails? Will Army morale stand up to the strain of the policy of sending an increasing number of British troops to Ulster to supply sitting targets to gunmen?

Will Mr. Paisley or the UDA get together with the Provos in order to drive Britain out?

(The first possibility does not matter, since, to an increasing extent, Mr. Paisley does not matter in Ulster; the second is a piece of rubbish deriving from the false assumption that, because UDA men are often working-class they must be, in the political sense, 'proletarians').

Nothing, for the purpose of conversation, is ruled out.

What moderate Catholics want is just as much of a mystery. They do not want the IRA; they do not believe in the immediate possibility of a united Ireland; they do not believe (when cross-examined) that the concept of a mixed administration (community government and the like) has any meaning; their political leaders certainly do not want absorption in a Tory-dominated House of Commons as a result of any policy of integration. But, since nobody believes that there is any limit to the price which Mr. Whitelaw would pay for peace, everybody feels free to demand anything. The result is open-ended anarchy, springing from and ending in despair and cynicism.

Yet the truth is that Mr. Whitelaw is an honourable, talented and sincere man, who is risking his entire political future to discharge the most difficult political mission which could fall to a British Cabinet Minister at the moment. Not to salute him for this would be as churlish as, in my judgement, it would be irresponsible to refrain from pointing out the understandable misjudgements which are driving him and Ulster to ruin. These misjudgements are two.

Mr. Whitelaw believes that it is going to be possible to carry on like this – just holding the situation, just waiting for somebody to crack (preferably the IRA) – without driving Protestant Ulster into a rebellion. He is leaning on the loyalty of Ulster Protestants and also, though less conspicuously, on their fear of a confrontation with the British Army. He will drive them to something for which by tradition they are not equipped, but from which they will not shrink – guerrilla warfare (less indiscriminate than that of the IRA) against the Catholic population. He is asking the Protestants to bear more than flesh and blood can bear. He is bartering the loyalty of the majority for an increasingly improbable victory over the hearts of the minority, a victory which will have no instant effect on the conduct of the IRA.

But his second misjudgement is even more fundamental. It is a characteristically British misjudgement: it is inspired by that healthy distrust of principle which becomes fatal when it becomes total. He believes that in the end good can come by trying to govern a community (over which, in the end, you propose to maintain your authority) by diplomacy rather than law.

All that Mr. Whitelaw now has to do to bring the Protestant barricades down is to assert, and to mean, that he will accept nothing but surrender from the IRA; that he will use the security forces to attack all forms of lawless behaviour from all quarters and that within a specific period of time he will reconquer all no go areas by whatever combination of force and guile may be required.

No man is in a better moral position to adopt and carry out this policy than Mr. Whitelaw, though he can do it only with the support of the British Cabinet. If he declines it, the choice before Britain will be between military government and withdrawal. The latter possibility would be morally intolerable unless it were preceded, in Vietnam style, by an attempt to restore to the people of Ulster their own means of defence, means of which Britain, when she insisted on the abolition of the B Specials and the disarming of the police, withdrew from her.

But to mention this last possibility as an immediately practicable policy is to fall into the anarchy of mind which has been created in Ulster. Let Mr. Whitelaw restore the limits of sanity.

Paisley waits in the wings

Sunday Telegraph, 14 October 1973

In October 1956, the still relatively peaceful politics of Ulster were suddenly disturbed by a minor crisis. The bare facts of the matter were not remarkable. A 15-year-old Belfast girl, Maura Lyons, had quarrelled with her parents, taken a beating from her father and run away from home. She was later discovered in England where, for several months, she lived in hiding and in disguise, passed from hand to hand by a chain of anonymous benefactors.

What lent colour to the story in Britain, and explosive quality to it in Ulster, was that the source of the trouble was religious. Maura's parents were Catholics; she herself, having from her earliest years been attracted by the notion of one day entering a convent, had suddenly fallen in with the members of a relatively new Protestant Church, had begun to attend prayer meetings, and had last been seen in the company of a minister of that Church.

In the eyes of Republicans, her disappearance was a clear example of abduction of a minor by a highly-organised and thoroughly unscrupulous religious sect. In the eyes of some Protestants, it was a proof of the intolerable oppression employed by Romish families to keep their young in slavery and superstition.

In the context of Ulster, the case was bound to have immediate political implications, and it was the subject of several debates at Stormont. Who, Republicans would ask, could be sure that a Protestant police force would do its best to protect Catholic parents from the ever-present danger of having their children kidnapped by Protestant clergymen? Who, extreme Protestants would inquire, could be sure that in these feeble modern times the State in Ulster would run the risk of political trouble to protect a helpless maiden convert to the Bible from the brutal reprisals of her parents?

In December, as feelings mounted, a vast concourse gathered in the Ulster Hall to be addressed by the head of the Free Presbyterian Church himself, a young preacher of rising fame and imposing stature, the Rev. Ian Paisley. He played to them what purported to be a recording of the girl's voice, announcing her conversion and explaining that she had fled from her parents of her own free will to escape incarceration in a convent.

Hymns were sung, prayers bellowed, and Mr. Paisley declared that if he knew the girl's whereabouts he would not reveal them to the police. 'Very well, I am committing an offence. I will do time for it. I will be proud to do time for Protestant liberty.'

In the event, the offer was not taken up. On her sixteenth birthday, the girl landed up at Mr. Paisley's house in Belfast. She was duly conducted by him and his solicitor to the police, who had meanwhile issued a warrant for her apprehension as a person in need of care and protection and, at the station, amid much weeping and recrimination, there ensued a characteristically Irish scene.

Her Aunty doused her in holy water and kissed her, her father hit Mr. Paisley's solicitor, in the belief, apparently, that this gentleman had something to do with the girl's disappearance, but, on discovering his error, apologised, and the girl was packed off to a local authority home pending the hearing of her case.

Eventually, the matter was resolved by an order of the High Court making Maura Lyons a ward and appointing her father, subject to certain stringent provisions concerning respect for her religious convictions, as guardian.

This affair reveals Ian Robert Kyle Paisley in a series of postures which have become thoroughly characteristic in the past 18 years. Paisley succeeded in placing himself at the centre of the Maura Lyons affair. It was he who produced the recording of her voice (the tape having allegedly been left on his doorstep with the milk), it was he who eventually produced her from hiding, and it was he who emerged in the eyes of Protestant zealots as her principal protector.

Observe, however, that he never at any point accepted responsibility for her disappearance and that, while offering himself for martyrdom, he was able when the affair reached its climax to display a marked degree of detachment.

The incident also shows clearly what Paisley's power-base is and always has been: it is a following of extreme evangelical Protestants, representing a tradition of Calvinism which elsewhere in the world is almost entirely extinct. It is easy, but neither particularly fruitful nor illuminating, to pour scorn on his religious credentials.

No one who reads Paisley's sermons and writings can doubt that he is both thoroughly grounded in the theological tradition for which he stands and capable of sustained and rigorous thought.

In the context of Northern Irish politics, however, what matters is that this tradition not only excludes altogether the possibility of reconciliation with Rome, but also postulates that faithful members of the Roman Catholic Church are under the dominion of an evil institution which must, in proportion as it is believed and obeyed, corrupt their lives.

When Paisley says, 'I have hated God's enemies with a perfect hate,' he refers to the Roman Catholic Church and more particularly to the Pope. He can express compassion for those he considers innocent dupes of the Church, and he makes much of his belief that Roman Catholics should enjoy full civil rights provided they respect the law. But he also makes no secret of his conviction that the only ultimate way to an ordered, Christian society is a mass conversion of Papists to the faith of the Bible.

The notion that a man's religious convictions could in any way be irrelevant to his political trustworthiness or social usefulness is clearly alien to him.

Until the middle 1960s Paisley's crusade was primarily a religious one, though its political overtones were obvious. It was aimed against two forces, both of which were making marked headway in Ulster as in the rest of the world – ecumenism and liberal theology. He appealed to the latent spirit of militant evangelical Protestantism, and he did so with fantastic success.

Yet, for all its success, Paisley's Free Presbyterian Church has always been in Ulster a minority movement, a fiercely anti-establishmentarian affair, utterly opposed not only to Rome but to all the regular Protestant denominations.

Socially, though it certainly has some rich adherents, the Free Presbyterian Church has drawn its support chiefly from the Protestant working classes and from the 'small men' – who feel themselves menaced by modernity.

So it is that in the 1950s and 1960s Paisley appears to the world as a religious fanatic and a formidable nuisance to the authorities, but in no sense as a competitor for real political power.

The world press begins to be entertained by accounts of his visits to Rome to put the Vatican Council in its place or to rebuke the Archbishop of Canterbury for whoring after the Scarlet Woman; he earns martyrdom, in the shape of a £5 fine, for helping to bust up a meeting of the Reverend Lord Soper, who came to Ulster to preach 'heresy'.

In 1966 Paisley at length secured a prison sentence as a result of another march ending in violence, this time against the General Assembly of the Presbyterian Church, which had to be chastised for 'Romish tendencies'. He served three months.

This was the first real test of strength between Paisley and the establishment; the establishment won, to the extent that the sentence was enforced, but the cost was a severe riot outside the Crumlin Road gaol. The reformist policies of

Captain O'Neill (now Lord O'Neill of the Maine) gave Paisley the cue for an open entry on to the political arena. Henceforth he was to pose as much as the repository of the neglected tradition of Unionism as he had as the repository of the neglected tradition of Protestantism.

It was, however, the famous civil rights march in Armagh, in November 1968, and the yet more famous civil rights march from Belfast to Londonderry in January 1969, which gave Paisley the opportunity to make his decisive contribution to the tragedy of Ulster. No one will now be disposed to deny what Paisley at the time contended – that the civil rights movement was already heavily penetrated by the IRA, alert as it always has been to every chance of making mischief.

What matters, however, is that at this stage the civil righters were both peaceful and feeble. The bulk of their not very formidable demands was about to be conceded. Had solid conservative-minded Ulster Protestants, repelled by the impudence of these ill-kempt children, marching about the place talking dangerous rubbish, been content to treat these demonstrations with the tolerant contempt shown by the middle-aged in Britain to student sit-ins, it is more than likely that the whole affair would have subsided.

As it was, the ferocious attacks on the marchers, and at Armagh (even more tactlessly) on ITV and BBC cameramen, had two instant and irretrievable consequences: it convinced large sections of the British people that Ulster was a fascist tyranny, and it terrorised many moderate Unionists into the belief that even modest reforms in Ulster could not be achieved without the risk of anarchy.

Paisley's second prison sentence, for his behaviour at Armagh, ended after a few weeks as a result of the general amnesty proclaimed by the new Prime Minister, James Chichester-Clark (now Lord Moyola). Paisley was now free to make his bid to control the establishment, which so far he had merely succeeded in injuring.

Benefiting from the general disillusionment with O'Neill and with British policy, he succeeded first in almost beating O'Neill at the General Election of February 1969, and then in taking O'Neill's seat at the by-election which followed his resignation.

The transformation of Paisley the rebel into Paisley the statesman had begun; but at Stormont it could never really succeed. There he was known, and in the society of his fellow Ulstermen he found it hard to control his manners.

When, at the Westminster General Election of 1970, he succeeded in beating his Unionist opponent Henry Clarke in North Antrim (benefiting substantially from Clarke's reputation in Ulster as 'a progressive'), Paisley achieved that change of scene which was essential if he were to wrest any lasting political advantage from his wrecking past.

At Westminster, by a combination of personal geniality, local colour, with punctilious respect for parliamentary etiquette, genuine oratorical gifts and, above all, bewildering moderation, Paisley has achieved an astonishing success.

To many, therefore, it came as a nasty shock to find this exemplary son of the Mother of Parliaments not only proclaiming his intention to wreck the new Northern Irish Assembly, but doing his best on the very first day of its meeting to accomplish that end by unlawfully installing his own candidate for the presidency in the Chair, and staging what was in effect an assembly of his own after the meeting had been duly adjourned.

The key to this unhappy contrast is a simple one which Westminster has never grasped. Paisley's power-base is still a fanatical section of the Protestant lower orders of Ulster society. He can afford moderation at Westminster, but not in Belfast, and he has, indeed, suffered acutely in recent years from the difficulty of reconciling his opposite roles.

In the last resort, Paisley cannot risk total conversion to the role of statesman. His power is a personal power, exerted over hysterical crowds and trembling religious penitents.

It is easy for such a man to destroy, but less easy for him to create. What is more, Paisley's one totally unshakeable conviction – the unbridgeable gulf between Catholics and Protestants – makes it impossible for him to make any practical contribution to a Northern Irish settlement.

He may vaunt the impartiality with which he treats his North Antrim constituents, but his principal organ, the *Protestant Telegraph*, pours constant vitriol on Rome and its adherents. Whatever its credentials as a system of theology, when it descends to the market-place Paisleyism becomes a gospel of hate.

Politically, it is not a philosophy or a programme at all, but a mode of protest against the errors and weakness of British and official Unionist policy. It is largely a direct product of the mistakes of Whitehall. Correct these mistakes and Paisley could be rapidly reduced to his natural and original role – that of a relatively trivial nuisance on the periphery of politics.

We could still integrate Ulster

The Daily Telegraph, 18 June 1974

In the dramatically changed state of Northern Irish politics which has followed the successful 'loyalist' strike, political parties in Britain and Ulster seem to be agreed on only one proposition – that, whatever constitutional settlement may eventually be achieved in Ulster, total integration in the United Kingdom is 'not on'. Nevertheless, there is much evidence, including a recent opinion survey conducted for Independent Television News, to suggest that this proposal has the support of a huge majority of Protestants and a substantial number (according to the poll more than half) of Roman Catholics.

To jettison this idea, without further thought about what it really means, could turn out to be the last and fatal blunder of British policy towards Ulster.

At the moment, politicians in Westminster, Dublin and Belfast are still gasping and floundering under the impact of what was in effect a totally successful, though almost entirely bloodless, 'loyalist' insurrection. Only one lesson has so far been drawn from this cataclysmic though perfectly predictable event – the lesson that the 'Irish Dimension' (the plan for a Council of Ireland with elaborate machinery and limitless potentialities) must be dropped. That fact is as clearly understood by Mr. Cosgrave as it is by Mr. Paisley himself.

The hope still lingers, however, that if all thoughts of institutionalised co-operation between North and South are indefinitely postponed it may be possible to resuscitate the other and more valuable ingredient in the Sunningdale agreement – executive power-sharing in Northern Ireland.

This hope I believe to be one of the most dangerous illusions by which British politicians have been afflicted in their approach to the Ulster question since 1968. Many a Protestant hard-liner will today assure you that he accepts the concept of 'power-sharing'. By this, however, he means (as innumerable conversations I have had recently in Belfast plainly showed) that he is not, or does not wish to be regarded as, a downright defender of perpetual Protestant ascendancy. Ask him whether he is willing to have executive power shared with any known Nationalist or Republican politician, and he will reply with an emphatic 'No'.

He will equally make it clear that he is not prepared for any settlement which confers on the British Government the power to vet Northern Irish administrations for the purpose of ensuring that they are representative of the communities.

The most probable result of further Assembly elections in Northern Ireland (and these cannot be put off indefinitely) is the return of a crushing majority in favour of the restoration of simple majority rule in Ulster. The greatest concession to power-sharing which could be expected from such an Assembly would be an undertaking to reserve a number of executive appointments for Roman Catholics who had not necessarily been themselves elected. Such an arrangement would obviously be acceptable neither to the Social Democratic and Labour party nor to the British Government.

Another and far more sinister version of 'power-sharing' is also conceivable – a coming together (such as is at present being plotted) of Protestant para-military organisations with one or both wings of the IRA.

This last horrific eventuality would spell the end of democratic institutions in Ulster. It would produce merely a truce based on the principle that those who have achieved local power in Ulster by direct action (frequently amounting to thuggery) shall be permitted to retain it.

Almost anything, therefore, which is allowed to arise spontaneously out of the present disposition of forces, almost anything which comes about as a result of applying the currently fashionable panacea of allowing 'Ulstermen to settle their own affairs', will mean the end of the Union.

The likeliest eventual outcome of such a policy is the creation of an independent Protestant Ulster within reduced frontiers and under extremist domination. Such an outcome would certainly involve a callous sacrifice of the silent and moderate majority in Ulster; it would condemn Ireland to decades of chaos and leave Britain with a permanent hot-bed of revolution on her doorstep.

Yet the only reasonable alternative to this – some brand of integration in the UK – in spite of the evidence for its popularity in both communities in Ulster is almost tacitly ruled out. In Dublin, it is still unnecessarily identified with the final and irrevocable denial of Irish unity, while in London it is shunned as implying a large, united and fanatical Ulster lobby at Westminster. My contention is that it is possible now, as it was not before, to construct a form of integration to which these objections would not apply.

The first element in such a scheme would be the raising of Ulster representation at Westminster to the level justified by the size of Ulster's population. By the standards currently applied to Scotland, this would involve the addition of seven or eight seats, and the establishment of an Ulster Grand Committee on the Scottish model.

There is, however, no reason why Westminster elections in Ulster should not be conducted on the basis now used for Assembly elections of the single transferable vote. This would effectively ensure a substantial representation of the Roman Catholic minority and, almost certainly, the return of some moderate Unionists and Alliance men as well as a fair sample of the hard-line 'loyalists' who now enjoy a representation disproportionate to their electoral strength.

There is, in the British constitutional tradition, nothing to authorise the dogmatic view that elections to Parliament must be conducted on an absolutely uniform franchise and by identical methods. Until 1950, Members for the Universities were returned by multi-Member constituencies operating a form of proportional representation. The arguments for an exceptional arrangement to secure special representation for minorities in Ulster are too obvious to need stating.

It would then be necessary to provide for local government in the province by transferring the local government powers only recently vested in Stormont back to county councils. This would involve the regrettable need to scrap the admirable local government structure designed by Sir Patrick Macrory, but it would not necessarily involve a return to a multiplicity of local authorities.

If Ulster were to be divided, for example, into three large local government areas plus Belfast, at least one of these areas would almost certainly be under the political control of the Roman Catholic minority. What is more, real power-sharing has proved far easier at the local than at the provincial level in Ulster.

There remains the need to write into these arrangements some effective recognition of Ulster's ultimate right to self-determination. This could be done, no doubt, by periodic plebiscites, but it could be done with far less dangerous drama by a built-in and permanent plebiscite – an arrangement under which, at each successive General Election, the elector, in addition to voting for a candidate, declared on a separate ballot paper his preferences about Ulster's constitutional status.

Possibly the greatest single source of opposition to any such scheme as I have outlined would be the Ulster political establishment itself. Ulster politicians have no great zeal for the prospect of being reduced to the status of county councillors.

If, as now seems to be the case, the only form of devolved government likely to emerge in Ulster is a thoroughly objectionable one wholly incompatible with the Union, the British Government cannot honourably avoid the duty of offering its own alternative to independence. That alternative must satisfy the demand of most Protestant Ulstermen for British standards in a British community; it must offer substantial participation in politics to the minority; and must give that minority what is now clearly essential to it, the protection of a prolonged British political and if necessary military presence in Ulster. What other sort of settlement could combine these objects?

Four ways the Irish show good sense

The Daily Telegraph, 30 June 1986

I have four reasons for rejoicing at the result of the Irish Republic's referendum on divorce. In the first place, it is another valiant assertion by this admirably old-fashioned people that the State is not just a machine for maximising material prosperity and otherwise allowing its subjects to do what they want with their lives provided they do not diminish each other's freedom. The State should, on the contrary, reflect such moral consensus as exists among the people and present them, however subtly and discreetly, with a vision of the good life.

Theoretically we still subscribe to that doctrine in Britain. Otherwise we would not have an established Church. However, we have allowed ourselves, largely by default, to become a secularised and materialistic society, and we are much more miserable for having done so.

My second reason for rejoicing is a strong conviction that the amount of human suffering which is produced by making divorce too easy is far greater than the very real amount which comes about from making it too difficult. Of course, one weeps for those unhappy people in the Republic who are condemned to marriages which have virtually no existence. Who of us in my generation does not remember A. P. Herbert's book *Holy Deadlock*? But it was that book which set us off on the Gadarene descent which has brought us so close to destroying the institution of marriage and saddled society with all the costly social evils which that has involved.

Of course, the Divorce Bill which Dr. Fitzgerald was going to introduce had he got away with the referendum was a very modest and sensible one. It would have authorised divorce only when a breakdown of marriage could be plainly demonstrated, and the only evidence it would have accepted for such a breakdown was a separation of five years. This is far better than the British system. We also now take our stand on the view that the breakdown of marriage is the sole ground for divorce; but in practice we have largely retained the principle of the matrimonial offence, so that many of those seeking dissolution still have to prove adultery or cruelty against their partners. Nothing seems to me to be more flippant or un-Christian than the notion that occasional acts of adultery (however trivial) are a reason for breaking up what is meant to be a lifelong partnership.

If Mrs. Thatcher were thinking of going in for a 'Moral Majority Ticket', she might do worse than consider something on the lines of Dr. Fitzgerald's Bill. But the Irish will have none of it, precisely because they think it would be the 'thin end of the wedge'; and who, in the light of our own experience, can say they are wrong?

My third reason for delight at this result is that, even if it will not contribute dramatically and instantly to the reconciliation of the two Irish traditions, it will certainly not operate against this end. A victory for divorce in the South would quite certainly have had that effect. Let me explain this paradox. Any idea that the Protestant population of the North is any more permissive in its attitude towards sex than is the Roman Catholic population in the South is rubbish. The definition of an Irish queer which prevails on both sides of the Border is one who prefers women to drink. The attitude of almost all Irishmen to sex is puritanical, prurient and hypocritical. If the two Irelands are ever to get together, it will be on the basis of puritanism of this order.

Of course, the Unionists in the North will herald the result of the referendum as a further proof that 'Home Rule means Rome Rule' and add that, as good Protestants, they do not think the State should interfere in private morality. What fraud! How loudly they supported Mr. Paisley's 'Save us from Sodomy' campaign!

But what would really have terrified Unionists would have been a victory for divorce. They would have seen this as evidence for the view that the Republic was prepared to go to any length in the harmonising of laws to achieve Irish unity. That would have made them really frightened and really mad.

My last reason for rejoicing is my genuine respect for decent Irish nationalism, the Roman Catholic quality of which is expressed in the Republic's Constitution. One cannot respect a nation which is willing to abandon all its distinctive characteristics simply for the sake of acquiring territory and unwilling subjects. May the people of Ireland North and South (from both of whom secularised Britain has so much to learn) remain loyal to their traditions and, in God's good time, find somewhat more friendly ways than they adopt at present of expressing their respective identities. 'Three cheers for auld Ireland', and 'No surrender' as well.

IRA shadow over the poll

The Times, 15 May 1987

Oddly enough, there is one respect in which the affairs of Northern Ireland, to be excluded by common consent from the British election campaign, are quietly dominating that exercise. I suspect that the precautions now being taken for the safety of British politicians, as they trundle round the country talking about everything except Ulster, are more elaborate than ever before. At any rate, I hope they are.

One does not have to be in an army or the victim of a particularly macabre imagination to realise that a successful IRA attack on one or more eminent participant in the election campaign would have an enormous appeal to the godfathers of Republican violence in Ulster. They would not be deterred, as the Brighton bombing attempt shows, by fears of the ferocious reaction which such an event might provoke. They have come to believe that the British people are fundamentally unprovokable in that when you try to kill their leaders the stock reaction of the political establishment, having duly deplored the atrocity, is to say that we must not act under the influence of panic or anger.

What constitutes the best protection of the British political establishment during the next few weeks is the immense efficiency of our police forces and, above all, the fact that there are few very safe havens in this country from which Irish terrorists can plot their crimes and in which they can take refuge when their crimes have been committed.

In other respects, Irish terrorists in Britain have a few things going for them. The chief of these is that the majority of the British do not believe themselves at present to be subjected to any terrorist challenge. They lack, therefore, a war mentality and the vigilance and militant feeling which such a mentality inspires. It is natural and inevitable that this should still be so, for Britons on the mainland have suffered comparatively little from terrorist assaults.

This is not so, of course, in Ulster, as a recent experience of mine vividly illustrates. Last weekend I went to the province to address a meeting of the Friends of the Union, in the company of my much more distinguished colleagues in that movement, Ian Gow, James Molyneaux and John Biggs-Davison. We met in the civic centre at Craigavon. Before a solid, middle-class, moderate Unionist audience, we rehearsed the argument for preserving the Union, modifying the Anglo-Irish agreement and refraining from the negative policies which so irritate the British. We have said it all before. They had heard it all before, and they listened with respect and only the slightest evidence of boredom.

Then, just as the meeting was about to end, a message was handed to our chairman and read out by him. It was to the effect that an attack had just been made on the police station at Loughgall and that (sic) 'six policemen had been murdered'. None of us thought to disbelieve it and suspect an error in transcription. We were all used to that kind of atrocity; it called for a gesture of respect for the dead, a prompt suspension of the meeting and a particularly solemn, and therefore outstandingly tuneless rendering of the national anthem. Then, as we broke up and chatted in grim voices, the true version of the event came through. It was not six policemen but eight terrorists who had been killed (we had heard nothing yet about the innocent passers-by).

Here then, it seemed to us, was an occasion for rejoicing, not mourning. It seemed to have been a splendid exercise and a brilliant victory for the intelligence service. Instead of being arrested en route and sent down for a few years for belonging to the IRA and carrying arms, the enemy had been trapped, beautifully and brilliantly, caught in the very act and wiped out. One felt the same kind of elevation that men of my age did when listening to the tally of German bombers shot down in the Battle of Britain.

You will say that all this shows how fighting a terrorist war corrupts the defenders of law and order. Did not every one of these terrorists have a mother? Were they not courageous though misguided men? Should we not think of the extent to which they were simply the products of an unhappy history? All this is true, and there will be a time and place for recording it; but a people confronted by a direct terrorist challenge must not allow its instinct of self-defence to be paralysed by such meditations. Warfare even against terrorists should be confined within the limits of propriety; we should not shoot prisoners as the IRA does, but we are under no obligation to take special pains to diminish enemy casualties.

As the book of Ecclesiastes tells us, there is 'a time to love, and a time to hate; a time of war, and a time of peace'. Inducing us to get these times mixed up is one of the deadliest weapons in the armoury of terrorism, designed as it is to atrophy our instinct for self-preservation. A final warning to the IRA: any attempt seriously to disrupt our affairs in the next three weeks will revive that flagging instinct in the British people in the most conspicuous manner.

The response of the Unionist community in Ulster to IRA terrorism is not the result of some Irish cultural oddity; it is the result of Ulster's having been subjected to years of sustained and ruthless attack. It is the characteristic response of the British when under fire. The difference is simply that the mainland British have not yet been under serious IRA fire and their patriotism and imagination does not yet extend, unhappily, to a proper sympathy with the feelings of loyal Ulstermen.

This was the last article Utley published. He died a fortnight later.

Whitelaw's doomed legacy

The Times, 7 June 1988

So the people of Northern Ireland, on top of everything else, are to be exposed not just to one more 'political initiative' but to two. One of them, obviously the more interesting, has been tentatively mounted by Charles Haughey, Prime Minister of the Irish Republic, who now hopes to open direct talks with the various Ulster Unionists who, in turn, seem moderately well disposed to talking to him. Any exercise on which Haughey embarks is extremely interesting, because it is likely to be conducted with great ingenuity and because, given adequate intellectual equipment and reasonable political insight, there is some hope of discovering what is actually behind it.

The other 'political initiative' now being undertaken is in the hands of Tom King, the Northern Ireland Secretary. It is, for that reason, less interesting, because there is no guarantee that it has any clearly thought out purpose and because one cannot be sure of anything about it except that it is bound to be extremely well-intentioned.

The word 'initiative' has a special meaning for Ulstermen and for those of us elsewhere who identify ourselves with the cause of that unhappy province. The 'initiative' *par excellence* was, of course, that mounted by William Whitelaw in 1972 after the institution of direct rule.

In the Northern Irish vocabulary 'initiative' at that time was not just an abstract noun. It described a grand apparatus of government designed, in the best colonial manner, to lead the benighted people of Northern Ireland back to sanity and truly English moderation.

Whitelaw's substantial figure presided over a vast imported staff. Eminent civil servants, who went over to give Ulster the benefit of years of vast and irrelevant experience; glossy secretaries seconded from the Foreign Office who picked up from their employers a deep sense of mission; many of them living, at vast public expense, in Belfast's top hotel, the Culloden. The girls used to complain bitterly that the cuisine (that particular variety of elaborate, rather stodgy continental food which Ulster produces when it wants to be regarded as sophisticated) was bad for their figures and ruinous to their digestions.

The Unionist populace treated all these representatives of the Raj with deep suspicion. 'Who's that pretty girl over there?' one would be asked: 'Oh! she's The Initiative,' one would reply. Voices would instantly become hushed.

As time went on, it became clear that almost the only exception to this suspicion of the 'initiative' was the master himself. William Whitelaw did almost everything conceivable to alienate the Unionist community, including talking for a moment to the IRA; yet his popularity as a man seemed to increase rather than diminish. Some attributed this, churlishly, to the fact that he was the only major politician to which the province had been exposed – apart from Edward Heath. Heath had become the yardstick by which the sensitivity of British politicians to Ulster's feeling was measured.

Others said that Whitelaw's miraculous popularity was due largely to the fact that he was not tainted by temperance, and to his extraordinary gift for making convincing apologies after perpetrating horrible mistakes. The truth was that his popularity was the result of his outstanding well-bred benignity.

This did not make him a successful Northern Ireland Secretary of State; it might, in other circumstances and with the benefit of strong colleagues, have made him a very good British Prime Minister.

Be that as it may, the great Whitelaw initiative was a flop. It ended by his accomplishing what he had misguidedly set out to achieve – the disintegration of the Unionist party – and with that went the political destruction of the most effectively liberal leader that party had ever had, Brian Faulkner. After the loyalist strike of 1974 had destroyed Whitelaw's power-sharing executive and torn to shreds the Sunningdale agreement, Ulster's politics became more nearly polarised than ever.

I remember long afterwards a characteristically friendly comment from William Whitelaw about my past disagreements with him. 'Utley,' he said, 'you always told me that I was driving Faulkner too far. My God you were right! But what a damned fool he was to allow himself to be driven!' Well, on that occasion, I was not wholly disarmed.

The disastrous Whitelaw initiative has remained the model for Tory initiatives in Ulster, though none of them has had quite the grandeur of the original gala performance.

Poor Humphrey Atkins had a shot at it, astute James Prior (who came to very sensible conclusions at the end of his tenure) was unaccountably sold the idea that he could reproduce what was essentially the Whitelaw blueprint successfully by simply adding the adjective 'rolling' to the word 'devolution'. All ended in failure, precisely predictable failure.

Of course, these Tory failures were nothing compared with the grandiose one achieved by hyper-intelligent Merlyn Rees. Instead of trying to discover and mobilise the centre in Northern Irish politics as Whitelaw had done, he set about trying to bring the extremists on both sides together, inventing in the process a concept called 'Ulster Nationalism'.

He got a short truce with the IRA which produced nearly disastrous consequences and gave that organisation even more encouragement than it had ever had from Whitehall during these troubles. Only good solid Roy Mason (the best Ulster Secretary of State we have ever had) avoided initiatives, though of course he had to mutter about them from time to time.

Well, what will happen to Haughey's 'initiative'? If it is to succeed at all the old horse dealer will have to agree to a much weaker Anglo-Irish agreement than he has got, and this will enrage and alienate John Hume, the leader of the SDLP, who looks to Haughey as champion and protector of the nationalist cause in the North. It is just possible that Haughey will do this because he is not a man of principle (for which one must be profoundly grateful when one considers how awful the principles would be if he were).

But on this favourable prognosis what happens to King's initiative in the North? The disappointed Hume will compensate by refusing to take part in any power-sharing devolved arrangement which does not give the Nationalists a real stranglehold on Northern Irish administration; in particular on the conduct of security policy in the North.

But, of course, long before this, the dangers to Unionism in these two initiatives will become apparent, and the only interesting question will be which of the Unionist leaders manages to nip out of the exercise most adroitly, leaving his brother in the ditch. I put my money on Ian Paisley.

During all these years, I and others like me have been very discouraging to all initiatives and I have continually been told I am a cynic who should give them 'a fair chance', and that in spite of the fact that I believed on all occasions that to give them such a chance would produce appalling consequences.

The predicted consequences have happened and, when I have presumptuously pointed this out, I have been told I am judging 'with hindsight'.

However, my shoulders, metaphorically speaking, are broad, and it would seem to be a pity to interrupt the rhythm of this dance.

6 · *Miscellany*

The illusions of affliction
Weekend Telegraph, 2 April 1965

To belong to any vested interest or to be part of any distinct group, however loosely organised, is a situation which no doubt carries with it grave temptations. In general, however, the rest of society is perpetually on the alert to point it out when anyone begins to yield to these temptations.

If you are inclined to religious fanaticism, your opinions on any subject, however remote from theology, will be diligently scrutinised for evidence of the hidden hand of sectarian intolerance; if you are a businessman or a trade unionist, your views on God will be ruthlessly examined for traces of economic interest.

Only one type of vested interest of which I am aware is immune from this kind of censure – it is that powerful, sadly numerous, highly organised and extremely self-conscious body of people, the disabled. Suspicions of the purity of their motives may indeed sometimes lurk in the minds of those who, in the characteristic phrase of the context, are 'more fortunately endowed'. An occasional speculation about the possible relationship between their physical limitations and the idiosyncrasies of their characters may sometimes be whispered, though by way, not of criticism, so much as of extenuation. For the rest, however, they are absolutely protected.

Absolutely, that is to say, with one generally insignificant exception which is the apologia for this article. From time to time, a disabled man may be allowed to get away with an outspoken criticism of the weaknesses or a searching analysis of the peculiar temptations of his 'brothers in affliction'. Good taste will not, of course, allow the disinterested reader to approve his arguments, but they may at least be cited charitably as evidence of a robust character, or overlooked compassionately as examples of the carping ill-nature sometimes engendered by unmerited suffering. Only the rest of the disabled will be free to denounce him for harshness or ill manners.

It is not clear from my experience how far this immunity extends to the representative of one type of disability who sets his spear against those encumbered by another. Prudence therefore requires me to say that such general remarks on the psychology and economics of disability as are made here spring from the experience of a totally blind man in his early 40s who has inhabited, albeit angrily and disloyally, what is odiously known as 'the blind world' since he was nine. Any extended application to which his view may pretend is made subject to correction and with apologies.

Personal experience is, of course, not the only body of evidence. A massive and constantly growing literature emanating from the disabled themselves is devoted to building up and sustaining their image.

These books, the production of which is in itself a valuable industry, appear, I have noticed, with special profusion round about Christmas time.

The brave men whom they describe (or more accurately who describe themselves through this medium) are invariably cheerful, frequently to the point of absurdity, dedicated to being 'normal' with a passion which can only be regarded as wholly morbid, and bitterly resentful of charity. A large part of their lives appears to be spent in repelling, with indignant insults, innocent offers of help from their neighbours; they frequently have wives – quietly brave and cheerful women who have evolved in conscious complicity with their husbands an extraordinary and complex pattern for the conduct of matrimony.

Its essence is the rule that the little woman should do much for her husband while persuading him that he is doing it for himself; oddly enough he, for his part, is obliged to be fully conscious of the subterfuge, quietly and bravely to assist it in little ways and pointedly to advertise it to the public at large. Spontaneity does not appear to be the principal ingredient in these matches.

It is armed or encumbered with this 'public character' that the disabled man must embark on the task of making, or at any rate getting, his living, and it is here that the economic interest of the subject appears. He has of course from the outset one overwhelming asset from which all of us thus placed derive enormous benefit: the charitable instincts of his fellow men. These of course are not wholly sterilised by the prudently unconvincing attempts of the disabled themselves to prove that they are not suitable objects for charity.

What many of the disabled undoubtedly assume is that they *should* have charity, but should in no circumstances appear to have it, and this is a basis on which the rest of the community is only too anxious to play; it fits in, of course, with all the fashionable hypocrisies and confusions about the nature of welfare.

Up to a point, indeed, a hard and fast line between economic employment and charitable assistance cannot properly be drawn. If the blind, the halt and the maimed can, at the cost of lavish public expenditure or private philanthropy, be equipped to earn at least part of their living, there is everything to be said on grounds of happiness for so equipping them.

If they can do some job moderately well, but not quite well enough to ensure that they would get it in an open market, there may be something to be said for the kind of statutory compulsion which now exists on employers to employ them. If they can be partly self-financing in sheltered workshops, it is better that they should so live than that they should be kept in idleness. What is essential is that the disabled, no less than their well-wishers, should be quite ruthlessly and unashamedly aware of what is and what is not economic employment.

The good taste which obscures this distinction sometimes falls very heavily on the disabled themselves. One obvious illustration is the case of the professional man who, in spite of some physical handicap, can in fact earn a moderately good living in the open market. One of the chief obstacles to his employment is undoubtedly the tacit, indeed carefully suppressed but deeply implanted, assumption of prospective employers that they are doing something charitable in employing him.

They would not, of course, say so for the world, but once people have got in the way of distributing what is in effect charity under the guise of economic employment, they easily pass to the habit of giving economic employment under the false assumption that it is charitable, and as such something to be kept carefully within the limits of financial prudence.

Another way in which the same category of disabled man tends to suffer from the benevolence of employers arises from the conspiracy to conceal that there is any respect in which the disabled in open employment work at an economic disadvantage.

In most cases, the necessary professional expenses incurred by disabled men in doing their jobs are inordinately great, and much too great to be met by the simple expedient of paying them inflated fees for their labours. Employers are aware of this, and feel that to employ such men while failing to compensate them for their inevitable disadvantage would be cruel.

I, for example, as a blind journalist, could not earn a penny without the constant help of a highly competent secretary-cum-research assistant.

In the early years of my career, however, I encountered on more than one occasion resistance to employing me because employers felt that this was a burden which I could not properly be asked to bear myself, and which they could not bear for me. It was only with difficulty I finally established the point that I preferred to ply my trade less lucratively rather than not at all.

On the whole, however, it is the community at large rather than the disabled themselves who suffer most from the moral confusions surrounding their position. One expression of these confusions is a device particularly favoured by the philanthropic for putting money into the pockets of the handicapped without insulting them, by employing them, at considerable expense, to conduct or preside over services for their fellow-sufferers.

I know some instances in which, by accident, the man most qualified to run, for example, an organisation for the blind happens himself to be blind.

On the whole, however, the objections to this sort of closed employment are formidable, and in so far as it encourages the disabled to think of themselves as a class apart, it does grievous damage to their prospects of ordinary employment. I certainly would find constant attention to the affairs of the blind a most embarrassing and depressing occupation. There is no mystery about the effect of most disabilities on a man's competence. The disabled themselves bravely assert this whenever they write or talk about their own condition, but are they really quite so loath as they seem to enjoy the prestige conferred by the false idea that nature has given them exceptional compensations?

'Well, I suppose, my memory is a bit better than the average; I can, for example, recite *The Daily Telegraph* verbatim after one reading; but you would be the same if you had to depend on your memory.'

Such words are only a slight parody of a distressingly familiar line of self-advertisement. They encourage the notion that the disabled are in some way miraculous and they win admiration; but in most branches of economic employment miracles are regarded as a little inconvenient to have about the place and not wholly to be depended upon.

To this extent, the propaganda of disability, with its refusal to admit the existence of any limitations or to allow any unheroic explanation of how these limitations are overcome, is a formidable barrier to the healthier ambitions of the 'less fortunately placed'.

Broadcasting needs heretics
The Daily Telegraph, 27 August 1976

Why was it thought necessary to precede and follow each instalment of Mr. Auberon Waugh's recent television *jeu d'esprit* about the class struggle with an explanation that he was only expressing his own view?

According to an official spokesman of the Independent Broadcasting Authority the reason was simply that researches had confirmed the IBA's impression that the viewing public, when unaided by such announcements, fails altogether to distinguish between programmes genuinely intended to be impartial and programmes which, in the language of the trade, are 'one-pair-of-eyes' (i.e. confessedly subjective) performances.

I must confess to a total sympathy with the viewing public. It had never occurred to me that the great majority of 'documentaries' on the civil war in Ulster, the trade union movement or the affairs of South Africa pretended to be anything more than honest expressions of prejudice and malice on the part of those providing them.

This however, apparently is not so: these programmes represent the facts not simply as seen by a number of individual reporters, but as weighed, tested and vouched for by the BBC or the IBA. What is more, a credulous public, if not specifically warned by these authorities against doing so, will take them as 'gospel'.

Just, then, as there are things which the vicar may discreetly say at tea but which it would be unsuitable for him to utter in the pulpit, so there are things which Mr. Auberon Waugh may tolerably say in casual conversation at a peak viewing hour which could not be suitably said by a member of the media priesthood officiating at some central sacrament like 'News at Ten'.

This priestly role conceded, it remains to consider what the doctrines are over which the broadcasting hierarchy stands guard.

They are not yet, let it be said, the doctrines of revolutionary Marxism; to suggest so is to fall into the kind of hyperbole of which Mr. Waugh is himself sometimes capable. They are rather those of liberal egalitarianism which may conveniently be abbreviated to the golden rule that all conceivably invidious distinctions between different categories of people – between blacks and whites, men and women, the clever and the stupid, the habitually law-abiding and the habitually criminal – are in their nature both false and sinful.

Though this secular religion lacks a systematic theology, it has already built up a majestic liturgy. What is more, the broadcasting ecclesia does not confine itself to preaching the word. In recent times, it has set up a comforting service of ghostly counsel and advice.

Night after night, this pastoral office is discharged by those humble but saintly priests of the media, the disc jockeys, who receive telephoned confessions from members of the public who cannot bring themselves to love immigrants or to forswear vengeance against vandals; and who, in return for their obeisance, receive not only just reprimand but discreet and practical hints on how to combat these temptations.

What the new religion so far lacks is a concept of blasphemy. This must await the time when its beliefs have been personified and it has achieved a company of saints and an army of martyrs whose names can be tremulously invoked by the faithful in moments of extreme stress. The four-letter word 'Foot' or the far more satisfying expletive 'Scanlon' have not yet entered the national vocabulary of oaths.

Yet, if blasphemy there is not, heterodoxy there certainly is. And, with that liberality which is the mark of ecclesiastical statesmanship, it is felt prudent from time to time to allow the likes of Mr Waugh to express it, provided that the public is duly warned of what is being done to it.

In all this, of course, there is nothing particularly surprising. No State on earth has ever felt that it could afford to give an equal tolerance to all opinions about morality and politics.

The doctrinal foundations of society change from age to age and place to place, but doctrinal foundations there must always be. What is remarkable about our new priesthood is that it should remain wholly unaware that it is imposing an orthodoxy at all and should continue to cherish the illusion that it is presiding, with superb impartiality, over an intellectual free-for-all with no holds barred. This is the more astonishing since the demands of the new orthodoxy are so stringent and comprehensive, leaving virtually nothing of the smallest human interest to the judgement of conscience.

But what is most astonishing of all is the evident amazement with which the IBA learnt that the public, far from being shocked out of its senses by Mr. Waugh, was thoroughly delighted by his performance. His particular exercise in social criticism (a most worthy successor in its wit and penetration to Matthew Arnold's essay on 'Culture and Anarchy') was admired, I suspect, not mainly for its novelty as television, but for the way in which it bridged the gulf between the media priesthood and their reluctant laity.

A large percentage of the daily conversation of ordinary Englishmen still consists in observations about the characteristics of different social classes. Social class is still regarded by them not only as an important but also as a thoroughly legitimate factor in the running of life. It is only within the sacred precincts of the broadcasting establishments that these obscenities are hushed.

Plainly, at any rate until Mr. Waugh came on to the screen, the IBA and the BBC did not realise that they are still essentially missionary churches operating in hostile and savage country.

In very rude health

The Daily Telegraph, 31 July 1984

Mr. Brian Hayes, an outspoken Australian, has run a phone-in programme on LBC, the independent London news station, several hours long and five days a week, for some eight years. As an elderly listener, I find phone-in programmes one of the most unappealing innovations of post-war broadcasting.

Some of them are designed to give ordinary simple folk the chance of talking directly to their rulers, like Mrs. Thatcher and Mr. Scargill (he, by the way, is on the Hayes programme today). The trouble about that is that the rulers have centuries of experience in the art of bemusing, seducing, over-awing, and generally seeing off ordinary simple folk.

This danger can only be averted by frequent interventions from some skilled practitioner, like Sir Robin Day, and these interventions can scarcely avoid sounding impertinent. It would be better to let the skilled practitioner get on with the interviewing task himself.

Mr. Hayes's programme, however, also seems to have another, and odder purpose. Morning after morning, scores of bewildered and averagely inarticulate housewives (Jenny from Putney, Patricia from Ealing and so on) ring him up for no other apparent purpose than to receive a good verbal clobbering, in which respect they are never disappointed.

'Well, Brian,' they cheerily begin, 'I wanted to say something about the pub hours, you know, what with the tourists and all that.' 'Do you want to talk about tourists or pub hours?' comes the sharp retort.

I suppose Mr. Hayes (a very accomplished broadcaster by the way, and a very civil man in private conversation) is teaching them how to think. The evidence is, however, that he does not make much progress in that direction, and to the casual listener the impression is that of a sado-masochistic orgy, French lessons by a strict disciplinarian. It is really very distasteful.

*   *   *

I have always thought that if there is doctrinal bias in BBC radio, it is to be found in religious rather than political broadcasting. I have in mind particularly Miss Rosemary Hartill, the BBC's religious correspondent.

Barely concealed in all her reporting is a consistent disposition to everything trendy; but she is a delightful broadcaster with the voice of an amiable and precocious 12-year-old, so that the listener has the pleasant sensation of being patiently rebuked by a friendly child.

She reminds me of that saint who, having been born, instantly delivered a sermon of several hours' duration, at the end of which he expired. Wisely, the BBC seems never to let her on the air for more than five minutes, a precaution which I hope will continue to be observed.

*   *   *

It is intriguing to speculate on the personalities behind the female voices (often modern and, by dismal Reith standards, sluttish) which Radio 4 employs for announcing and news-reading.

Pauline Bushnell – warm, generous, slightly fussy? Harriet Cass – a trifle haughty and probably tall? Laurie Macmillan –

mildly cynical? (her family probably regard her as an intellectual) and Kate Moon – perfect.

I have for long vainly sought from the BBC an opportunity to meet these ladies: could this last desperate public appeal succeed?

Commentary

The Daily Telegraph, 24 December 1984

At Christmas, one writes either about God or ghosts. When I was a young man, I used to work for *The Times* (another newspaper published in London). It was part of my duty to write the annual Christmas leader.

Now *The Times*, whatever it may have been at various points in its history, was not at this time, in the ecclesiastical sense, 'an establishment newspaper'. Its Christmas leader, as I remember it, used in those days to be a carefully drafted diplomatic convention, which had to be widely examined before publication and approved by the representatives of various denominations on the staff.

There was Mr. Iverach McDonald, a stout Presbyterian, Mr. Stanley Morrison, a rather extreme Papist, and even (though he may not have been taken into direct consultation), Mr. Kent (the Manager), a Plymouth Brother.

This is not to mention my greatest friend at that stage of my career – Horner, the Editor's driver. He could drive from the gates of Printing House Square to those of All Souls in 45 minutes flat, not only preserving himself and his passengers intact but also preventing several other accidents which might have occurred through unreproved careless driving. He once confided to me, on this question of the Christmas leader, that 'the trouble with this office, Sir, is too much chapel.'

What I remember most about the exercise, however, is an annual letter I used to receive from a sort of inverted religious maniac – a reborn atheist, resident (I would judge from its extraordinary literacy) in some expensive lunatic asylum in the south-east counties. Once, I recall, his letter began with these words: 'Sir, I see you have used Christmas once again as a pretext for mentioning Jesus Christ.'

*   *   *

Still conscious of this admonition, I shall write about ghosts; and particularly about the disgusting inequalities which this professedly civilised and humane society still tolerates in respect of the distribution of opportunities for posthumous apparition and intervention in our affairs.

Let me make my position clear: I regard the opportunity for such appearances and interventions as a privilege rather than a punishment. I do not take Hamlet's father's view. For example, I regard it as possible though barely conceivable, that, when I have been long below the sod, this newspaper will develop policies on subjects dear to my heart which I cannot approve. In those circumstances, I should like to be free to make some judicious intrusion – an apparition before the Editor at some critical moment; if that fails, a little mischief on the stone (for which there must be precedents) and, failing that, some poltergeist activity in the local hostelry.

This matter of the gross inequality which now disfigures our society's arrangements in relation to supernatural phenomena was first brought to my attention by a gentleman who, some years ago, mounted a campaign in favour of more working-class ghosts, observing correctly, that, in this class-ridden community of ours, ghosts are drawn almost exclusively from the ranks of the rich and privileged.

But, to my mind, there is an even more damaging injustice: it is the almost total absence from our affairs (at least so far as I can judge, on the basis of extremely inadequate research) of political ghosts.

Not even Spencer Perceval (a Prime Minister murdered in the lobby of the House of Commons) haunts the place. Some fire watchers during the war did hear a strange noise in Westminster Hall, but it was proved to have been produced by a pigeon in the rafters. A good story about Churchill, shortly after his appointment as Prime Minister in 1940, having received valuable counsel from his long-lamented father, is sharply dismissed by Dr. Martin Gilbert.

Yet politicians, who are so apt to rise from their purely political graves to give romanticised versions of what Britain was like in their day, must surely pine for posthumous activity, particularly as their names are so often taken in vain by their successors. There is a case for a right of reply.

Ghosts are, by nature, diffident. All they need is a little judicious encouragement from a quango with a small subsidy, which could be prudently supplied by cutting the money now spent on discouraging sexual and racial descrimination. Years ago, I had the distinct impression that Edmund Burke's statue outside Trinity, Dublin, extended a hand to me in a warm embrace; but my ten-year-old daughter who accompanied me failed to corroborate; indeed, described my account of the matter as 'a frigid lie'.

Not that I have not seen a ghost in the most incontrovertible circumstances. I did so many years ago and shortly afterwards went blind but, 'these are matters of which I shall not speak on this side of the grave' or, at any rate, until this column is faced by an even thinner day than today.

*   *   *

The Irish Information Partnership has written to offer me a regular supply of highly accurate and thorough information about all aspects of Irish affairs. My confidence in its offer would have been even greater than it is had it not been addressed to 'Mr. Charles Utley, Editor of *The Daily Telegraph*'!

Commentary

The Daily Telegraph, 6 January 1986

I have never myself served on a jury. This I do not regard as an exceptional boon, but rather as an extreme and humiliating deprivation of civil liberty.

I was summoned twice for jury service. On the first occasion I wrote an elaborate letter explaining, in reasonably modest language I think, that I could not imagine anyone more suited by intellect and character to the task; but that I had to reveal that I was entirely blind and that, therefore, I would be incapable of correctly estimating visual evidence. I got a statutory reply to the effect that my 'application for remission of jury service' had been accepted.

In response to the second summons, I waxed more eloquent and less modest about my unique fitness for the duty, adding, by way of wit, that 'it should be recalled that justice herself is notoriously blind.' However, I got the same reply.

I do not think these experiences have soured me. The truth is (and I offer it as a confession) that I have never been wholly convinced of the virtues of the jury system, fundamental though its importance is in the English legend.

The English view of the matter is expressed at its most eloquent and sentimental by G. K. Chesterton:

'Our civilisation has decided, and very justly decided, that determining the guilt or innocence of men is a thing too important to be trusted to trained men . . . When it wants a library catalogued, or the solar system discovered, or any trifle of that kind, it uses up its specialists. But when it wishes anything done which is really serious, it collects 12 of the ordinary men standing around. The same thing was done, if I remember right, by the Founder of Christianity.'

Now, up to a point, I am on Chesterton's side. It is extremely important that people should not be convicted of crimes which they have not committed. This has to be achieved at the cost of failing to convict some people who have committed crimes. Nevertheless, the administration of justice is a moral, not simply an expedient, activity. It is better, in the old maxim, that 99 guilty men should go free than that one innocent man should be falsely condemned. In so far as the jury system is directed to that end, I approve of it.

Nothing is more significant of the decay of our political culture than the prevailing view that justice is something which can be supplied on a production line. Like most of our current evils, this is the result of liberal humanitarianism. The theory is that the deterrent to crime is not punishment but conviction; get as many of them as possible convicted, one way or another, and then you can afford to be lenient about punishments. The opposite view is that it is crucial to get the verdict right, and that, if this involves the risk of failing to catch many guilty men, the balance must be restored by punishing such as you do catch with extreme severity. This is not a 'reactionary' view; if I remember rightly, Jeremy Bentham supported it.

My difficulty is that I do not believe that 12 good and true men (and women) selected at random are the best means of establishing the facts. Remember that the principle is that the judge declares the law and passes sentence, while the jury establishes what actually happened according to the evidence. It has always seemed to me that this is an extraordinary distribution of duties.

Ordinary, commonsense people are quite good at deciding what should be done to proven criminals, whether they should be treated mercifully or severely. This calls for moral sense and human understanding, qualities in which many very sophisticated judges have lately shown themselves to be extraordinarily deficient.

Deciding what actually happened in any given case, however, is a highly sophisticated operation for which average mankind is wholly unsuitable. Ask any two people who have witnessed the same road accident what they saw, and you will get my point. The judgement of fact according to evidence demands clinical detachment, a complete sterilisation of prejudice and compassion and acute powers of accurate observation. These are the prerogatives of the élite; most human beings are totally destitute of them.

Special juries, recruited from people of high professional station who are known to be able to read and write (they have now been abolished in deference to egalitarian madness) have much to be said for them; ordinary juries have little to be said for them.

*   *   *

A word for Sir Gordon Reece: journalists who spend their entire lives urging politicians to improve their 'public images', are not well placed to be snooty about the remarkable achievements of a man who has devoted so much of his life to this task. Helping to make political virtue prevail under the conditions of democracy is an extremely irksome and squalid task, like maintaining the sewers. Those humble men who are prepared to dedicate their lives to it deserve a mark of royal favour. Sir Gordon is unlikely to get ideas above his station, since the effect of his elevation seems to have been to convince most people that he is Mrs. Thatcher's hairdresser.

Commentary

The Daily Telegraph, 18 February 1985

Mrs. Thatcher beat Galtieri; she is about (I think) to beat Scargill and, after tonight's debate, I believe she will be seen to have beaten Kinnock. Why is it, then, that (unless I am entirely wrong) she is about to yield in a thoroughly feeble way to the most ridiculously pretentious institution in the land, the BBC?

It is not that she likes the place. Its self-assurance, its pomposity, its flagrant bias all appal her. What is more it spends money lavishly. It is the perfect victim for her abrasive, intelligent, economical mind. It is demanding that the licence fee (the impost which it imposes on the British people for listening not to BBC programmes but to any programmes at all), shall be increased by 41 per cent to £65. She will not give it this boon, because she realises that it has asked for more than it is prepared to settle for; but she will (possibly) cave in at about £55, for which it will be very grateful indeed. She may also pluck up the courage to say that it is to have it for only two years rather than three. In essence, however, the BBC will have got away with it again.

There is a reason for this in the Prime Minister's otherwise balanced nature; she has an inordinate love of accountants. She was once wistfully heard to remark that the reason why Cecil Parkinson was essential to the Cabinet was that he was the only accountant in it.

So it was that, when she decided to tackle the BBC, she made an accountant, Mr. Stuart Young, its chairman. This expedient failed because Mr. Young, like all his predecessors, was soon completely sucked in to the warm, self-congratulatory atmosphere of the organisation. He became the spokesman of his staff.

She also sent Peat Marwick in to do a sort of time-and-motion study designed to establish whether the BBC was spending its money prudently and, inevitably, the report was fairly favourable. But the question is not whether the BBC is doing what it sets out to do as economically as possible, but whether it ought to be doing what it is doing.

This is the question which the staff of the BBC has so far successfully averted. It rests its case on the proposition that 'public service broadcasting' is a seamless garment which includes entertainment, education, news and everything else.

This, to put it politely, is mysticism; to put it bluntly, it is fraud. There is relatively little cross-fertilisation in the public broadcasting service; how many disc jockeys on Radio 1 bring their invaluable insights into the nature of broadcasting to the service of the Third Programme?

Nothing is plainer than that much of the BBC's activity could be financed perfectly well out of advertising; I certainly can see no fundamental difference in cultural quality between the programmes offered by the Corporation and those offered by Independent Television; as an inadvertent listener to Radio London, I also observe that the BBC's local broadcasting stations do their best to supply the genuine entertainment value of advertising by slipping into their intervals jazzy little commercials for their own programmes.

To put it in a nutshell, the BBC, no longer a monopoly, is using immense sums of public money (on breakfast television, on local radio and on a number of ancillary activities like the selling of computer software) to expand its territory. It resists the principle that the State should only support what cannot otherwise be provided efficiently and responsibly, because it believes that this principle would lead to the dismemberment of its empire and would expose it to the same sort of public scrutiny as is suffered by the Arts Council.

The BBC has become almost insanely competitive. For example, this revealing note appears in the minutes of a recent meeting of the Overseas Programme Liaison committee: 'The possibility of a revised audience figure was discussed now that the VOA [Voice of America] claimed an audience of 110 million.'

The External Services (financed by the Foreign Office) are undoubtedly the most respectable and valuable part of the Corporation, but surely no one can accurately estimate their audiences, and the guess certainly cannot be legitimately influenced by the claims made by a rival organisation.

The BBC is very wily, possibly the best organised vested interest in the country. If it is to get even part of the money it is asking for, the nature of its exercise should be reviewed, not by some huge Royal Commission or the like (the BBC is adept at bamboozling such bodies) but by a small committee appointed to act rapidly and consisting in part of ex-members of the Corporation's staff who are up to all the tricks. The aim should not be to annihilate 'public service broadcasting', but to discover what, in modern conditions, its limits ought to be.

Commentary

The Daily Telegraph, 4 March 1985

One must not bang on. The prosecution's case against the BBC has been stated and defending counsel (assisted by innumerable juniors) has replied, ponderously and, in my judgement, most unpersuasively. The Government will make up its mind.

But one by-product of this controversy seems to me to be of enough general interest to warrant further comment. What I have in mind is the increasingly prevalent tendency of the very young institutions (50 years old or so) to seek to arrogate to themselves all the deference and piety which properly belong to ancient institutions – like the Crown, the Church and the older universities.

Such genuine parts of the historic Establishment may properly claim respect, even at times when they provoke. The claim does not lack rational foundations. If one generation after another subscribes to a certain way of doing things, it is not unreasonable to believe that there is something to be said for that system and to be reluctant to destroy it or amend it save gradually and for overwhelming reasons.

Even when the reasons seem to be overwhelming, there may still be a case for pausing, on the ground that the established practice is firmly lodged, so to speak, in the national subconscious and that disturbing it too rudely could have traumatic and unpredictable consequences.

This is not what Lord Dacre is pleased to call 'highfalutin', abstract, Germanic' mysticism, it is plain English common sense. But nowadays there is an ever-growing tendency on the part of parvenus to muscle in on this innate, English conservatism. The result is that interesting, revolutionary experiments like the National Health Service are scarcely born before they start claiming the reverence due to grandfathers and implying that all who presume to criticise their functioning or suggest modest reforms in their operation are iconoclastic hooligans.

Hear, for example, the words of Mr. David Watt, about the BBC: the most important group of its enemies, he says, consists of those who have a visceral objection to the BBC 'as the perfect embodiment of the old establishment, the paternalist expression of traditional middle-of-the-road consensus'. Plainly, somebody has been telling Mr. Watt about 'the New Right', and it is to this concept of the pseudo-academic imagination that I must now briefly turn.

I know all about this because an endless succession of highly talented and often quite delightful young men and young women who are writing theses on the subject ask my advice about it. They have got hold of the idea that in this country (I cannot speak of the United States of which I know nothing) there is a new sort of Right-wing militancy – aggressive, intellectually vandalistic, doctrinaire, contemptuous of tradition, fanatically devoted to the free economy on the one hand, and to jingoism, racial discrimination, Draconian punishments and anti-permissive legislation on the other. If this 'pressure group' exists, I hardly know where to find it, though I do know that it is emphatically not to be found in the entourage of the Prime Minister.

I tell my pupils that the Conservative bias in favour of free enterprise dates at least from the days of the great Marquess of Salisbury (though of course it has always co-existed with other themes of Conservative thinking) and that the Tory party's belief in strong policies for national defence, public order and the judicious preservation of whatever national consensus exists about personal morality is as old as the hills. To mistake this balanced philosophy for a new kind of counter-revolutionary fanaticism is absurd.

I hope that, as a result of my counsels, this myth about the New Right will shortly be exploded in a number of learned treatises which will spare us a great many ill-informed and tiresomely repetitive newspaper articles about the sinister activities of the 'Tory intelligentsia' at the court of Mrs. Thatcher.

Expressing Royal emotion for posterity

The Daily Telegraph, 5 May 1986

What, then, is remarkable about the love letters of Edward VIII and the Duchess of Windsor which are being displayed to public view and, largely I suspect, also to public contempt?

Well, the answer is nothing much. These letters are specimens of a genre of writing which is governed by extremely rigorous conventions, and they observe those conventions to perfection.

Consider the chief elements in this branch of the literary craft. It is necessary for the lovers to invent a private language (eanums and WEs and all that); this task often requires extreme mental effort (I almost said 'intellectual' effort); it is often very painful. Then there is the device for conveying sentimental messages, too blushmaking to be delivered directly, through the medium of pet animals to which the power of speech (though not entirely of reason) is fictitiously attributed.

Then, there is the process of fraudulent rejuvenation to which middle-aged lovers feel obliged to submit themselves – 'a boy is holding a girl so very tight in his arms tonight. He will miss her more tomorrow because he will have been away from her some hours longer and cannot see her till Wednesday night.'

Now, these mercilessly rigid rules spring from an obvious psychological need. Those in love constantly doubt whether the strength of their feelings is adequate to the occasion. In modern England, the view is that syntax is the enemy of sincerity. Any idea that a man or a woman can feel strongly and yet express the feeling in a disciplined and precise manner is powerfully discouraged. You must be slipshod, childish and incoherent if you wish to be regarded as spontaneous.

I will wager that among the stable, often quite mature and splendidly literate readers of this column there are very few who have not written such letters and even kept them in suitcases or shoeboxes. I would dearly like to make a personal confession in this respect, but alas! I cannot. I have written but one love letter in my life – to my wife on the verge of our marriage.

Being blind I had to type it and, such is my manual incompetence, it turned out to consist mostly of numerical fractions. It will, happily, find its place in no anthology; I say 'happily' because I suspect that it was written in something resembling (though not too closely) the style of Edward VIII.

No: what is surprising is not that these letters should have been written but that the Duchess should have wished them to be published even posthumously. Perhaps she had no firm faith in life after death; if she had, she would surely have spared herself and her lover eternal blushes. I suspect, however, that her decision can be easily explained. Just as lovers are always preoccupied with the need to convince themselves and each other of the power and integrity of their feelings, so the Duchess had an equal wish to convince posterity of the beauty and integrity of her relationship with King Edward. What other way of doing it than to display these carefully contrived banalities to the world?

I do not suppose that when Edward awoke from his 'drowsel' in the Royal bed at Fort Belvedere or wherever, he snatched a pen and paper and wrote his immortal words in five minutes flat. They must, I think, have taken him quite a time, and I have enough respect for him to suppose that they must have induced a brief spasm of nausea.

I do not know whether he ever thought of their subsequent publication, but that is quite conceivable.

On the other hand, I am quite convinced that when his great predecessor Henry VIII wrote to Anne Boleyn, he had no expectation that his words would eventually appear in that beautiful anthology edited by Antonia Fraser called *Love Letters*. His letter vibrates with passion, but passion controlled by grammar. So do most of the letters in this great collection.

Now, I am not saying that King Edward and Mrs. Simpson were insincere (after all, she fared a lot better in the end than Anne Boleyn); I am merely saying that it is a great error to suppose that what is said with elegance and precision necessarily lacks spontaneity. Is there any human emotion which does not become deeper and truer for being exactly defined?

My much lamented friend Stevie Smith once asked me to write a love story for one of her magazines in the manner of a *Times* leader (old style), as she thought this to be the only form of spontaneous expression of which I was capable. Well, if this 'boy' ever feels constrained to write another love letter, it will not be modelled on Edward VIII, but expressed quite straightforwardly in the language of this column.

An amateur in South Africa
The Times, 16 March 1987

I have always had the greatest sympathy, amounting almost to admiration, for that stalwart friend of President Reagan, the former Judge William Clark. He exposed himself, you will remember, to almost universal ridicule while being examined by the Senate foreign relations committee in 1981 to establish his fitness to be deputy to Alexander Haig, then Secretary of State.

The committee held the view that it would be advantageous to Clark, in this new capacity, to have some knowledge of foreign affairs. They asked him, therefore, a few elementary questions. For example, could he name the Prime Ministers of South Africa and Zimbabwe. On both counts, the judge failed, and bore his failure manfully. Of the first he simply said he did not know; of the second that he could venture a guess but was not willing to do so. In spite of the great amusement he gave to the *bien pensants*, Clark was admitted to the administration and then, it seemed, proceeded to acquit himself admirably. His defence was that he could acquire these interesting bits of information as he went along, but that he was being employed as an administrator and man of general intelligence, not as some miserable computer crammed with ephemeral facts.

Facts are, of course, important to the making of political judgements. They are to be acquired, used, forgotten and rediscovered whtn it is necessary so to do. They are, however, no substitute for thought, and too much concentration on retaining them can be an encumbrance to thought. The essential facility with which education is supposed to equip a man is the ability to summon them up at short notice and arrange them with a proper regard to their significance. The media, incidentally, do a great deal to obscure this truth by running programmes like *Mastermind* in which contestants are invited to compete with each other in displaying their command of obscure information, thereby putting the intellectual establishment and the privileged classes generally to shame. I once knew a man who had won such a competition; his knowledge was obviously immense, his understanding seemed to me far from remarkable.

In free societies, politicians and journalists are in the business of being amateurs. They should cling to that status. They bring to their task a body of general prejudice, a few items of ill-remembered knowledge and, if they are competent, a faculty for concealing their inadequacies. If freedom is to be preserved, they must cling to this role and absolutely decline to become experts.

But alas, I protest too much. The reason for this is that I am about to make my first visit to South Africa, a country on which I have already expressed many strong opinions. I think it would be natural to expect that my first experience of the place would bring about at least some small change of mind. As it is, I will return here in three weeks' time and announce, I hope with reasonable humility, some conclusions. These you will be disposed to dismiss as the off-the-cuff reactions of an ignorant journalist who has spent a short time examining a question of infinite complexity and immensely tragic proportions. Like Judge Clark, I will try to learn as I go along.

However, it would seem to be only fair to start with a general restatement of the prejudices from which I begin. These are extraordinarily gloomy. To my mind, it is virtually inconceivable that there is any discoverable 'solution to the South African problem'. There are some interests in politics that can safely be pronounced to be incompatible with each other; the demand of the black population for one man one vote and the wish of the white population (Afrikaners and English) to maintain not just their supremacy but their very existence, come into this category.

I cannot conceive of any way in which a bridge can be built between these two positions. Benevolent liberal-minded attempts to build such a bridge (the actions of Dr. Denis Worrall, for example), do not seem to carry much hope. President Botha's fate illustrates once again de Tocqueville's maxim that the moment when an authoritarian régime is in most danger is when it begins to reform itself.

The questions that remain to be answered are whether white supremacy can be maintained at all and whether, in terms of human cruelty, the cost of maintaining it would in any case be too high. The second question is largely nullified by the amount of human cruelty that would almost certainly follow from the abandonment of white supremacy in favour of majority rule.

If I were a South African I am pretty sure that I would now feel that, in terms of morality, the supreme need was to maintain public order, that this need would justify curtailment of the freedom of the press and of civil liberty generally, and that the moment was wholly unripe for the consideration of constitutional reform of a fundamental kind. I am, however, an Englishman, and all these conclusions go against the grain, though at present I can see no way of resisting them.

I hope my views will be changed by my actual experience of the place. Anyway, I have stated them in advance and, if I play the game fairly, you will at least be able to judge whether (as they say) 'his holiday did him good'.

South African realities

The Times, 13 April 1987

Writing in *The Times* on 16 March on the eve of my first trip to South Africa, I listed the prejudices with which I set out: 'If I were a South African,' I wrote, 'I am pretty sure that I would now feel that in terms of morality the supreme need was to maintain public order, that this need would justify curtailment of the freedom of the press and of civil liberty generally, and that the moment was wholly unripe for the consideration of constitutional reform of a fundamental kind.'

How far have these prejudices survived their first brief contact with reality – a visit of three weeks, two of them spent as a guest of the South African Government, one as the guest of an old friend, an eminent retired South African diplomatist of strongly liberal inclinations and very little sympathy with President Botha and the National Party?

In one respect my prejudices have been fortified. I did not realize the full extent of the power of the South African republic to sustain itself and to maintain by coercion what in Ireland is known as 'an acceptable level of public violence'. Last May, the Eminent Persons Group was predicting a steady acceleration of disorder which would end in a bloodbath.

I can find no one in South Africa, on the Right or Left, who now supports that thesis. The Government's emergency measures, whether you like them or not, have achieved their immediate object. A supporter of the United Democratic Front admitted as much to me: 'Nothing fundamental in the way of reform will happen for the next ten years,' he said. 'After that, it is possible that the system will collapse.'

This remarkable approximation to a restoration of public order has been achieved by a massive policy of administrative arrest and a display of overwhelming public force. In the process, I have no doubt there has been some physical brutality, though I have no doubt either that its extent has been exaggerated. Even liberal South Africans welcome the result, though they cannot approve the means.

In relation to the press, the government is paranoid, and this aspect of the state of emergency has become thoroughly ludicrous. Newspaper editors have to have lawyers sitting constantly at their side to avoid breaching some of the many regulations; but this does not protect the Government from perpetual attacks by the English-language press and damaging little notices declaring that newspapers have been produced under conditions of censorship.

The whole thing has the proportions of a considerable nuisance, rather than those of tyranny. What is more, the editor of one liberal newspaper told me that he thought the government's restrictions on the televising of violence were justified; television, he said, had become an incentive to disorder.

The essential point is that South Africa is not a banana republic constantly under the threat of political convulsion. It is maintained by a white army of indubitable loyalty to the State and by a massive civil service which at present is equally loyal. It is just possible to imagine a Right-wing coup but it is not possible, for the foreseeable future, to imagine a Left-wing coup. The speculations of progressives in the West about the imminent disintegration of the South African State are simply silly.

The strongest fortification of the State is, of course, the determination of the Afrikaners to survive. They believe that a unitary democracy based on one-man-one-vote would destroy them and destroy South Africa. They have no 'mother country' – they feel no sentimental allegiance to Holland, nor do the Dutch particularly like them. Unlike the English, they do not believe in the wisdom of concession. They are there to stay or to die.

This difference between the British and the Afrikaner approach to politics can scarcely be exaggerated. The essence of the English political tradition is the belief that the art of politics consists in discovering what is inevitable, and then bringing the 'inevitable' about as smoothly as possible.

This particular technique is applied with special alacrity to white colonial populations, like the Southern Rhodesians, who can be sacrificed with little inconvenience to the electorate at home. To do them justice, however, the British also apply it to their own country – for example, in the 19th century, by enfranchising large numbers of illiterate people in the belief that it would all turn out right in the end and that anyway we could now set about educating our masters.

No such blithe irresponsibility prevails among the Afrikaners or indeed among the majority of first-language English whites in South Africa. They believe, with substantial justification, that one-man-one-vote tomorrow would mean a national ruin to which any other fate would be preferable.

With these feelings I strongly sympathise and I do not believe that the coercive measures in which they are at present expressed are for the most part morally indefensible.

But, in another respect, which I shall explore tomorrow, my prejudices have been altered.

Let Botha get on with reform

The Times, 14 April 1987

The South African Government, with the overwhelming support of the white population, is resolved to resist the imposition of a unitary democratic State based on one-man-one-vote. It believes, rightly, that to accept such a settlement would amount to political suicide.

It will have at its disposal, for the foreseeable future, the physical means necessary to avoid yielding to this form of constitutional radicalism. If it succumbs to any sort of coup (which at least for ten years or so is unlikely) it will be a Right-wing not a Left-wing coup.

So far, then, my prejudices have been confirmed; but in one signal respect they have been destroyed. The case for constitutional reform in South Africa rests not on morality or the need to accommodate arrangements to the prejudices of the civilised world, but on sheer fact. By the end of the century, the population of South Africa will be 45 million of which 35 million will be blacks. The economy of South Africa is now virtually stagnant. By the year 2000 there will be huge unemployment unless current economic trends can be radically reversed.

The drift from the homelands to the towns will accelerate, because the homelands cannot sustain such a population and because whatever economic future South Africa may have will depend on the availability of trained black labour. It is inconceivable that this migrant population can be contained in black townships and deprived of all political rights save those of self-government at local level. Apartheid is collapsing not primarily as a result of moral pressure from outside but because of its own internal contradictions.

These truths are at least as well perceived by intelligent Afrikaners as they are by enlightened people in the Western world – hence President Botha's attempts at reform and hence also the revolt of the Stellenbosch Afrikaner academics against his failure to do more. Reform is essential, but what kind of reform?

Innumerable constitutional models are now being advanced – confederation, federation, consociation. Confederation seems to the outsider to be a rearguard action designed to reintroduce apartheid by the back door. The recipe is to carve the place up into a large number of autonomous states so constructed as to ensure that some are controlled by blacks, some by whites, some by Indians and some by Coloureds. If blacks find themselves working in white states they will be regarded as immigrant labour and therefore not clearly entitled to political representation there. This is a chimera.

Federation is a different matter: there would be a number of states in which an attempt would be made to secure a balanced representation of distinct ethnic interests. The model for this is the programme of the KwaZulu/Natal Indaba which has proposed a complex system for the government of that region in which a balanced representation will be given to blacks, Indians and whites. This, of course, involves racial discrimination, though the fact is concealed by the use of euphemisms such as 'group-interests'.

The guts of the matter, however, are these: however important decentralisation may be for the future of South Africa, the place must have a central Government; someone must control the army and the police, and have a final say in the distribution of resources. There must be a central legislature in which blacks as well as Coloureds and Indians are represented, and some sort of balance must be struck between their respective constitutional powers. The notion of race must be preserved in the Government of South Africa. The alternative, as my liberal friend put it, is 'one-man-one-vote for one minute: after which there will be a one-party State, probably controlled by Marxist blacks, and therefore both tyrannical and disastrously incompetent'.

So everybody ends by saying that there must be negotiation; but negotiation with whom? There would now be much to be said for removing the ban on the African National Congress, summoning it to the conference table and engaging in a long parley. Let us be clear, however: the object of that exercise should be to demonstrate that the ANC, Marxist-dominated and committed wholly to the principle of one-man-one-vote in a unitary State, does not entirely represent South African blacks. By the same token, it would be sensible to release Nelson Mandela: he would not of course be a free agent when released and it would probably be necessary to re-arrest him when he continued to advocate violence. That also would make a point. It would be part of a process designed to isolate black radicals and prove that they were not the authentic representatives of majority black opinion.

What, then, prevents these arguably sensible measures? They are prevented largely by sanctions (the only rationale of which is to destabilise South Africa and promote a bloody revolution) and by the belief that any concession made to those who impose them will lead to further demands. At present, sanctions are ineffectual and will merely increase black unemployment and divert energy from the supremely important task of developing the economy and improving the life of the black population. What they do otherwise is to intensify the opposition of whites (and particularly relatively poor whites) to any sort of reform. It is possible that President Botha when re-elected will not continue with reform; it is also probable that he will. The existence of sanctions makes the first possibility vastly more likely. My final message: for God's sake, leave them alone!

For pedantry read purity

The Times, 29 June 1987

One of the few signs that, with the election out of the way, it is now possible to give a scintilla of attention to serious matters is provided by the publication last week of an excellent pamphlet on the teaching of English (*English our English*, £3.90 from the Centre for Policy Studies).

Written by John Marenbon, a don at Trinity, Cambridge, it is a comprehensive attack on 'the new orthodoxy' which has infected the minds of English teachers and Her Majesty's Inspectors of schools on the question of what English is and how it should be presented to pupils at every stage of their careers. Roughly described, 'the new orthodoxy' starts from the premise that English is not, in the normal meaning of the word, a 'subject' – that is to say it has no precise limits and enjoins no authoritative techniques.

This ideology is opposed to grammar, save as a descriptive science with no imperatives, is 'child centred' in the sense that it maintains that teaching should be dominated by what interests those subjected to it and is obsessed by the principle that all languages are equal and that all dialects are also equal, both to each other and to standard language.

Its total effect is to reduce English lessons to periods in which the young are encouraged to while away their time in talking about whatever gives them enjoyment or, to put it more pompously, on whatever is likely to develop their moral imagination and to encourage them (as Mr. Marenbon points out) not to think too highly of the Prime Minister.

You may well say that all this is familiar enough. The battle for the purity of the English language has gone on throughout the whole of my lifetime. Its conspicuous generals include Sir Ernest Gowers, A. P. Herbert and my much lamented father-in-law, Dermot Morrah, who edited *The Times* style book.

Those of us who have taken part in this campaign do not seem to me to have got very far. We are swimming against the tide, and what destroys us is one lethal weapon, the charge of pedantry. We have recourse to the argument that we are not pedants at all but are simply concerned to preserve the language as a vehicle of accurate communication and therefore something of practical convenience.

My childhood was haunted by a nightmare conjured up by a preparatory school master in the mid-1930s who was concerned to convince me of the lethal consequences which can sometimes follow from an inadequate attention to grammar. He told me a story (which most of you over 60 were also probably told) of an unfortunate foreigner visiting this country who was drowning.

Lacking the advantages of an expensive education in English, this unhappy man cried out to the people standing on the shore: 'I will die: you shall not save me'. Naturally, his wishes were observed, and he was borne away *on a watery bier* (another joke of my childhood). Had he had the advantages of a decent education, he would have cried: 'I shall die; you will not save me'. *Shall* following *you* is an imperative. *Will* following *I* is an imperative.

I was never wholly convinced by this story. It seemed to me that much would depend on the particular emphasis which the victim gave to the words *shall* and *will*. It also seemed to me that much depended on the context. There might be those on the shore who were more impressed by the general circumstances than by the drowning foreigner's attention to grammatical detail.

Certainly the avoidance of ambiguity is a proper function of language, and the argument that people will know what you mean from the context is very undependable, people being what they are. The abuse of the word 'disinterested' (which used to mean free of all corrupt motive) is a case in point. Its confusion with 'uninterested' (meaning not bothering at all) can cause doubt. 'Anticipate' is another classic case in point: was it not A. P. Herbert who pointed out the difference between saying 'John and Mary expected to get married', and 'John and Mary anticipated marriage'? Of course, morals change, and the distinction is not quite so important as it used to be; but it is still worth preserving.

The case for absolute precision in English does not rest wholly on practical convenience. There is, I maintain, an intrinsic virtue in saying precisely what you mean. Abandon this principle and the case for decent English has gone.

Another preoccupation of 'the new orthodoxy' is 'appropriateness' – you should not use the same sort of English to your mistress as you do to your bank manager. Well, I doubt this. 'Appropriateness' is one of the chief reasons why the language is declining. As an obituaries editor, I suffer from it particularly – from what, I think, Virginia Woolf described as 'the true biographical style'. This prescribes, for example, that no dead man should ever have helped to found an orphanage; he must have been 'instrumental in founding an orphanage', thereby emphasising the majesty of death.

I shall go on trying, but with little confidence.

Why I shrink from 1988

The Times, 28 December 1987

Why do I enter the New Year (that arbitrary division in history) in a spirit of almost unmitigated gloom? For two reasons, one of which concerns foreign policy and the other our domestic affairs.

The first reason is that the Western world has now surely embarked on a process which may well prove to be irreversible and of which the conclusion will be to leave it prostrate and helpless before the military might of the Soviet Union. There is no mystery about how this came about. We emerged from the last war convinced that in the 1920s and 1930s we had made the unpardonable error of putting national prosperity and domestic comfort before national defence. We resolved that we would never make this mistake again, and, of course, we proceeded to do so.

It was not a recognisable mistake, because it consisted not in disarmament but in the acquisition of new weapons more devastating, but also rather cheaper, than any which had been known before. As soon as the Soviet Union developed similar weapons, we found ourselves committed to the principle of mutually assured destruction. We would allow our national survival to depend on a threat which, if ever we carried it out, would infallibly lead to our own destruction. This was a grievous error, and grievously we have repented it. Not so grievously, of course, as we might have done. The expectation that the West might react to Soviet aggression in Europe by using the nuclear bomb very probably has helped to preserve peace. Had the Russians called our bluff (for bluff it largely was) disaster would have ensued in the shape of Western capitulation.

As it is, however, the West is clearly being induced to abandon its nuclear deterrent. The process will be a long one, but I cannot see how at any point it will be interrupted. The revulsion from these weapons, the perception of the total absurdity of continuing to pile them up will prevail, and the result will be the acceptance by the West of the Russians' vast preponderance of conventional weapons in Europe.

We shall lie at their feet. It could be that they will not in fact assault us. That is Mr. Powell's view, and there is much in Russian history to support it; but it could also not be so. If an amiable relationship is to arise between the West and the Soviet Union, some conditions will have to be satisfied. One of these is that the West will have to abandon its moral arrogance. It will have to stop prattling about human rights and implicitly encouraging the satellite countries in Eastern Europe to rebel. But this is part of the essence of American foreign policy and it is also part of the moral conviction of Mrs. Thatcher about foreign policy.

If we had Salisbury running our affairs, recognising that there are Soviet spheres of influence and British spheres of influence, we might be all right. But that is not who we have. What we look like having is an absolute abandonment of power and no corresponding reduction in moral pretensions.

We shall have, in fact, the worst of all worlds – military weakness and universal moral arrogance. Some of this difficulty will be overcome by hypocrisy – by pretending that things are all right behind the Iron Curtain when they are not; but that will not be very good either. I find it to be a gloomy and, indeed, a horrifying prospect.

At home I am not much happier. I deplore the end of Thatcherism. What Thatcherism meant was that we would depend as far as possible on the spontaneous forces of society operating within the rule of law. Its implication was that we would not know what kind of a society would result from this; but it would be the right kind of society because it would have been created rightly; it would be the best sort we could get, because no other method could be better. We might be rich or poor, but we ourselves would have decided which.

I see this faith disappearing. I see a Government which thinks it knows exactly how many engineers, poets and anchorites the country will need, and sets about producing them. I see a Government which is attacking the independence of our universities and doing very little that is rational to ensure the independence of our schools. It is really rather a Heathite sort of Government – a Government which has lost faith in freedom because freedom did not produce the results it wanted. I also see a Government which is inspired by no other object than the impossible one of preserving its own existence infinitely.

What is most distressing about it, however, is its reliance on blatant, brutal, unlawful authoritarianism to improve the Queen's subjects. The way in which it has permitted random breath testing which Parliament has not approved, to be introduced by the abuse of legislation is a case in point. This is not a Government which believes in anything but its own preservation, and it is wholly unworthy of its leader.

A happy 1988 to most of you.

Other-worldly broadcasting

The Times, 11 January 1988

It is a pity, but a fact, that those who take up the cudgels against bias in broadcasting almost always end by looking ridiculous. This was the case with Mr. Norman Tebbit. He had an excellent argument and his motives were unimpeachable; but he nevertheless failed.

I think there are two reasons for this sort of misfortune. The first is the assumption, almost always made by the critics of this section of the media, that there is a conspiracy in operation. The idea is that a bunch of fanatical producers and editors get together for the purpose of abusing their power to corrupt society, subvert government and undermine Mrs. Thatcher. I do not believe this to be true.

Let me illustrate my point. From time to time the television services seek my advice on some question on which they think me to be well informed. The normal procedure is to send round to me an amiable young woman with a pleasantly sluttish voice and a 2.2 degree from a modern university. She is called a researcher. I give her a drink and we talk, and later I sometimes receive a rather insulting tip. I remember one such visitation from a girl who was compiling a programme on Christianity and Conservatism. The assumption underlying the exercise was that I was a museum piece, too frail and antique to be exposed to direct contact with the public but worthy of being described. After I had bored on for a bit the child politely interrupted me with this practical question: 'Could you just tell me exactly when it was that people began to say that it was possible to be a Christian and a Conservative?'

I explained, to the best of my ability, that throughout most of European history it had been widely believed that Christianity required a passive acceptance of the social and political order and that, therefore, it was only in comparatively recent times that the notion had grown up that one could be a

Christian without being a Conservative. I went on to point out that this relatively modern development – this view that you could be opposed to the established order and determined to destroy it (a view which had certain historical antecedents to which I sought to introduce my interviewer) was a very good thing. The young woman was perplexed beyond belief. She, plainly, had always believed that the idea you could be a Christian and a Conservative had been invented by John Selwyn Gummer.

These people mean no harm. They are not consciously exercised in importing bias into broadcasting. They just do not know about anything that happened before 1917, and that is putting it generously. It is we who are to blame for having failed to educate them while giving them an overwhelming impression that they have been educated.

The second trouble with the critics of broadcasting is that they assume that there is something intrinsically wrong in the broadcasting services expressing any kind of consensus. Such a consensus is inevitable. These semi-monopolistic institutions are in existence to reflect contemporary culture. They should not do that exclusively, of course; they should always reserve some time for those who are attacking the accepted view. Nevertheless, they cannot keep up a universal debate in which every possible opinion is expressed. They must reflect the times in which they live.

This is precisely what they're not doing at the minute. The broadcasting establishment has a view of Britain which is frozen in the 1960s and immortalised in the memory of Sir Hugh Carleton Greene. He invented the idea that the BBC was not just a mirror, but an estate of the realm, appointed to the task of criticising and reforming society. It was a most discreditable attitude. He spawned a generation which still survives and dominates broadcasting. It is, indeed, expressing a consensus, but it is the establishment consensus created a quarter of a century ago.

The broadcasting authorities must find some way of bringing themselves up to date, of living in the real world. One of the fundamental objections to them is not that they are 'biased' but that they are not contemporary. They are striving earnestly to preserve something which has gone. Thereby they cause offence and anger and may also do a little harm, but, in bringing themselves up to date, they should not forget their duty to give a platform to the critics of the current establishment.

I am prompted to these thoughts by a brilliant lecture given by Ian Curteis to the Edinburgh television festival last August, and now published in *The Salisbury Review*. He was a staff director in the BBC's drama group in the 1960s, and later the author of a play about the Falklands, which the BBC rejected. His theme is the way in which BBC drama has been captured by the Left, by the critics of the historic establishment. He thinks that this is a legitimate theme for BBC drama, but that the other side of the coin should be exhibited as well. He also believes that the BBC should get in touch with the world as it is. All this makes him a more formidable critic than Mr. Tebbit.

7 · *Three Conservative Political Centre pamphlets*

Utley's formidable reputation as a popular Tory philosopher was in part based on the series of pamphlets he produced for the CPC and other Conservative 'think-tanks' at regular intervals throughout his career. The profundity of his thought was recognised by successive generations of Conservative Ministers who sought his counsel.

The Conservatives and the critics

1956

> '*I do not resent criticism, even when, for the sake of emphasis, it parts for the time with reality.*' – SIR WINSTON CHURCHILL

It is natural for Governments to be criticised and it is a sign of weakness if they should appear to resent criticism. It is even a sign of weakness if they should fall back on the familiar argument that criticism is unjustified unless accompanied by positive proposals; for this is by no means a universal rule. There are occasions when it is legitimate to say to a Government, 'You are making a mess of this for the following reasons; I don't know in detail what you ought to do but I know for a fact that what you are doing is not the best that could be done.' That sort of criticism is all right so long as the reasons alleged are valid and so long as the critic, without necessarily going into detail, can satisfy himself that a better policy than that of the Government is physically and politically possible.

I am not a practising politician and I am therefore not concerned here to argue that everything the Government has done is right, or that no improvements in its policy are possible or desirable. As an amateur political philosopher, my interest is rather less in what ought to be done at any given moment than in the kind of question which you should ask in order to find out what ought to be done. What concerns me are the methods by which political judgements and decisions ought to be made. It is for this reason that I am now writing about the Government's critics. For they appear to me to display an instrusive confusion of mind regarding not only the present state of the country but the whole nature of politics.

No doubt, their practical importance is not quite so great as they would have us believe. A good many of them are journalists, and what a journalist writes about politics is as likely to be determined by the desire to have a brighter press as it is by the desire to have a better country. I am not condemning my profession; there are plenty of tried Lobby correspondents and political journalists who have acquired, in the course of years of diligent observation, a vast knowledge of the apparatus of government and a profound understanding of the habits of politicians. In this respect, the British press is uniquely served. But there are others, who live in a peculiar journalistic world, as remote from politics as is a Trappist monastery, and who tend to judge politics entirely by the standards of literature. They have allowed themselves to escape from reality to the extent of thinking of politics always in terms of a good story, of thinking of politicians always as characters in novels and of supposing that their behaviour can be deduced from theoretical prepossessions. There is nothing they cannot do with a political scene when they come to write about it.

If, therefore, I appear at times to be giving undue emphasis to journalistic criticisms of the Government, I hope I shall be acquitted of the charge of suggesting that these criticisms necessarily have any practical importance. I am using them, as I shall use the other specimens of criticism to be discussed here, primarily as illuminating illustrations of how not to think about politics. I shall try to show in the process how I think politics ought to be thought about. If I do all this in the context of our current political and economic affairs, it is because I do not believe that even the methodology of politics can be satisfactorily discussed out of relation to a concrete historical situation.

There are broadly two types of opposition to the Conservatives, although these must later be subdivided. There is in the first place the official Opposition, the people whose regular business it is to criticise; that is to say, the Labour or Socialist Party. They can be kept for later consideration since, like the biblical or Malthusian poor, they seem always to be with us. But there is, secondly, a miscellaneous bag of critics, who are not Socialist and to whom it is tempting, but quite inaccurate, to apply the word 'Poujadist'. It is quite inaccurate to apply this word to them because the people who are commonly called 'Poujadist' in Britain, unlike the supporters of M. Poujade in France, do not always appeal to any clearly definable class or even appeal to any known tradition in British political thought. They consist, in fact, of two categories: those with a literary grievance against politics, and those with a real grievance against the domestic policy of the Government.

LITERARY CRITICS
In the first category, I would place Mr. Malcolm Muggeridge, the brilliant editor of *Punch*, and his able disciple Mr. Henry Fairlie. Mr. Muggeridge is a humorist, a characteristic which befits, but in the past has not always distinguished, his office. Up to a point, he is performing for democracy a service which the wielders of power always urgently need. The great and powerful in all generations (and this applies to them even when they are also the numerous) need court jesters as much as they need priests. One of the great aspects of the Christian literary tradition in Europe is its emphasis on the importance of making fun of the mighty. It is good for any society to be reminded of the vanities by which it lives; it is as good for the leaders of the Welfare State as it is for queens and emperors. This function of satirising temporal authority is morally very important, irrespective of its motives. A political satirist should always behave as though everybody in politics were

wrong, and may be excused if he behaves as though every-body were equally wrong.

It is one thing, however, to be a professional political humorist, and quite another thing to represent your jokes as serious contributions to the science of government or sensible suggestions on how to do things. It is this which is wrong with Mr. Muggeridge: he does not know his place. Hence, he finds no difficulty in imagining himself as Chancellor of the Exchequer for the purpose of contributing an article to that extremely unhumorous organ the *News Chronicle*, and, in that capacity, in proposing that the Government should direct labour and forcibly limit profits. Now a parson, or an editor of *Punch*, is eminently justified in pointing out to the rich at all times that they are too much devoted to money, and to the working classes at all times that if they want the advantages of a highly organised economy they should themselves be prepared to submit to organisation in the public interest. But for a practical Chancellor of the Exchequer in the piping days of peace to announce the institution of direction of labour combined with the forcible limitation of dividends would assuredly produce two effects. In the first place, it would produce a general strike, and in the second place, it would produce whatever the British entrepreneur's equivalent of armed revolt may prove to be if ever he is tempted so far. Whether the two movements would join up to form a popular front against Mr. Muggeridge, thereby creating national unity, may be doubted. It is in any case irrelevant, since the speed with which the object of the movement could be realised would soon remove all reason for its existence. Government from Bouverie Street might be pure in intention and inflexible in aim, but as a practical expedient it is rather worse than theocracy.

I do not think Mr. Henry Fairlie might be a priest in another incarnation as Mr. Muggeridge supposes that he himself might be. They are also different in the sense that Mr. Fairlie has a book knowledge of the working of British politics in the past. Mr. Fairlie, however, is a referee turned centre-forward; like most other Liberal journalists, he is most at home at a standpoint of morally superior detachment. When he decided to come down on to the field, the only thing which he found it in his heart to do was to play both sides at the same time, using his referee's right to declare either of them offside when they got in his way.

I do not profess to be able to describe Mr. Fairlie's philosophy of politics as a consistent whole, because I do not think that it is a consistent whole. The nearest approach I know to a codified account of its content is a pungently obscure article in the March 1956 issue of *Encounter*, from which I thought I deduced the following propositions: (i) that it is a great error to suppose that the British have a genius for compromise since they are best in a state of conflict; (ii) that the trouble with both political parties is that they agree with each other too much; and (iii) that the middle classes are 'effete' and that it would be no bad thing if a new class from which political leaders could be recruited were to arise.

I will take these propositions in order. As an essay title for a university scholarship examination the proposition that 'The British have no genius for compromise' might be very good indeed, and I can imagine Mr. Fairlie distinguishing himself in writing for that proposition. He could do it by the same tactics as were used by the undergraduate who immortalised the spirit of youth with the affirmation that 'The French have never had a revolution'. It is doubtful, however, whether there is much advantage to be had in adult life from facing such questions even in the columns of intellectual monthlies. The answer is too simple and too prosaic: the English are very good at not quarrelling bitterly when they have nothing of substance to quarrel about; they are very good at avoiding quarrels; and the chief characteristic of their genius for conducting them consists in their instinctive perception of when to stop and the shortness of their memories when they have stopped. There is really nothing much to be done even by immortal youth when confronted with the simple arithmetical calculation of the number of our revolutions compared with other people's.

The second proposition, however, brings Mr. Fairlie on to safer ground, for it concerns not what the English do but what the English ought to do, and is to be tested therefore not by facts (which are a notorious burden to literature), but by the unfettered exercise of the moral imagination. It would be good, Mr. Fairlie says, if we were to disagree with each other more. Now, it is perfectly true that we run our politics on a basis of two political parties, each trying to get power, and that the Opposition is doing its forensic duty in exposing the Government's policy at any time to the most searching criticism possible. It is also true that when there is a real issue of principle in politics it is a good thing for it to be debated as such. But it is a bad thing for it to be pressed to the point of endangering the life of society. Always, a political party must bear in mind that when it comes to power it will be legislating not only for those who share its principles but also for those who oppose them.

It is clearly impossible for Mr. Fairlie or anyone else to say whether there is too much or too little conflict in the State at any given moment without specifying the sort of thing which he would like to see either or both of the political parties doing. If Labour went in for full-blooded Socialism it would alienate its trade union supporters and annihilate itself; if the Tories went in for uncontrolled deflation and mass un-employment they would alienate the electorate for ever. It is forgivable to recommend either of these policies on grounds of national interest – forgivable though misguided – but it is unpardonable to recommend both on the ground that politics would then be nice and dialectical. If these obvious extremes are rejected, it is hard to see what other extremes can be suggested in their place. As it is, there is a marginal but extremely important measure of disagreement between the parties, and there is absolutely no case for gratuitously widening it. There is, that is to say, no *political* case for doing this; but fundamentally, Mr. Fairlie's arguments have no-thing to do with politics. They are aesthetic preferences in favour of a particular kind of journalism, which imposes the melodramatic view that everything everywhere is being managed with the greatest possible degree of stupidity or corruption or both.

The third point, the accusation that the middle classes, from whom our political leaders are alleged to be recruited, are 'effete' altogether defies analysis. As a contribution to the amenities of class warfare, it might be objected that no section of the community deserves less reproach, for whilst Mr.

Fairlie has only a literary grievance the middle classes have a real practical grievance, and one which up to now they have suffered with commendable restraint.

MIDDLE CLASS CRITICS

Already, during the period of Socialist Government, Mr. Herbert Morrison was saying that the middle classes had borne a sudden change in their standard of life with praise-worthy patience. Since then, things have not got very much better for them. There is a strict limit to which a community can live by the exertions of a talented minority while making life as difficult as possible for that minority; and what is happening to many members of the salaried classes, and in particular to many pensioners of the salaried classes, is at the very least almost as bad as it is represented to be. The assumptions on which their whole economic lives used to be based have been revolutionised. They can no longer save. It has become inevitable that they should abandon the task of protecting their savings. The bank managers who would give them overdrafts on the strength of their securities will now, in obedience to Treasury directives, oblige them to sell their securities rather than see them through difficult times. Though their salaries have increased, if they are still earning them, they have not, over the period since the war, usually increased proportionately with the cost of living. They are conscious that their ingenuity presides over the production of wealth, and that they themselves play an important part in devising and maintaining the machinery by which their wealth is confiscated and distributed to others. They cheerfully contribute to the education of other people's children, and bear with comparative indifference the charge that they are wicked to depress their standard of life in order to educate their own children.

For the first four years of Tory rule, these grievances were suppressed, first and foremost because every class, including the middle class, benefited from Mr. Butler's success in curbing the rise of prices and from the reductions in taxation which he made. The Government has certainly not done yet everything it can do, or everything it ought to do, to improve the lot of the middle class; and it is fair to add that, judged by its public pronouncements, the Government is as uncomfortably conscious of this as are its critics. The middle class is right to press for better treatment, and there seems little cause to doubt that if it presses hard enough it will get it. My argument is not that it should be dissuaded from pressing hard, but that it should be dissuaded from pressing in the wrong direction – the direction in which it would be led by its self-styled friends who now pose under such grandiloquent titles.

Unconsciously, many people have supposed that the Conservatives, like the Left, have their Utopia, and that this Utopia was a kind of middle class heaven. They have supposed that the first four years of Tory rule were a period during which an anaesthetic was being administered to organised labour in preparation for a surgical operation designed to induce such Utopian conditions in the economy. It is not, however, the Tory aim to create a Utopia; there is no such thing as 'the Tory society', and the phrase ought never to be permitted to be used. The aim of Toryism is a national policy designed to reconcile as equitably as may be the interests and wishes of the various classes of society, not to impose on society as a whole a class ideal.

One essential question has faced this country since the war: shall a state of things which may roughly be called 'full employment' be maintained by deliberate acts of Government policy? The question has been there all the time, but the answer to it has been a foregone conclusion. It has been a foregone conclusion because a powerful and highly organised section of the population, organised labour, has determined that it shall be answered affirmatively; because full employment is a necessary consequence, as well as in part a cause, of the policy of maintaining a minimum standard of life below which people are not allowed to fall; and, above all, because British public opinion has resolved that the cost of prolonged periods of mass unemployment (even when they may be held to express accurately the economic facts), is materially and morally too high.

It is, of course, the natural vice of democracy to elude the truth that anything which is worth having is bought at a price. So the fact that this full employment, which is the dominant feature of our economic and political life, carries with it certain evils has until lately been sedulously suppressed. It is clear, however, that one of its effects is to give a large and disproportionate power to organised labour in deciding the nation's financial policy, and that power will be used by labour as power is always used by everybody, largely to its own advantage.

One of the Government's problems in these circumstances is to help the middle classes without endangering full employment and the essential fabric of the Welfare State. This does not exclude substantial tax relief, but it does exclude massive tax reductions set off against lavish cuts in Government social expenditure. Even if more modest policies are attempted, they encounter difficulties. A state of full employment tends, as we now all know, to inflation unless it is accompanied by some restraint in wage demands. It is always very difficult to get a voluntary restraint of wages. But it is politically impossible to get one if at the time trade unions are being asked to restrain themselves, middle-class people and shareholders are being given an easier time. It is only necessary to understand the politics of the nursery to grasp this fact. Whatever the Government deliberately does for one section of the community must be paralleled by something which it is doing for another section. Hence, if the Government cuts a food subsidy, it must also make it difficult for the private shareholder to get an increased dividend. What, indeed, would happen if the Government altogether ignored this rule? The answer is an unfettered rush for higher wages and a steepening of the inflation, which would eat away by price increases everything that the middle classes might gain by tax concessions.

Accordingly, the Government has made its first aim to call a halt in inflation through monetary and fiscal measures, to let production catch up a little on consumption, to create a state of affairs in which it is possible to permit some eventual relaxation all round. It is now a question of a supreme effort in voluntary restraint.

The answer that is commonly made to all this, particularly since the 1956 TUC Congress, is that the restraint will not be forthcoming. That may prove to be the case, and, in proportion as it is not forthcoming, the Government may have to fall back on one or other of the extremes of more rigorous deflation or public control. My contention is that either would be so great a calamity that a Government which had not made the attempt to avoid both would be culpable.

It is one thing to point the finger of condemnation against abuses of power perpetrated by organised labour, and to press for the equitable treatment of the salaried and professional classes. It is quite another thing to indulge in that characteristic heresy of the 20th century in politics, the heresy that treats government as an instrument of a party or of a class rather than as the guardian of a nation. Politics is the art of conjuring a national policy out of the conflicting ambitions of classes and the incompatible wishes of men. To think of it otherwise is to become a votary, however tepid, of Jacobinism, and the proper symbol of that political philosophy is the guillotine, not the British oak.

ECONOMIC CRITICS

I have distinguished two broad categories of opposition to the Government, the opponents with a literary grievance and those with a real grievance, and distinguished these in turn from the official Opposition whose proper business is to oppose. It would be remiss not to say a word about another class of critic, which has distinguished itself as much by its outstanding accomplishment as by the limited range of its wisdom. I mean a certain school of financial journalists, of whom Mr. Graham Hutton is the most vigorous and widely informed and Mr. George Schwartz the most amusing. They are all luminaries of the journalistic profession whose writing, by virtue of being conducted under the discipline of reality, has unsurpassed clarity and force. It is very important, therefore, that laymen should understand what they are up to.

Their attitude was brilliantly exemplified in a recent anonymous article for *The Times Literary Supplement* entitled 'The Dynamic Society'. They represent a revival in the great classical science of economics, a return, albeit partial, to the assumptions about human psychology which the makers of economic science first stated and, more especially, to the assumption that one of the governing motives of human behaviour is the love of profit and the fear of loss. They have tended to take their stand on one broad principle, the principle that the only effective alternative to a fully controlled economy is an uncontrolled economy; for, since economic behaviour is governed by rewards and penalties, the rewards and penalties must either be automatic or imposed by authority, they cannot be simply non-existent. This has led them to deplore the attempt to achieve a mixed economic policy and any kind of middle way. It has inevitably made them critical of both political parties, and particularly of the Conservative party which they regard as the unworthy heir of the traditions of economic Liberalism, in which last respect, of course, they are mistaken.

Now the belief in 'economic man', like all rationalist abstractions, is an illusion. No practical statement can be made about man as such. He likes profit and dislikes loss, but either feeling may be overcome by religion, patriotism, class consciousness or a thousand other non-economic causes which become determinants of economic behaviour. Above all, different men have profoundly different views about how to look after themselves. Underlying the belief in free enterprise there is usually to be found a doctrinal prejudice in favour of independence; underlying the belief in collectivism a doctrinal prejudice in favour of association. Some men are persuaded that they stand the best chance in open competition, others that they stand the best chance in comradeship with those who share their interests, others that the only way to get on is to make marks on ballot papers. These psychological factors are factors in economics.

The 18th-century Rationalists who invented economics based themselves, as is now generally recognised, on an over-simple psychology. This psychology became particularly out of date with the social developments of the next century, which brought men ever closer together in ever larger social units. They believed, however, that they were describing human nature; they would have never denied that the validity of their conclusions depended on the validity of what we now believe to be the inadequate conception of man's nature which they formulated. The 20th-century partial renaissance of classical economics has converted it unwittingly from a descriptive science into something much more like a system of moral beliefs, and these beliefs though they coincide with the interest, the tradition and the outlook of the property-owning class, conflict at many points with the interest, the tradition and the outlook of a large section of the unpropertied class. To object to this statement on the ground that it is Marxist in character is to adopt the naïve fallacy that the connection between a man's opinions and his station in society was never discovered until a German intellectual found it out by reading in the British Museum. There *is* such a connection, though it does not afford a complete explanation of life.

I do not deny that there are certain elementary truths which politicians who are not economists are apt to neglect. One of them is that the minority upon whom all vast increases in production depend are peculiarly susceptible to the influence of profit, and that this need to stimulate exceptional talent by exceptional reward is an indefeasible limit on the practical sovereignty of the electorate. This truth has been rammed into us by the financial journalists and by the leading articles in *The Economist*, and it is a kind of instruction which public opinion needs. But it is not in itself a sufficient guide to political action. The desire for individual profit and the fear of individual loss are extremely powerful motives. But such things as a belief in some measure of equality and a desire for some certainty in economic matters are also powerful motives, and these are commonly under-rated by the economists or too arbitrarily dismissed as non-economic factors.

It would be tempting to say that these economic critics, who have done incalculable good, are right about economics but wrong about politics, but this would be to accept a dichotomy which is false. It is a perfectly arguable proposition, for example (and one which these economic critics could accept), that, if the Labour party were to be returned to power tomorrow, the effect, regardless of anything which the Government might do, would be an immediate collapse of the pound simply as a result of the loss of foreign confidence. If this is so, the error of trying to separate economic and political considerations for the purpose of any argument about either is patent.

SOCIALIST CRITICS

There is, after all, only one practical choice before the country at the moment, and it must now be stated. It is the choice between the Government and the Opposition.

The Labour party is at a very crucial stage in its development and it is facing a problem which frequently afflicts so-called progressive parties in this country, the problem of trying to decide what to do next after all of their social objectives which the country can be expected to endure have been achieved. It is the same sort of problem that faced 'Finality John', Lord John Russell, after the great Reform Bill in 1832. Lord John Russell had both quieted the fears of his opponents and confirmed his own faith by thinking himself into the position that once this reform was carried out Utopia would have arrived. But once Utopia has arrived what becomes of the 'party of progress'? If you live by the doctrine that heaven is round the corner, you must be very careful never to get there.

So it is with the Labour party today. They got into power in 1945 having saddled themselves with a clear-cut programme of nationalisation, most of which it proved possible to carry into effect before the public's patience was finally exhausted. They went on with the assurance of a somnambulist, nationalising one industry after the other with a valiant disregard for all the distracting circumstances of life like inflation and the dollar gap, and then they went to the electorate with the proud assertion, 'We are a party that keeps its promises.' Of course, they were immensely surprised when the electorate responded with the ungracious but characteristic exclamation 'Would to God that you weren't!' (The electorate is an exacting mate; it often finds fidelity more trying than caprice.) What was the Labour party to do? Was it to say 'The glorious revolution has arrived, it is our business to defend it', or was it to think up a new destination towards which to proceed? The first course was out of keeping with the vocation of the 'party of progress'. But the second course also presented acute difficulties: it is all very well to go forward in politics, but 'forward' is not a political term, it is a description of a spatial relationship, and if the only direction you know about is blocked by a sullenly indignant sovereign people, you have to think up a new direction.

This is what the Labour party has been trying to do. In the process, because of its rationalist tradition, it has to preserve its reputation for intellectual consistency. Socialists think that politics consists of meditating in the abstract about what is good for Man, and then having a quick glance at the world as it is in order to find out how much of this you can persuade particular men to put up with. The Socialist, therefore, does not improvise gracefully. When something goes wrong, he goes back into the study, gets down the books, refreshes his mind as to his eternal principles, has another quick glance at the world and decides what the current expression of these principles should be. So it was with the Labour party when, after one narrow defeat and then a big one, it started to appoint committees to debate such fascinating intellectual questions as the nature of personal freedom and social equality. Labour does not fiddle while Rome burns; it sits down to write a thesis for its doctorate of music by the light of the flames.

First of all, Labour has tried to put itself right with the electorate by announcing that it is against Big Brother Bureaucracy. It has obliged young Mr. Wedgwood Benn to write a series of fatuous letters to Government departments (without revealing his identity) in order to complain of their being treated in a manner more appropriate to the outpourings of other institutions than the House of Commons. Subsequently it has published the view that civil servants should behave politely.

This done, the Labour party has asserted its belief in equality as distinct from nationalisation. It has for long been apparent that the only possible way of approaching more nearly to equality of income was to penalise still further those who earn reasonably high rewards by actual service to the community, the already much depleted £2,000 to £4,000 a year group. This most Socialists know to be fatal, so they have had to content themselves with a series of obscure but official threats, and for the rest, with magnifying abuses further up the scale. The *New Statesman and Nation*, for example, thinks that too much money is spent on chocolate cake for the royal garden parties and that too good a time this season has been enjoyed by débutantes; and then, of course, there is always the conspicuous consumption of some industrialist's wife to decry. As Mr. Anthony Crosland admits, if all these supposedly offensive perquisites were divided up among everybody, it would amount to nothing ('To make the rich less rich would not make the poor significantly less poor', he pointed out in the July 1956 issue of *Encounter*); so the case for equality is now openly a case for levelling down.

Another device is to suggest that the Tories have a wicked plot for creating new inequalities which must be anticipated. Mr. John Strachey, in his very honest book *Contemporary Capitalism* (Gollancz, 1956), tries hard but unsuccessfully with this; being obliged to admit, with some understatement, that Sir Anthony Eden, Mr. Butler and Mr. Macmillan are not the counter-revolutionary types. He is, in fact, unable to find any more awe-inspiring thugs to engage the attention of militant democracy than Lord Percy of Newcastle and myself. I am accused on page 271 of having demonstrated 'the scope and width of Conservative anti-democratic reaction', though Mr. Strachey has the grace to add that this reaction is as yet confined to the 'highly intellectual circles' in which he pays me the ambiguous compliment of supposing me to move. What I have said about democracy, and what, over a far longer period and with infinitely more distinction Lord Percy of Newcastle has said, is that it cannot be assumed to be infallible, to be exempt from greed, envy and stupidity, and that it needs criticism as much as any other form of government. As targets of the new social revolution, we are not a patch on the débutantes.

Thus, in the end, the Labour party has been driven back on the one thing it knows about, nationalisation. This is to be accomplished without consulting the electorate, by taking over shares in industry in lieu of death duties.

Honesty requires the admission that it cannot be assumed that in practice the Labour party would get far with this policy. It is also the business of an Opposition to have a policy and it may be excused for looking hard for one. It is not my business to play Mr. Gaitskell's hand for him, but like all believers in parliamentary government I have an interest in his hand's being played well, and the reason why it is not being played well is largely as follows. Mr. Gaitskell has seen that the world has changed, so he has gone back to his study and consulted his books, and, not surprisingly, he has found in them an outmoded principle. His flexibility is confined to calling it a new name ('mutualisation' or 'municipalisation' or something odious of the kind) and thinking up a new way of putting it into practice without being noticed. This is a pity. He should not have retreated from reality; he should have submerged himself in it.

The dominant reality about our politics and our economics today is this: we must have full employment or something near it, and we must have much less inflation and much steadier prices than we have had in most of the post-war years so far. There are some who say that these two requirements are incompatible, and that one of the factors in the problem (full employment) should be crossed out, and resort made to the self-regulating economy. There are others who say that these two can be reconciled only by applying the principle of social organisation sufficiently, and having a powerful State armed with and deploying the kind of controls we became accustomed to in war. My contention is that both these sets of people – the whole-hogging capitalists and the whole-hogging Socialists – are not merely wrong, but are committing the ultimate offence against the free society. They are forgetting that a free society in its very nature consists of everlasting tensions and conflicts, and is, in its essence, an attempt to strike a balance between incompatibles. The Conservative party has been faithful to its tradition in trying to prove both these sets of arguments wrong, and in trying – by the right mixture of fiscal controls and voluntary restraint, and the right timing – to create a state of affairs where the choice between an economic free-for-all and a bureaucratic tyranny will not have to be made.

I am not saying that its policy has always been right in detail, or that it has always presented its policy with sufficient clarity and authority. I am saying that its policy has the right theme, and that it is being attacked in the main by bodies of doctrinaires who want politics to be very simple and by a handful of aesthetes who want it to be very exciting.

Liberty or equality

Published in *Liberty in the Modern State*, 1957

Equality is an idea which must have considerable emotional appeal at all times and in all places. There will always be inequality, and there will therefore always be people who would benefit by a greater degree of equality. Envy being a universal emotion, there is, in all states of society, something to be said for putting forward an egalitarian political programme. This is the first reason for the Labour party's policy statement *Towards Equality*. The second reason for it is that politicians always find it useful to generate a vague feeling that there are an awful lot of abuses going on, even though you cannot put your finger on them. The third reason is that it has now become absolutely essential for the Labour party to find something to talk about instead of nationalisation.

There is no political party and no group of political thinkers, however remote from reality, which supposes that you can achieve absolute flat equality in any respect or sphere. The traditional, academic definition of equality, the only intelligible meaning which the word can be given, is the absence of irrelevant distinctions. The problem upon which the discussion of equality hinges is how to apply the proper test of what consitutes irrelevant distinctions. There are two general views about this. One view is that you must have a single, sovereign, universal principle of selection which will tell you where everybody ought to be in society and how long they ought to stay there. The other view is that society is of its nature complex and human beings are various, and that accordingly no society which tries to build itself on one single principle of selection can prosper, or in the last resort even survive.

It is the second of these views which we as Tories maintain, and it is the first of these views which, in all their successive incarnations, the so-called 'progressives' in English politics have maintained. At the beginning of the 19th century, it was the 'progressive' view that lucrative posts and all the plums should be reserved for people who had shown that they could buy in the cheapest market and sell in the dearest. Nowadays, the 'progressive' view, as you will see if you analyse Mr. Crosland's recent articles in *Encounter*, is, in effect though not in words, that the great principle of equality is that lucrative posts should be reserved for university dons. Each generation of 'progressives' produces its own acid test for choosing the social *Herrenvolk*, its own simple, sovereign principle for organising society and apportioning its rewards properly. If you are anything of a sceptic, you must doubt very much whether any one of these principles is likely to be universally and generally valid.

Of course, none of this appears on the surface. For a great deal of the time, in fact, this Socialist pamphlet on equality is trying to pretend that there is no need for any principle of selection in society. The argument, in the long section it contains on education, is that it is very wicked to choose people by a competitive examination at the age of eleven. Thus the Labour party publicly resists the assertion that what it means by equality is the imposition of a uniform test. It does so because it is appealing to the underdog, and even in a society based on equality of opportunity the majority of people will still be in the category of underdogs; the only difference is that their superiors will claim that their superiority is founded upon ampler talent and virtue, never on accidents like inheritance or so on. That may be more offensive or less offensive to the common mind, but the thing will remain as it is.

This question has very little to do with the amount of economic inequality which is permitted. You all know how much we have been able to progress towards the ideal, or the trough, of complete economic equality of income under a formally capitalist economy. Under a formally capitalist economy you leave your saving to be done by private persons, and you then take the rewards of it away from them in the interest of equality. Under a Socialist economy you have your saving compulsorily organised by Government departments, and civil servants are paid for controlling the national policy of investment. A Socialist economy is capable of very considerable degrees of inequality, not only of inequality of income, but what is more important of inequality of power. A capitalist economy is capable of being organised by the operation of taxation in such a way as to produce a substantial measure of financial equality.

The question, then, is whether you have one means of choosing your élite, or whether you have several; whether you have a world in which everything is reserved for people who have passed a particular competitive examination and then subsequently advanced from the cradle towards grave responsibilities on the civil service model, or a world in which there is a variety of different means of getting to the top. That really is the problem of equality in a nutshell. It is to conceal that formulation of the problem that 'progressive' propaganda in every age is devised; our task is to expose that propaganda by putting these comparatively simple considerations forward.

Now if you are trying to achieve equality, by which, as I have shown, I mean a regulated system of inequalities governed by a single principle of selection, you can only do it by an extension of public authority. The extension of public authority is the one idea the Labour party has got. It is a bad idea. It is electorally a hopeless idea, and they recognise this. But it is really the only idea they have. They all hoped for something more; they appointed all these committees to see what more there might be. But they have shown in their pamphlet on equality just how intellectually bankrupt they are. For towards the end of that pamphlet, when you come to the peroration against inherited wealth, you will see a proposal to the effect that, in order to destroy this monstrous source of unearned privilege in society, the Inland Revenue, instead of taking death duties in money, should be able to take the death duties in shares and land. In other words, that they should be able to nationalise the industry of the country piecemeal and to do so in such a way as will avoid the possible embarrassments of parliamentary discussion. That is really the only thing in the way of a concrete proposal which emerges – the proposal that the State should gradually extend, in oblique and indirect ways, which will be protected from the danger of public controversy, its control to an ever-larger sector of the national wealth.

Of course, any thorough-going Socialist is perfectly right to make this proposal, because if you really want to organise society in such a way as to apportion all its rewards and settle all disputes within it according to one sovereign principle, then the only way to do it is to have one sovereign power applying that principle, and that power is the bureaucracy. You reduce yourself again to what dear old Sir Waldron Smithers used to say, that it really was a choice between one thing and the other.

Now it is not a stark choice, because in politics there never is, and in the politics of free societies there never ought to be, a stark choice. But it is an important intellectual decision to make. Do you want your society to be organised in accordance with some single governing conception, although that conception may only be the result of an intellectual fashion lasting for fifty years? Or do you want it to be organised on a much more complicated basis with a much greater degree of variety? If you want order, and if you want simplicity and the application of a single principle, then it follows as the night the day that you must have the authority, and that, in proportion as you wish to impose that principle, you must vest in those who are charged with interpreting it very large powers over the rest of the community. The ultimate reason of most true Liberals for being Liberals and of most Conservatives for being Conservatives is that they do not want that degree of uniformity thus imposed.

When we come to the question of what we mean by liberty we might (particularly if we had been brought up in this university and not in the other one), let ourselves in for a great deal of metaphysical speculation and such fascinating questions as whether people should be forcibly prevented from crossing bridges which it is known will break under them, and so forth. But if, like Edmund Burke, you detest the very sound of these metaphysical things, what you will ask yourself when you come to the definition of liberty is: What are the characteristics of a free society? We have arrived at one negative characteristic already, namely that it is not a society based upon uniformity imposed from above. What are its positive characteristics? Here, I think, there are more difficulties, because some of the positive characteristics of a free society make demands upon the character and are, therefore, not particularly popular. One of the perennial characteristics of a free society, for example, is that there are tensions within that society. If you are constantly feeling that you want to live in the kind of world where there are no disputes or none which cannot easily be settled by a straightforward administrative organ, then you will not want to live in a free society. If you want to live in a free society then you have to reconcile yourself to an apparently never-ending series of perpetual tensions. The whole business of government will be to hold the reins and to see that these tensions are properly and peacefully managed, and that one group or class does not establish its ascendancy over the rest. This imposes upon statesmanship a very heavy burden, and it imposes upon citizenship an extraordinarily difficult task of tolerance and restraint. So there are always excellent temptations for not wanting to belong to a free society; and it is always profitable in politics to give the impression that you can get a free society without having these inconveniences and these tensions and these problems of statesmanship.

But you cannot; because one of the most outstanding permanent characteristics of a free society will undoubtedly be the fact that its people want incompatible policies simultaneously. If you are a journalist, you can make a living by writing articles every week pointing out that the things that people want are not reconcilable with each other, and that if only people were intelligent they would not want these incompatible objects. But that is not a useful exercise in statesmanship at all. The beginning of wisdom in statesmanship, the essence of having breathed the air of politics at all, is to know that this thing is natural, and that this is what it will always be like.

Look at England since 1945. The real problems which have beset this country have had nothing, or very little, to do with the problems that have been publicly ventilated; on the contrary, the real problem which has beset this country since 1945 is a problem which, by common consent and as part almost of the very foundations of the British Constitution, it has until yesterday been improper to mention in public. That problem is whether you can reconcile the aims of the Welfare State, which implies and demands full employment, with an efficient economy, including the absence of inflation (without which, in the last resort, the Welfare State itself cannot be sustained). This has been the real dilemma. The point which I am putting to you is that such dilemmas, such incompatibilities of demand, are things which have to be managed in a free society, and that however we get round them it will not be simply by trying to abolish them.

This is not, at the moment, a particularly fashionable view among intellectuals. There appear, as far as I can see, to be three main trends of intellectual thought about British politics going on at the moment. First of all, there is the attitude which was so brilliantly represented in a recent anonymous article in *The Times Literary Supplement* called 'The Dynamic Society'; it was the old *laissez-faire* argument very ably stated. And do not suppose that this old *laissez-faire* argument is something which is simply an easy way out for the rich: it is not. Capitalism is a religion which makes extremely earnest demands on people, whether they are rich or poor; and if *This England* likes to have that comment next week it can do so, because it is perfectly true. When you talk to somebody, for example, in the motor industry who has just had to sack a lot of men and feels that the credit squeeze is pressing him out of business, he immediately blames the Government for this situation. Capitalists are always ready to invoke State power or to criticise the abuse of State power when they are in difficulties. It is very easy to throw overboard the pure doctrine of capitalism which makes immense demands. In order to believe in unfettered capitalism you have to be a person who prefers chance and enterprise to security, and this is one of the rarest of human qualities.

I am not commending this pure capitalist approach; I am merely saying that it is one of the approaches offered by an intelligent wing of opinion at the moment, and this intelligent wing of opinion says, though in infinitely less transparent words: 'Look here, it is absolutely incompatible to have full employment and an efficient economy without inflation.

Therefore cross out one of the factors in the problem. Cross out full employment, get back to reality, and to an automatic self-regulating economy'. This type of person argues in favour of what you might call an abstract view of the nature of man and his relationship to the economic organisation of society. These people think they know the things to which man responds, profit and loss, and they have a universal scheme.

At the other extreme there are those who say that these incompatibilities of a free society, such as this demand for full employment, on the one hand, and for efficiency and an absence of inflation on the other hand, can only be reconciled by applying the principle of social organisation sufficiently and by having an all-powerful State directing the economy as it did in war-time. There are people on the Left of the Labour party who believe that, and those people also are exponents of an abstract and universal doctrine. They know about Man; they know the principles which will provide a clue to the solution of how man's economic activities are to be organised.

My contention is that both these sets of people are committing the ultimate offence against the free society; they are forgetting that a free society in its nature consists of contending groups and, in its nature, is an attempt to strike a balance between incompatibles. They are committing the first sin against politics; they are trying to impose order, simplicity and, in a naïve sense, rationality on affairs to which none of these things properly applies.

There is another group to which I must briefly allude, which consists of those who rely neither upon the capitalist solution nor upon the Socialist solution but who want both, in the sense that both are aesthetically attractive. In that group I put all those people who do not really mind what happens so long as it is good fun, so long as we are all at each other's throats in a really exhilarating way with none of this namby-pamby nonsense of all trying to agree and stop revolution and civil war. That is an approach to politics, but it is not one which is likely to achieve a very wide acceptance; it is an aesthetic view, a view of persons who are not soiled with power; it is essentially a view of people who are there to watch. But the two serious views, the view that you do it all by free enterprise, and the view that you do it all by State control – those are the two which are incompatible with the nature of a free society.

The Conservative party has been faithful to its tradition in trying to prove both these sets of arguments wrong, and in trying – by the right mixture of fiscal controls and voluntary restraint, and the right timing – to create a state of affairs where the choice between an economic free-for-all and a bureaucratic tyranny will not have to be made. It is an extremely difficult task. But there seems to me to be one thing about which the Conservative party ought not to make any mistake. If we fail in this effort to find the middle way which is essential to the free society, then we will not get the solution of unfettered free enterprise instead; we will get the opposite solution. We will get some sort of an economic crisis overtaking us, and in such a situation the really easy thing to do always is to resort to the brute force of the State and have controls back again.

From all this I would draw a holy trinity of morals. First of all, equality, as understood by 'progressive' persons, means in practice the imposition of a single test of social selection instead of the allowance of several. Secondly, liberty can be preserved in the management of the affairs of a society, which in its very nature is divided and the subject of tensions, only by compromise. Thirdly, if the Conservative party, which traditionally from Burke onwards has acknowledged this second truth, should ever forget it, we shall get, not some glorious free enterprise Utopia, but the Socialist bureaucratic tyranny which we have been trying to avoid.

What laws may cure
A new examination of morals and the law
1968

> *Of all the ills that human hearts endure,*
> *How small that part which laws may cause or cure.*

Those lines, widely and falsely attributed to Samuel Johnson and in fact written by Oliver Goldsmith, used to represent one of the most important ingredients in Tory thinking. Today, most Tories would feel inclined to qualify them. Laws may be capable of doing little good, but we have learnt that they are powerful engines of evil, of consequences which their authors never intended or foresaw but which press hardly and deeply into the lives of ordinary people.

By a curious convention of British politics, those ordinances which affect most intimately the life of the subject are least likely to have been authorised by any kind of popular mandate. We assume nowadays that politics should normally be concerned almost exclusively with the distribution of wealth. At regular intervals, we present the public with more or less clearly defined choices about how the balance of payments crisis should be tackled and about what type of taxation system we should have. On such points, the organised political parties take up their stands, publish their manifestos and offer more or less coherent alternatives to the electorate. It is between these alternatives rather than between the individual merits of candidates that electors decide when they cast their votes – and woe betide those politicians who, having got themselves to Westminster, deviate from the commitments of their party as interpreted by their party's leaders on such matters as these. Deviations there are, but they must be authorised and enforced from above. By this means, the electorate is given some kind of intermittent control over one part of its own destinies. It may decide wrongly or it may be wantonly deceived, but it gives the imprimatur of its approval to certain broadly described policies, and it always has the chance of eventually taking revenge on any who have fraudulently secured that approval. In these spheres, there is a discernible element of popular consent.

In striking contrast to this, laws affecting the more intimate areas of life – the relations of married couples, the rights of men to make physical love to each other and the rights of unborn children – are almost wholly removed from popular control. All the political parties classify such matters as issues of conscience to which it is improper to apply the party whip. When such questions arise at Westminster, the MP suddenly becomes possessed of an unaccustomed freedom. He can speak and even vote as he likes.

It is true, of course, that he still has his constituents to contend with. They may write him rude letters and threaten to withdraw their support from him at the next election. In practice, however, the electoral fate of comparatively few MPs is decisively affected by their views on these questions of private morality and of the proper relationship between it and the law. When polling day comes, the central question, defined by the political establishment on both sides, will dominate the scene, and the maxim that votes should be cast for parties not men will in general prevail.

As a result, vast areas of legislative activity are effectively removed from popular control. The House of Commons, acting independently of the electorate and with the now only negligible restraints imposed by the Lords, can revise the conditions of marriage, the laws affecting homosexual behaviour, the rules which determine who can and who cannot be legally given an abortion and the institution of Sunday observance.

When the history of Britain since 1964 comes to be written, it may well be judged that, during this period, the quality of English life was changed less fundamentally by the nationalisation of steel or the activities of the Prices and Incomes Board than by a number of Private Members' Acts which have received no kind of sanction, however oblique, from the sovereign people. It is certainly true that most of this legislation would not have been possible without some measure of aid from the Government in supplying time for its discussion in Parliament and even in applying to members the moral pressure which arises from the knowledge that a bill is unofficially approved by most members of the administration. In matters of morals the prevailing trend of Socialist opinion has been permissive, and this has been an important factor in our affairs. Neither Government nor Opposition, however, has formally committed itself to either side in this great national controversy. Could it not be fairly argued that, for better or for worse, the English allow those of their laws which most closely affect their private behaviour to be settled by an oligarchy?

Some of the dangers of this arrangement may be inevitable. It may well be that Members of Parliament, so easily coerced over other matters, will not abandon the few remaining areas in which their consciences are respected. It may also be that our legislation about private morality is infinitely more intelligent and humane than it would be if it arose spontaneously from popular prejudice instead of embodying the views of a relatively civilised minority. Yet there are perils in the gulf which could easily arise between laws and the moral sentiments of the people who have to obey them. May there not also be practical advantages, at least to the Conservative party, in trying to achieve, if not an enforced orthodoxy on these matters, then at least a broad consensus informed by the many relevant elements in its tradition of political thought?

THE CONSERVATIVE DILEMMA

Certainly, that task will not be easy. In these matters, as in so many other respects, the historic Conservative party speaks with two distinct voices. The principles it proposes are complex and often apparently self-contradictory. There is, in the first place, the old voice of Tory paternalism which may be heard in the prayer-book petition that the Queen and her magistrates shall receive the divine Grace which they need in order to execute justice 'to the punishment of wickedness and vice and the maintenance of thy true religion and virtue'. The language comes from an age in which Church and State were regarded as different aspects of the same entity, and in which the law assumed that all loyal subjects were by definition conforming members of the established Church. Yet, its echoes can still be heard in contemporary controversy. The notion that, if the function of the State is not precisely to make men good, then at least it is to establish the conditions in which they will be helped to be good and to present them constantly with a pattern of what constitutes good living, is far from wholly extinct. Today, it receives less direct and more sophisticated expression in such maxims as these: society is not just a collection of isolated atoms, but is held together by a common moral tradition which the law must express and maintain. How can the laws be obeyed if they are not loved, and how can they be loved if they flout or even fail to assert the deepest moral convictions of the people? Or, on a more practical plane, there are such complaints as these: 'A few years ago, I could tell my son as he went away to school that homosexuality was an offence so terrible that the State sometimes punished those who committed it with life-long imprisonment. Today, I can only tell him that it is something of which old-fashioned people like myself strongly disapprove. Can anyone doubt the profound effect which this change in the law is going to have on human behaviour?'

On the other hand, there is the equally strong authentic note struck by the liberal elements in the Conservative tradition represented, for instance, by Burke's admonition to Government that it must tolerate frailties until they have festered into crimes. How can a party which is so deeply concerned with the dangers of State interference in economic affairs look with favour on the intrusions of government into far more intimate sectors of life? If freedom in the conduct of wage negotiations is sacred, how much more sacred is freedom in the conduct of love affairs? What right have men to impose their own standards on each other? Even on the highest view of the ends of government, what scope would there be for true virtue in a society which enforced all moral obligations under pain of imprisonment or death? Have not the worst tyrannies in history, like Calvin's Geneva, been the work of men convinced that it was their divine duty to enforce goodness and punish wickedness?

The truth is that there are very few sane and moderate men who honestly consider these things today without being painfully torn between these conflicting traditions. There are of course the professional extremists – men who think that there is a simple choice between maintaining the traditional virtues and opening the flood-gates to a moral revolution which will install sexual promiscuity, homosexuality and obscenity and blasphemy in speech and conversation, as the normal social conventions. There are also extremists who believe with equal passion in the virtues of moral innovation and who, starting from the dogma that the supreme aim of government is to preserve individual freedom, are in practice conspicuously less concerned with the freedom of those who favour traditional ways than with giving unlimited rein to moral experimenters. As a result of both these extremes, it has become fashionable to speak as though there were a clear-cut choice between favouring tradition or permissiveness, as though a man who favours legalising homosexuality between consenting adults is in logic bound also to favour abortion by consent or the free provision of contraceptives to adolescents. This dichotomy is unreal, and repugnant in particular to the whole spirit of Conservative thinking. The criteria for deciding when the State should and should not interfere in private morals are of a far more subtle and complex kind.

LIBERTY AND LAW

To an extent which is not generally realised, current controversy on the whole question of the relationship between legislation and morality is still dominated by the thinking of the 19th-century liberal intellectual, John Stuart Mill. Mill started with the simple, clear-cut proposition that human actions could be divided into two categories, self-regarding and other-regarding. In the first category came all those actions which affected only those who took them; in the second, actions which produced an effect on society. Since liberty was a good wherever possible to be preserved, it followed that self-regarding actions were wholly outside the proper sphere of the State. A man's liberty could only reasonably be curtailed in order to protect the liberty of others. It could never be right to coerce him for his own good.

Mill spent much of his life painfully exploring and struggling with the difficulties which this beautifully simple doctrine presented as soon as he attempted to apply it to concrete cases. Could it really be assumed utterly wrong in all circumstances to restrain a man's actions for the sake of safeguarding his own interests? Is it proper to prevent a man from crossing a bridge which one knows would collapse if anyone stepped on it? Is the right to commit suicide a natural right?

The trouble was that liberty is not a simple concept. An individual's acts of free will often contradict each other. The passionate desire to get drunk and equally passionate wish to avoid a hangover are often irreconcilable: which should take precedence? It is common to find individuals voluntarily limiting their own freedom, submitting to some kind of external authority which, on the whole, they believe will promote their own happiness more than it would be promoted by the instant gratification of each of their inclinations. Is the freedom of a drug addict really more curtailed by submitting him to a compulsory cure than by allowing him to become incurable?

The difficulties of drawing a line between what affects the individual and what affects society proved equally hard. It is scarcely possible to conceive of any act so private that it produces no impact on others. If the impact is sufficiently damaging, there will be a case for State intervention. Many have started with Mill's principles and found that, without ever contradicting them, it is possible to justify vast public intrusions into private life.

Mill was inspired by the worthy idea of keeping legislation within reasonable bounds. He soon found, however, that there were large areas of life which, though they seemed quite unsuitable for legislative interference, could not tolerably be abandoned to the competition of private whims and interests. He fell back on the idea that what the State could not suitably do in such cases might be done by the pressure of public opinion. Clearly, much useful social behaviour arises neither from spontaneous devotion to society nor from fear of government, but rather from fear of social disapproval. As Mill's critics pointed out, however, this did not really help much with the problem of liberty. The psychological pressures exerted by neighbours could be just as tyrannical and far less predictable than those exerted by governments acting through known laws, interpreted by impartial courts.

What the majority of Mill's critics found insupportable, however, was the suggestion that his principles could be used as a bar to the prohibition of certain kinds of gross vice, the effects of which could not possibly be confined to those who practised them but which must spread like a contagion through society. The emotions which this aspect of his thinking aroused are well illustrated in this quotation from one of the sternest and most acute of his opponents, Sir James Fitzjames Stephen, who thus parodies Mill talking to a pimp:

> Without offence to your better judgement, dear Sir, and without presuming to set up my opinion against yours, I beg to observe that I am entitled for certain purposes to treat the question of whether your views of life are right as one which admits of two opinions. I am far from expressing absolute condemnation of an experiment in living from which I dissent (I am sure that mere dissent will not offend a person of your liberty of sentiment), but still I am compelled to observe that you are not altogether unbiased by personal considerations in the choice of the course of life which you have adopted (no doubt for reasons which appear to you satisfactory, though they do not convince me). I venture accordingly, though with the greatest deference, to call upon you not to exercise your profession; at least I am not indisposed to think that I may, upon full consideration, feel myself compelled to do so.

This parody is of course grossly unfair. It shows, however, the impatience of a highly intelligent and practical man (an Indian administrator, a judge and a historian of the criminal law) at Mill's view that it was possible to construct a philosophy of government starting from the premise that individuals were isolated beings and going on to the view that the whole art of statecraft consisted in delimiting little areas of privacy within which they could be allowed to cultivate their own garden. Stephen believed, on the other hand, that every society has its own conception of the good life and that it was proper to use political power to promote that conception. He was fully conscious, however, of the dangers of extreme authoritarianism which such a doctrine carried. How did he deal with them?

In considering legislation on an issue of private morals, he argued, the State should ask precisely the same kind of question and make the same kind of calculation as in legislating about any other subject. Obviously, the first consideration was whether the end which the new law promised to promote was in itself a good or bad end. The second consideration was whether, assuming it to be good, it was so good as to counteract the inevitable disadvantage of making a new law at all, i.e. the disadvantage of restricting the sphere of freedom and enlarging the territory of social life subject to coercion.

WHO DECIDES?

It seems to me that these principles should be the starting point of all our thinking about legislation to do with the conduct of private life. There are moral ends which it is perfectly proper to defend or promote by the use of legislative power, and some of them are of a kind which concern extremely intimate activities. It is not true that the happiness of the people and the quality of a society's life is wholly unaffected, for example, by such factors as its marriage customs or the extent to which its members are addicted to drug taking or homosexual practices. It may be that marriage is a bad institution, that drug taking and homosexuality are either morally neutral or positively virtuous activities, but it cannot be said that these things belong to a department of life which produces no social effects and which is consequently and obviously outside the legitimate sphere of State activity. We shall think much more soberly, rationally and constructively about all these controversies if we begin by ridding ourselves of the temptingly simple solution which Mill offered.

Yet, it is clear that there are particular difficulties in legislating about personal morals. To begin with, who is to decide what morals should be enforced? This is indeed only one part of the large and perennial question in political thought. Who has a right to decide anything? No doubt, the constitutional answer is that in a democracy the decision rests with the majority; yet, particularly where deep and highly personal convictions are concerned, the democracy must do its best to respect minorities. An unusually large consensus of opinion is needed to make legislation on such matters tolerable or even practical. To take a practical instance: a politician faced with the problem of whether or not to support Mr. Steel's recent Abortion Bill cannot, even in the first instance, confine himself to asking whether his conscience tells him that abortion is or is not acceptable. He must consider what the general public body of opinion is on this subject. He must consider himself rather as the interpreter of the national conscience in so far as there is one than as the people's moral mentor.

Morals are not static. We are all tempted to confuse them with ethics. The most rigid of practising Christians, for example, is bound to admit that the teaching of the Church on such questions as the legitimacy of usury has changed drastically throughout the centuries. What is more, if he is a rational man, he must also admit that these changes have not necessarily been the result of human weakness and fallibility so much as the result of the perennial need to adapt constant principles to changing circumstances.

Even when the rule does not in itself change, the precise degree of importance which attaches to the breaking of it may not remain constant. *Pace* the Bishop of Woolwich, it is hard to see how a Christian, without gross infidelity to the sources of his religion, can take the view that pre-marital unchastity need no longer be regarded, in an absolute sense, as wrong. Yet, there is no reason on earth why a Christian should not admit that the moral importance of this offence has been considerably altered by the invention of effective contraceptive devices. Those who legislate about morals, even those who preach about morals, ought to look closely at the societies for which they are legislating or which they are exhorting.

Suppose, however, that a firm consensus of opinion on the extreme importance of discouraging some private activity deemed to be immoral has been discovered. Suppose that it is widely felt that the continuing practice of this activity damages the whole quality of social life and causes ever-growing human misery. Other conditions have still to be satisfied before a wise legislator can decide to bring the brute force of law to bear on those who persist in defying social convention.

He has in the first place to ask himself whether any law he may decide to make can be enforced, or enforced with enough impartiality and constancy to stop its becoming an intolerable affront to the principle of legal equality. Failing this, he has at least to be sure that the presence of this unenforceable law on the statute book will in fact produce a favourable effect on human behaviour, that it will perform the functions of a sermon rather than a threat. If the law is to be made, it must also be established that the cost of enforcing it in terms of human happiness and virtue is not so great as to offset the merits of enforcing it.

These calculations are never easy and can seldom be made with complete certainty. An even harder judgement is involved in distinguishing between activities which can be safely regarded as wholly deplorable and those which, however much they may offend current sentiment and however bad their contemporary effects may be, may nevertheless contain potentialities for good. Most experiments in thought and living are initially somewhat grotesque in character; society has often come to value things which it originally regarded as destructive and abominable. What liberals who assert this principle often forget, however, is that the innovations which have survived and sometimes come to be regarded as valuable elements in civilisation are those which have withstood the test of popular criticism. We remember the heresies which have matured into orthodoxy, the experiments which were once persecuted and have come to be revered. We forget the numerous aberrations, absurdities and quackish remedies which have fallen by the wayside and which, but for the sometimes healthy force of public intolerance, might have destroyed society or stultified progress.

ISSUES OF PRINCIPLE
These principles are abstract enough, but it is my purpose here to indicate the questions to be asked about this particularly

delicate and complex kind of legislation rather than to prescribe the answers they should get. The one fact which surely does emerge clearly is that legislation about morals, which so often raises passionate controversy, is peculiarly unsuitable for the attentions of either confirmed, professional 'reactionaries' or confirmed, undiscriminating 'progressives'. We could, I am convinced, have spared ourselves a good deal of emotion and reached, on various matters, much sounder conclusions had this truth been recognised.

Take, for instance, the controversy which ended with the passing of the Sexual Offences Act 1967. There can be very little doubt that there is in this country a strong consensus against homosexuality; the practising homosexual is still regarded with some degree of instinctive horror, and there are virtually no parents who would not go to almost any length to ensure that their sons did not become homosexuals. Had the object of legalising homosexual acts been to promote the practice of homosexuality as an experiment in living, the Bill would have been unimaginable.

As it was, the question was whether the old law did anything to discourage homosexuality and, if so, at what cost this was achieved. Sexual inclinations once formed do not easily respond to even the direst threats of punishment. One object of punishment, the reform of the criminal, could in this case be said to be positively frustrated by the kind of punishment imposed. What better way of fostering spreading homosexuality than incarcerating those who are addicted to it in one-sex prisons! The cruelty and ineffectiveness of the punishments were equalled only by their arbitrariness. It was a scandal that some, aided by good fortune, should be able to practise this vice with impunity while others went to prison for it. The homosexual was also particularly exposed to blackmail, and the old law, in failing to suppress one sort of corruption, encouraged another.

Only one respectable argument against the Bill was ever raised. It was felt that the very presence of the old Act on the Statute Book was a token of public abhorrence of this vice and that, in the course possibly of decades, its removal would produce a slackening in private morals. Since the Bill also provided for a considerable increase in the penalties for seducing the young, it seemed to Parliament that the rather nebulous and long-term objection to it was overwhelmingly offset by the amount of useless and corrupting misery which it would prevent. I am sure that Parliament was right.

I do not think the issues of principle were nearly so clearly considered in the case of Mr. Steel's Abortion Act. This arose at least in part from the unwillingness of many of the Bill's supporters to formulate clearly the main question which it presented – is abortion acceptable on social as distinct from medical and technically psychiatric grounds?

The Bill had three distinct aims. The first was to make the responsibilities of doctors and their liabilities much clearer than they were as a result of Mr. Justice McNaughton's famous judgement in the 1930s. A law which imposes severe penalties ought certainly to be predictable. The second was to end the state of affairs in which a rich woman could get an abortion competently performed while a poor woman could not, a state of affairs which was objectionable on grounds of legal equality. The third and closely related object was to put an end to what are believed to be the vast numbers of illicit abortions dangerously carried out by amateurs.

These were in themselves worthy objectives, but it is not clear that the Act will fulfil them. How can a court be expected to decide whether a doctor has acted in good faith in deciding that an abortion is necessary 'to the mental and physical health' of other children in the family? Do we think that abortion should be acceptable purely on grounds of social convenience, and how should that phrase be interpreted?

It is not at all clear that as a result of this reform doctors can be any more sure of their rights than they used to be, nor is it clear that illegal abortions will diminish. There is still far too much confusion about which ought and which ought not to be legal. It may be that the lines of demarcation cannot be laid down precisely by the law itself. In this case, there would have been much to be said for an amendment favoured by the House of Lords which proposed that abortions should be sanctioned and carried out only by a panel of approved doctors.

It is equally doubtful whether the principal moral question presented by the reform of the Divorce Law now being proposed has been properly put. That question is whether we regard marriage merely as a contract between two individuals to be terminated by mutual consent when it is no longer desired by either, or whether the community as such has an interest in preserving the institution. There can be no doubt that public opinion is still overwhelmingly in favour of life-long marriage as the normal social rule, and that the institution of the family is still regarded as an essential element in our social arrangements. Equally, it is clear that public opinion is now predominantly in favour of allowing the dissolution of marriages which have irretrievably broken down when dissolution can be brought about with proper regard to the interests of both parties. It may well be that a separation of five years does constitute proof of irretrievable breakdown, even when one party still wishes to assert his or her rights over the other. It is quite indefensible, however, to suggest that two years' separation accompanied by mutual consent is proof that there is no future in a marriage. What, in such intimate circumstances, really constitutes free consent? Even if it could be established that in the present conditions of the law most couples who had been separated for two years never came together again, it certainly cannot be established that if the marriage bond could be legally dissolved by such separation many a couple who at present succeed in sticking together would not accept defeat long before it had really happened.

Yet another principle is involved in the current controversy over the right to buy and use soft drugs. Respectable medical and sociological opinion is still divided over the question of whether the use of such drugs leads inevitably or generally to the use of hard drugs. What is certain is that the current craze for drugs is part of a general movement of cultural protest, a movement which seems to even relatively unbiased observers to protest against society itself. It may be (though I am inclined to think that it is not) that some elements in this protest will eventually be recognised as valuable and will become incorporated in the culture of civilised countries. In its present manifestations, however, this movement is something which no one concerned to maintain any kind of social cohesion can regard without horror and abhorrence. It may be that in 50 years time marijuana will have proved a healthy substitute for alcohol. Like other experiments it must pass through the sieve of popular criticism. To legalise it today would be an act of insanity.

CONCLUSION

It is part of the State's business to promote morality. This can sometimes be done by enforcing morality. Persistent and pettifogging interference with privacy, even when undertaken in apparently good causes, defeats its own end. In our society much of this interference is undertaken in defence of causes, such as the control of drunkenness on a massive scale, which have ceased to be relevant to contemporary life at all. One of the most important tasks of the wise legislator in the field of morality is to do away with unnecessary restrictions which merely discredit authority.

In the end, it is not government which supplies the content of morals or even plays the main part in conveying them from one generation to the next. In Western civilisation it is the function of the family. How to strengthen that institution by emphasising instead of persistently diminishing its responsibilities is one of the main questions now facing us. Though it is much too large to be debated here, one aspect of this question must be briefly mentioned.

The relationship between the law and parental responsibility is extremely subtle. It is hard to expect parents to stop their children from acquiring anti-social habits which the law appears to regard with indifference. Strong laws can support parental authority. On the whole, however, parental discipline of the young is almost always more humane and effective than that administered directly by the law. Keeping delinquent children out of court ought certainly to be one of our main legislative aims. But in the process parents should not be made to appear as publicly maintained vigilantes hand in glove with the authorities. They are there as much to protect their children against the law as to insist that they obey it. In this respect, the Government's recent White Paper on Young Offenders shows a good deal more common sense than the former proposal for a partnership between parents and welfare workers exercised through family councils.

For the Conservatives to emerge today either as the committed enemies of social and cultural change or as its indiscriminate supporters would be equally out of tune with the party's tradition. The Tory party stands both for social cohesion and for social evolution. Nowhere is the maintenance of a sane balance between these two aspects of Conservatism more important than in the debate about law and morals.

Memorial service address by Colin Welch

St. Martin's in the Fields, Monday 24 October 1988

Colin Welch, a distinguished political commentator and former Deputy Editor of The Daily Telegraph, *was one of Utley's closest friends and longest-serving colleagues.*

When the composer Meyerbeer died, his nephew composed a funeral march in his honour. He showed it to Rossini, who said, 'very fine, my boy, but what a pity it wasn't you who died and your uncle who wrote the funeral march'.

When Brigid and the Utley family asked me to compose a march in Peter's honour, they did me the greatest honour of my life and set me a daunting task. I feel inadequate. Why daunting? Well, think for a start how well Peter spoke on all occasions, grave and gay. *His* eloquence came naturally to him. Wit and paradox were his constant companions and faithful servants. He was in perfect command of his thoughts and feelings, his heart and mind, master always of that sonorous, clear, dignified and old-fashioned style, in which alone, I think, can profound and humane wisdom be expressed.

The least pompous of men, he was nonetheless a marvellous mocker of pomposity. One of his most irresistible comic ploys was to expound in richly Johnsonian terms the most trifling or base matters, the earthiest of advice, the raciest of gossip, the most ludicrous anecdotes, very often at his own expense.

Many fine writers are rotten speakers. The two modes of expression came alike to Peter, were indeed for him the same.

All he wrote was first spoken – perhaps that's why it read so well – normally dictated to Brigid or to one of that succession of lovely secretaries who helped him so much and whom he helped tirelessly in return.

Many people, from the founding aunts who brought him up onwards, helped Peter in various ways. They rejoiced to do so, and can have no regrets. They were richly rewarded, got more than they gave and can take pride in having helped to sustain an irreplaceable and bounteously creative life, by which we have all been enriched. Not only Peter and Brigid were in their debt, but all of us. As Peter's parish priest put it so movingly: 'in common with everyone who knew him, I was better for having known him.'

Peter of course spoke perforce without notes. Yet to say so is terribly misleading. No one in a sense had more notes, was better prepared. His speed of composition was prodigious. This was in his case the mark of a mind not shallow and facile but richly endowed and stocked. Kindly souls sometimes thought it cruel to ask a blind man to produce a 500-word leader on a subject not specially his own in half an hour or, say, to report from Ulster. His handicap was in fact made good, not only by the eyes of Brigid and others, but by that superb organising and generalising intelligence which, presented with a few facts, could at once by insight, logic, imagination and experience, by the application of good principles firmly held, grasp a wealth of truths not readily accessible to the sighted.

Another factor obviously daunting to me was the number, nature and distinction of Peter's friends. Look around you here: *si monumentum requiris, circumspice*. Among this throng could be found many more eloquent than I. Yet I must please emphasise that most of Peter's friends were not eminentoes. People who mattered a great deal sought his counsel and company. So did people who didn't in a worldly sense matter at all, except to him and God.

All were welcome at his feast of reason. I was about to say all except fools and bores, but they – or we – were gladly suffered and welcomed too. His court was catholic at what has been called that vile pub, the Kings and Keys. Bless me, it wasn't vile when Peter and his family and circle were there! It heard some of the best talk in London, not so much a saloon as a salon.

Another daunting factor for me was the flood of beautiful, sincere and moving tributes – often affectionately and appropriately amusing – which saluted Peter's death. Mrs. Thatcher spontaneously and most justly honoured his courtesy, rightly seeing in this no mere ornament but an expression of the great spiritual quality she discerned in him. From another angle, Frances Hill, one of the secretaries, lovingly recalled reading Evelyn Waugh's *Scoop* to Peter on the top of a bus, he helpless with mirth, soon the whole top deck helpless too. And so on: who could excel all these?

Peter must have been pleased to note how many of these tributes came from younger people who were grateful to him for teaching them, among much else, how to think and write. Yet in a sense he *taught* nothing. He was the least didactic of men, the least inclined to mould or reshape the young he loved. If we all learnt prodigiously in his company – and we did – it was from his presence and example, from the standards of intellectual rigour and lack of cant which he imposed upon himself rather than on others.

From Peter's *courage* too we learnt – learnt, for instance, not to complain about trifles – not anyway to do so without shame. This too he did not teach. Many people who have overcome great handicaps, who are in this sense self made, become conceited and harsh, unsympathetic about the lesser misfortunes and struggles of others. Not Peter, on the contrary.

Peter's courage was exemplary and unfaltering in the face of, at times, disappointments, difficulties and seeming betrayals which would have sunk lesser men. He treated them all with a serene and gallant insouciance, confident that God would provide. One fine tribute to him spoke of his bitter disappointment at losing an election in Ulster. I hope it isn't nit-picking to assert that such a man could never have felt bitterness about any such earthly temporal setback. He met it with his invariable humorous fortitude.

Also exemplary and unfaltering was – indeed is – Brigid's courage, different I think from Peter's, not less, perhaps even more. It is of a more defiant and combative sort, perhaps more realistic and earthy, battling always to keep the family craft afloat no matter what waves broke over it, facing always the storm, determined always somehow to provide whatever God in his wisdom had withheld, and to provide it lavishly too, plenty for others. The bank manager might groan, but so did Brigid's hospitable board. To praise Peter is inescapably to praise Brigid too: every word adds to her glory. Without her the story would have surely been very different, and sadder.

Peter was a great family man. His family brought him comfort and just pride. Some family men find in the family all they need, become a bit narrow, content to restrict their affections to that circle. Not Peter. While lavishing warmth and interest on his own, he also went radiantly outward with warmth and interest for others, as if we were all his family.

May I end on a personal note? I went to see the old boy in hospital, where he was unconscious or supposedly so, a bit restless but not, I think, in pain. I cannot speak of the desolation I felt to see him thus, to miss the loved familiar inevitable admonition, 'Colin! Have a drink!' – though the family soon made good the want. Ollie Knox told an excellent joke. Peter's mouth opened, his feet twitched. Was he still with us? Was this for him his last earthly joke?

As I left, I kissed him on the forehead and said, 'Goodbye, my dear old friend.' 'Goodbye for a time,' I added quickly, in hopeful respect to his hard unshaken Christian faith, the greatest faith one of his disciples thought he'd ever encountered.

Now, if a mind and soul of this quality has faith, who are we lesser mortals to doubt? Perhaps already in another place another voice has said to Peter, *'Well done!'*.

Index